MW00737836

GLOBAL MEDIA AND STRATEGIC NARRATIVES OF CONTESTED DEMOCRACY

In order to better understand how the world viewed the US 2016 presidential election, the issues that mattered around the world, and how nations made sense of how their media systems constructed presentations of the presidential election, Robert S. Hinck, Skye C. Cooley, and Randolph Kluver examine global news narratives during the campaign and immediately afterwards.

Analyzing 1,578 news stories from 62 sources within three regional media ecologies in China, Russia, and the Middle East, Hinck, Cooley, and Kluver demonstrate how the US election was incorporated into narrative constructions of the global order. They establish that the narratives told about the US election through national and regional media provide insights into how foreign nations construct US democracy, and reflect local understandings regarding the issues, and impacts, of US policy towards those nations.

Avoiding jargon-laden prose, *Global Media and Strategic Narratives of Contested Democracy* is as accessible as it is wide-ranging. Its empirical detail will expand readers' understanding of soft power as narrative articulations of foreign nation's policies, values, and beliefs within localized media systems. Communication/media studies students, as well as political scientists whose studies includes media and global politics, will welcome its publication.

Robert S. Hinck is an assistant professor in the Department of Communication Studies at Monmouth College. His expertise is in rhetoric, strategic narrative, and political communication.

Skye C. Cooley is an assistant professor in the School of Media and Strategic Communications at Oklahoma State University. His research centers on Russian political communication, global media and digital democracy, as well as developing and testing platforms for civic deliberation online.

Randolph Kluver is the Dean of the School of Global Studies and Partnerships at Oklahoma State University. He has published widely in the fields of new media, Asian politics, the internet in Asian societies, public diplomacy, and international communication.

ROUTLEDGE STUDIES IN GLOBAL INFORMATION, POLITICS AND SOCIETY

Edited by Kenneth Rogerson, Duke University and Laura Roselle, Elon University

International communication encompasses everything from one-to-one cross-cultural interactions to the global reach of a broad range of information and communications technologies and processes. *Routledge Studies in Global Information, Politics and Society* celebrates – and embraces – this depth and breadth. To completely understand communication, it must be studied in concert with many factors, since, most often, it is the foundational principle on which other subjects rest. This series provides a publishing space for scholarship in the expansive, yet intersecting, categories of communication and information processes and other disciplines.

GLOBAL MEDIA AND STRATEGIC NARRATIVES OF CONTESTED DEMOCRACY

Chinese, Russian, and Arabic Media Narratives of the US Presidential Election

Robert S. Hinck, Skye C. Cooley, and Randolph Kluver

Routledge
Taylor & Francis Group

NEW YORK AND LONDON

First published 2020
by Routledge
52 Vanderbilt Avenue, New York, NY 10017

and by Routledge
2 Park Square, Milton Park, Abingdon, Oxon OX14 4RN

Routledge is an imprint of the Taylor & Francis Group, an informa business

© 2020 Taylor & Francis

The right of Robert S. Hinck, Skye C. Cooley, and Randolph Kluver to be
identified as the authors of the material, and of the authors for their individual
chapters, has been asserted in accordance with sections 77 and 78 of the
Copyright, Designs and Patents Act 1988

All rights reserved. No part of this book may be reprinted or reproduced or
utilized in any form or by any electronic, mechanical, or other means, now
known or hereafter invented, including photocopying and recording, or in any
information storage or retrieval system, without permission in writing from the
publishers.

Trademark notice: Product or corporate names may be trademarks or registered
trademarks, and are used only for identification and explanation without intent
to infringe.

Library of Congress Cataloging-in-Publication Data
A catalog record for this title has been requested

ISBN: 978-0-367-25778-1 (hbk)
ISBN: 978-0-367-25779-8 (pbk)
ISBN: 978-0-429-28980-4 (ebk)

Typeset in Bembo
by Taylor & Francis Books

CONTENTS

TABLES

ACKNOWLEDGEMENTS

When starting this project in the summer of 2016, we hardly imagined the extent to which the presidential election of that year would impact US politics and US foreign policy around the globe. While we knew from our previous studies that the news stories reported within foreign media often told diverging narratives, depicting a variety of changing geopolitical issues and new international economic alignments, we hadn't expected the depth of reflection and juxta-positioning of US democratic governance to each region's own system of governance.

As we pulled and analyzed our data, it quickly became clear that US and global audiences were closely tuned into the political drama surrounding the 2016 presidential contest, and, at times, both fascinated and discouraged by what they were seeing. In reading these news reports ourselves, we began to witness the narratives of the US election moving beyond simply discussing US policy to include larger reflections, and challenges, regarding the merits of democracy itself. After completing this project, we believe now more than ever in the importance of seeking out and understanding global perceptions and stories about key events, as well as the need for careful reflection of American audiences' own reporting of events regarding our own political system.

As noted above, the ground work for this study largely began in the summer of 2016 with coder training and data analysis running until Spring of 2017. During this time, we benefited from the dedication of numerous undergraduate and graduate students, and other collaborators. Specifically, we would like to thank Yikai Zhao, Yongrong Shen, Peixin Dong, Leah Lagoudis, Brandon Gindt, Jala Naguib, Ashley Rossini, Julia Berg, Ethan Stokes, and Hannah Conrad, among others, who underwent extensive coder training, and retraining. Without their patience and determination this project could not have been completed. We acknowledge and appreciate the role of

Natalie Khazaal for her work in helping us to understand the Arabic findings. She is the principal author of chapter four.

We also want to thank our many colleagues who supported our work, including the College of Liberal Arts at Texas A&M University for usage of the Media Monitoring System, and the colleagues at BBN Raytheon for providing support for that system. Likewise, we would like to thank the coordinators of the Third Annual International Journal of Press/Politics Conference where we presented a shortened portion of our findings. Furthermore, we must express our gratitude to the anonymous reviewers and their feedback, as well as the editorial staff at Routledge.

Finally, we would like to offer our acknowledgment and gratitude toward our each of our families. Robert would like to thank Sara for all of her support, behind the scenes labor, and conversations throughout this process. Skye would like to thank Asya and Indiana for their patience and making the entire process an absolute joy. And Randy thanks Pam, Zachary, Sean, and Joel for keeping this academic grounded in real life.

As recent events and news reports suggest, we are currently experiencing a new age of global contestation. From accusations of election meddling, the advent of fake news, and even the implementation of misinformation campaigns from state and non-state actors, one can see the ongoing importance and battle over how we make sense of the truth claims, values, and beliefs undergirding our own political communities, as well as those abroad. We hope that readers of this book will walk away understanding one facet of this battle, as seen through the lens of foreign media narratives. We believe that by examining the stories told by other nations' media we can come closer to understanding their own aspirations, perceptions, interpretations of what issues matter most to them, and their reasonings as to why. More importantly, we believe that by taking on the perspectives of others we afford ourselves a lens to reflect and evaluate the stories we find ourselves telling.

Author's note: Chapter four was co-written by Natalie Khazaal and Robert Hinck. All of the other chapters were co-authored by Robert Hinck, Skye Cooley, and Randy Kluver.

1

STRATEGIC NARRATIVES OF THE 2016 US PRESIDENTIAL ELECTION

Contestations of US, Chinese, Arab, and Russian Soft Power Constructions

Introduction

The 2016 US presidential election was of tremendous interest to citizens of the US, as well as to observers around the world, with coverage being front page news for most news outlets around the globe. According to a commissioned study by CNN, 85% of survey respondents globally felt that the election mattered to the world, with 75% saying that it mattered personally to them. As Rani Raad, President of CNN International Commercial, stated, the report "shows the unprecedented interest in this year's US Election—it has global reach and a mix of policy debates that have the potential to affect the world at large" (CNN, 2016).

There are many reasons for the global interest in the election. Obviously, the US president is the most visible symbol of the US to much of the world, and the policies that the President brings to the office have global ramifications. The US also has one of the world's most robust media infrastructures, providing an almost limitless amount of content for other global media outlets. In addition, the US often sets the pace for electoral politics in other nations, with US style political campaign practices being replicated elsewhere, spread not only by widespread media awareness, but also by an army of US consultants who advise campaigns overseas. Finally, the specific policies of individual administrations potentially have important diplomatic, economic, and/or political significance, not just to the global order at large, but to individual nations. This is true whether the nation is an ally, rival, or even a neutral actor towards the US. With the possible exception of Britain's royal family, there is no other political process that is more globally followed than the US presidential election.

But perhaps more importantly, the US election is not understood as merely a singular event. Rather, it is a symbol of US political values and processes, and global discussions on the merits of "democracy" often are framed in reference to what is modeled in the US. As McClory (2017) notes, the US is the only country in the world that places its former and incoming leader on a stage for millions to see, with the "Peaceful Transition of Power" being the very symbol of American democracy watched around the world. The US election process, in its entirety, is a demonstration to both internal and external audiences on how Western democracy functions, and its viability as a model for the rest of the globe.

The ramifications of global coverage are many, in that global perceptions of the US, its citizens, its political system, and its global role are often driven by media coverage of the US. As Joseph Nye (1990, 2004) argues, a nation's soft power is very much impacted by perceptions of the political values and policies of a nation. If a nation's political values are seen as admirable, then that nation's "power of attraction," or its ability to lead other nations, is enhanced. Likewise, when the nation's political values are seen as dishonest, corrupt, or dishonorable, that nation's influence in the global order declines. Because of this centrality of attention, the US election becomes a fulcrum by which to affirm, contest, and/or alter the existing global order, and the role of the US in that order.

Soft power, then, cuts both ways, capable of enhancing one's image or hurting it. Furthermore, as a tool for international influence, it can also be turned against others. Indeed, soft power can be "surprisingly aggressive" (Price, 2015) and even viewed by target states' elites and broader societies as hostile intrusions capable of threatening their own established societal norms (Szostek, 2017a). And, while the US has lauded the ideational supremacy of its democratic liberal values since the collapse of the Soviet Union, that vision of world order is being increasingly contested. Closely tied to this has been the significant investment by non-Western nations in particular to advance their soft power capabilities by developing their own international news agencies to both combat the dominance of Western reporting, as well as augment their own international influence (Hayden, 2012; Powers & Gilboa, 2007; Gill & Huang, 2006; Hartig, 2015; Saari, 2014; Soldatov & Borogan, 2015). This restructuring of our international media ecology has reshaped the arena, both internationally and domestically, on how global events are reported, consumed, and contested. And yet, with all of this, there are few studies that explore how non-Western media systems package and explain US politics to their citizens in order to affirm, contest, and alter perceptions of US soft power; furthermore, the information that US voters receive about global perceptions on its election process are typically anecdotal, incomplete, and arise from Western news reports. How then do other countries come to understand the issues, characters, and practice of US democracy? What stories are told about the US election and how do those stories impact domestic audiences understanding of their own politics? Finally, what implications might this hold for US global leadership and soft power? These are but some of the questions this book sets out to answer.

In order to better understand how the world viewed the election, the issues that mattered around the world, and how global media systems constructed presentations of the US presidential election, we examined global news narratives about the 2016 US presidential election during the campaign and immediately afterwards. To do so, we utilized the theoretical construct of strategic narratives (Miskimmon, O'Loughlin, & Roselle, 2013, 2017) to demonstrate how the US election was incorporated into narrative constructions of the global order, analyzing 1,578 news stories from 62 sources within three regional media ecologies (China, the Middle East, and Russia). We chose this method because the narratives that are told about nations are in many ways more important than the actual facts or truths about that nation. Truth, or validity, from this vantage point is considered as societally constructed and shared through story and is less concerned with attempted determinations of an objective reality. As rhetorical theorist Walter Fisher (1984, 1989) argued, humans are best understood as *"homo narrans,"* or the storytelling species. We use narratives to make sense of the world, to define ourselves and our values, to define our rivals, enemies, and friends, and to explain our actions, values, beliefs and, ultimately, to create truth.

Our analysis demonstrates how the narratives told about the US election through national and regional media provide insights into how foreign nations construct US democracy, and reflect local understandings regarding the issues, and impacts, of US policy towards those nations, while also offering views on their own perceptions of the international order and projections of national strength. In this sense, our analysis goes beyond framing and agenda setting analyses typically employed by international news research covering election reporting in that frames and discourse analysis lack the temporal and causal features that narratives possess (Miskimmon et al., 2013). Narrative analysis provides us with a sense of how these political communities draw upon past occurrences to make sense of the present 2016 election, as well as what policies are trajected to be most attractive, or unattractive, in service to their future aspirations and understanding of world order. As Roselle, Miskimmon, and O'Loughlin (2014) argue, the concept of strategic narratives provides researchers with a new perspective to understand soft power by focusing on when influence occurs or fails to do so, especially with regards to how influence works in our new global media environment.

However, beyond introducing the concept of strategic narratives as a more fruitful means to understand soft power, Roselle et al. (2014) leave us with little understanding, and empirical evidence, of the role regional media ecologies play in crafting and projecting these narratives. Indeed, as Flew, Iosifidis, and Steemers (2016) argue, the forces of technology and globalization have given increased importance to global media and their narratives, raising the imperative for scholarship aimed at better understanding the linkages of strategic narrative construction and the implications for soft power. Rather than globalization becoming a homogenizing factor of media, new technologies and the forces of globalization have strengthened the power of local, national, and regional media. These findings are supported by studies of international news coverage which argue that news providers are primarily organized as national news providers (Papathanassopoulos et al., 2013) with foreign news presented through the prism of national interest and identity (Nossek & Kunelius, 2012;

Mody, 2010) leading to how foreign news is reported which varies greatly around the world (Aalberg et al., 2013). Thus, states, and their media systems, have increased power to pursue positive, or negative, regulatory interventions that help them control and manage media narrative in ways that better shape the story they want to see constructed on of a given event (Flew, et al., 2016). Consequently, we can expect that, rather than converging in meaning, a global event will increasingly take on drastically differing narrative forms depending on how it serves a local media system. This is especially true in countries adopting closer state-media relationships such as the ones our project analyses.

Even so, state actors are limited in their ability to project their strategic narratives in complete isolation from outside input in that strategic narratives operate "in a discursive terrain where the agencies of elites and masses are mutually constitutive" (Liao, 2017, 111); the narratives propagated by government officials or elites can fall short of effective influence if they fail to resonate with their target audiences, whether they be domestic or international. In this sense, strategic narratives are not simply one-way vehicles of mass manipulation onto a population, but rather rely on the complexities of shared meaning within an entire society in order to build a collective story that relays the truth of an event over to the population.

In a fundamental way, then, we take issue with the common definition of strategic narrative provided by Miskimmon et al. (2013) as first and foremost a rhetorical act, i.e., a narrative set forth to achieve a strategic goal. Our definition considers "strategic" as less about intention, and more about the role of a narrative in shaping the geopolitical worldview of an audience. In so doing, a strategic narrative defines the geopolitical reality, i.e., who are we? Who are our friends? Who are our enemies? What are our values? It is questions like these that provide meaning to geopolitical competition or cooperation, and define our ability to engage geopolitically at all.

As an analogy, the difference between a "strategic" weapon and a "tactical" weapon is that a strategic weapon is used to undermine an opponent's ability to conduct war at all, usually targeting industrial infrastructure, command structure, and the like. In contrast, a "tactical" weapon is one for local, immediate utilization on a battlefield, and is not designed, or expected, to undo an opponent's ability to conduct war at all, just stop an immediate attack. Likewise, a strategic narrative is a narrative with the ability to shape the geopolitical terrain, as it were, in defining the nature of the geopolitical world. A "tactical" narrative is one that is used to shape perceptions of an immediate issue, whereas a strategic narrative is much more foundational in shaping the perceptions of audiences as to the nature of the world itself. For example, a narrative about enemy soldiers conducting atrocities in a village is tactical, in that it undermines immediate perceptions of the current actions. As an example, in July of 2014, Russian news channels broadcast a false narrative about a young boy crucified by Ukrainian soldiers so as to portray Russian intervention in the Donbass region as a noble intervention. That narrative is tactical, in that it undermines any goodwill that Russians might have for Ukrainian nationalists.

By contrast, a narrative which posits that the current battle is part of long and epic war between "our people" and "the enemies of freedom" is strategic, in that it shapes the terrain on which the tactical battles will be fought; that of geopolitical worldviews. A narrative that demonstrates the century-long struggle of the Ukrainians to remove the yoke of the oppressive Russians is strategic, in that any particular event just reinforces the worldview.

A narrative about an event, then, is "spin," i.e., it seeks to shape the understanding of a particular event at a particular point of time. A strategic narrative, by contrast, provides the context and meaning for interpreting not just a single event, but all events, in that it allows us to interpret the actions of a geopolitical actor not just by *what they do*, but by *who they are*. Was Russian intervention in Syria in the fall of 2015 an attempt to uphold an ally and preserve stability in a region that was quickly crumbling by years of civil war and US interference, or was it an attempt to undermine the US dominance of the region, as yet another example of Russian attempts to undermine the US-led world order? The definition of events is driven by the worldview the audiences hold as to the nature of the geopolitical world.

As Schumacher (2015) argues, the function of narratives relies on the public acceptance of policies and policy action whereby elites' advancement of foreign policy narratives depends on more enduring structures of national identity discourse in which those narratives must be grounded. Although construction and dissemination of these discourses originate from elites in one or several states, they are expressed and codified in their media systems, thereby providing perennial boundaries for policy. Understanding the impact of strategic narratives in the formation of soft power, then, requires careful consideration of how these are expressed in national media, because "mainstream media simultaneously function as actors that voice particular narratives and as a conduit (and sometimes as a filter) for narratives put forward by a host of actors (including smaller media and new media organizations)" (Arsenault, Hong, & Price, 2017, 204). Thus, "it is in these mediated spaces that narratives are validated, contested, and ultimately made into reality" (Arsenault et al., 2017, 204).

Therefore, in the context of the 2016 US presidential election, this book sets out to contribute to the emerging field of strategic narratives in international relations and communication by conceptualizing strategic narratives as a means to exercise soft power at home and abroad through its focus on the role of national media systems as the source of narrative constructions in countries more antagonistic to US policies that possess closer-state media relationships. We focused our attention on three areas that are outside the club, as it were, of the Western media system of press agencies, outlets, and governments, and instead drew our data from two countries (China and Russia) and one linguistic region (the Arabic-speaking region of the Middle East) that do not typically share the political, economic, or cultural traditions of the West, and are thus likely to have starkly differing views of the US and its political processes. In doing so, we help overcome the gap in studies of non-Western media that exists in current international communication research (Kluver, Campbell, & Balfour, 2013), as well as advancing our understanding of the role media plays in strategic narrative influence.

It is an error, of course, to argue that "the world" has one opinion about anything, especially anything as contentious and controversial as US politics. Not only are there great differences in the perceptions and perspectives of nations around the world, within any nation there are likely to be tremendous differences in the likability of a potential US president, the value of proposed US policies, or the likely impact of any president on ties between the US and that nation. Nevertheless, it is helpful, and conceptually necessary, to try to develop a broad understanding of the range of opinions within nations and among nations about the US election process and its outcomes.

It is equally an error, we think, to argue that global perceptions are irrelevant to the US and its citizens. As has been suggested by a number of scholars, international public opinion in some ways functions as a "new superpower" (Castells, 2008; Arquilla & Ronfeldt, 1999). It is true that non-US citizens do not vote, but US actions in the world are doomed to failure if other nations, and the political leaders and citizens of those nations, do not to some extent understand the rationales, beliefs, and values that drive US policies. On the other hand, even if US citizens do not consider the interests of other nations to be as important as their own, they should at least be willing to understand how other nations perceive the US and its policies. Failure to do so can be incredibly short-sighted and misguided. As long as other nations, their leaders and citizens, are distrustful of US intentions and actions, it matters very little what the US hopes to accomplish in its foreign policy, as those efforts are likely to fail. A starting point towards bridging and overcoming such mistrust starts with understanding how others see the US and its political processes which we argue can be done through examination of the constructed strategic narratives concerning the US through regional media systems and consideration towards the implications those narratives have for US soft power.

Global News Coverage and Public Opinion

There is a long line of literature outlining the dominance of the US and other leading Western nations in terms of global news coverage. Most of these studies cite systemic factors, including political and economic strength, cultural similarities, and geopolitical ranking. A number of important studies (Aalberg et al., 2013; Gerbner & Marvanyi, 1977; Kariel & Rosenvall, 1995; Wu, 2000; Golan, 2006) have confirmed the unbalanced representation of foreign countries in US news media. Core countries (particularly the US and Western Europe), their international affairs, and their interchanging opponents or enemies have always been at the center of international news. Peripheral countries rarely, if ever, catch global attention, or only do so when defined by terms of larger major powers. Indeed, a number of studies of media coverage of global elections focus on just these core nations, with little attention to peripheral nations (e.g., de Vreese & Boomgaarden, 2006; Aalberg et al., 2013).

Furthermore, the extensive body of literature on the relationship of media coverage to political knowledge, attitudes, and opinion points to a strong relationship between how media outlets cover political personalities, events and issues, and subsequent voter (or non-voter) opinion (de Vreese & Boomgaarden 2006). However, there is a much smaller set of studies focusing on how international coverage of national level politics is interpreted and made sense of by foreign publics. As Farnsworth, Lichter, and Schatz (2013) argue, international coverage of US politics is particularly important: "today's persuader in chief speaks to a global audience … that global audience has grown increasingly skeptical of White House motives as a result of media reports that often condemn US leaders and policies" (2).

Analysis of news content beyond those of Western nations is particularly important today given the recent investments in communication technology and infrastructure, as well as the increased media savvy of nations such as China, Russia, Saudi Arabia, Qatar, and non-recognized actors such as the Islamic State. All of these efforts are designed, in part, to combat Western media dominance, pushing us to a new age of global communication contestation.

Reflective of this development, research into international news and elections raise questions as to whether we have entered into a new global village, or whether there exists a transnational public sphere, or some hybridization of news coverage. These studies tend to rely on theories of agenda-setting or framing to demonstrate the dominance or plurality of news flows. And, while agenda-setting has been found to inform audiences of what issues are important, it doesn't explain what specific views audiences come to hold about them. Research on framing analyses alleviates this, in part by demonstrating the means by which elites attempt to influence how publics come to view a specific issue and mobilize public support for their cause or policy. However, as Coticchia (2016) argues, these frames are more tactical in nature, providing only snapshots of events to serve the short-term purposes of elites. The idea of narrative, on the other hand, helps us go beyond the concept of framing. Narratives, through their inclusion of temporality, are strategic in that they focus on deeper, long-term sense-making of events. Thus, while frames may serve as the bricks helping to compose a narrative, narratives help shape our understanding of the world because inherently they are stories dependent on pre-existing, shared societal constructions of reality. While frames reflect snapshots of the world, by tying in questions of identity, as well as latent social values and cultural myths, narratives help us understand how societies make sense of the world around them.

The difference between narratives and framing may best be understood by considering the Islamic State's media strategy. As Heck (2017) argues, ISIS media served to propagate three narratives designed to legitimize its existence and justify its terrorist attacks. These narratives included descriptions of the Islamic State's worldview claiming that the West had subjugated Muslims, which the establishment of the Caliphate aimed to protect, constructed ISIS's identity by establishing the religious supremacy of its interpretation of Islam, and included ISIS's future vision of world order through its aspiration for global dominance. In this case, the strategic goal of the Islamic State's media engagement was not the tactical framing of specific events so much as interpolating its audience into a larger worldview to mobilize support for its imagined Caliphate. As such, we would not consider ISIS's media strategy as one composed of framing, but rather narrative construction and projection.

Returning to how national elections are covered in international news, Curran, Esser, Hallin, Hayashi, and Lee (2015) argue that there are moments when national media do project unified meanings to international events, with international elections being one example when crystallizing moments in international media might occur. In their study of Chinese, Japanese, Germen, UK, and US media coverage of the 2012 Greek, Chinese, and US elections, they found that, although the US election received the most coverage, confirming research into "elite nations" dominance in international news coverage, all three elections were reported on by all leading television news programs and websites in all five countries. This shows that some news events receive attention from national media around the world because they are viewed as being inherently newsworthy in terms of international news norms or are deemed globally influential. However, they also found that national spin was deployed to interest or relate overseas news reports to national audiences; and yet, despite the Greek and US elections being framed differently than the Chinese elections, the authors determined that there was more uniformity in coverage than difference. They concluded that convergence of international coverage of elections was not a consequence of a Habermasean global public sphere, nor of a McLuhan-esque global village, but reflected the "interplay of power in which privileged access of governments to the media, the hegemony of market liberal thought, the dominance of a small number of news agencies and the legacy of the Cold War, all play a part" (14). These findings establish the importance of power, whether it be access or values, but do little to help explain how nations come to combat or strengthen their relative influence in international media.

As noted earlier, globalization has strengthened the power of local, national, and regional media. That point is of further importance to this discussion because it means that states have increased power to pursue positive, or negative, regulatory interventions that help them control and manage media narrative in ways that better shape the story they want to see out of a given event (Flew et al., 2016). Rather than converging in meaning, a global event can increasingly take on drastically differing narrative forms depending on how it serves a local media system. Thus, any consideration of a global event from purely a Western media coverage standpoint is outdated, with Western media largely possessing its own localized system, rather than a force of global narrative dominance.

The study by Boudana and Segev (2017) of "provocation" narratives provides further evidence of these localized media systems. In their study they found that news coverage from four nations (the US, UK, Germany, and France) all established very similar narratives of provocation, typically pitting the US and its allies against a handful of other nations, including North Korea, Russia, and Iran. They argued that "provocation narratives are similarly used by all outlets [across all countries and news outlets] as a framing device to divide between good and bad actors, as well as to assign praise and blame to each side" (329). They conclude that, in spite of very different national press cultures, access to information, and political orientation, Western press outlets tend to follow similar narrative structures, at least in the case of narratives of provocation.

For these reasons, it is important to understand how nations outside the club of Western countries are reporting on US politics, and particularly events like the 2016 US election. As the studies reviewed above suggest, there likely are significant differences among non-Western nation's narratives of the 2016 election from those of Western countries. Whether they share the same narrative constructions of the US election and projection of US soft power is unknown, and our comparative analysis takes the first step in addressing this gap. While this dichotomy of the "West and the rest" can be problematic, in the context of the 2016 US election, we expect that those nations with more authoritarian or less developed liberal democratic institutions than Western-liberal democracies will have a different view of "the meaning" of the 2016 election. As a site of contestation over legitimate models of governance, analysis of the 2016 US election allows us to see how competing versions of legitimate governance come to be strategically defined in support or in contestation of the US led world order and how non-Western nations attempt to augment their influence in international media through the projection of such narratives. The means by which this occurs, as our next section goes into more detail, are strategic narratives.

Strategic Narratives

In their most basic sense, strategic narratives are compelling storylines describing events in convincing ways (Freedman, 2006). They contain actors, agents, scenes, instruments, and intentions (Burke, 1969), and serve to connect apparently unconnected phenomena around some causal transformation emplotted over time (Miskimmon et al., 2013, 2017). Communication scholars have long recognized the importance of narratives in shaping our sense of reality. Indeed, the rhetorician Walter Fisher (1984, 1989) argued that we as a species are *"homo narrans,"* or the narrative species, and suggested that a narrative paradigm was a better explanation for human decision-making than what he termed the "rational world paradigm," which holds that our decisions are grounded in some sort of exercise of formal logic, structured upon clear lines of argument, evidence, and rules-based logic. Fisher thus proposed an understanding of human rationality grounded in narratives, in which people make and justify their decisions in credible narrative accounts, rather than the traditional forms of logic prized by logicians. Story thus being the most important means by which human beings explain and understand their conditional reality in relationship to, and with, others.

More recently, the idea of narratives has garnered greater attention by international relations scholars (Schmitt, 2018), with Freedman (2006) introducing the term to the field of international security to describe compelling storylines which would explain events convincingly. Building upon the importance of narrative, Miskimmon et al. (2013, 2017) proposed the idea of "strategic narratives," which are "representations of a sequence of events and identities, a communicative tool through which political actors—usually elite—attempt to give determined meaning to past, present, and future in order to achieve political objectives" (5). Central to their idea is that political actors use "strategic narratives [to] integrate interests and goals—they articulate end states and suggest how to get there" (5). These strategic narratives operate on three levels: a) international system narratives describing how the world is structured; b) national narratives describing the story of the state, including its values and goals; and c) issue narratives describing why a certain policy is needed. These three levels can overlap, as Roselle (2014) states, thus "Strategic narratives at one level will be strengthened by resonance with narratives at other levels" (101).

From this perspective, Miskimmon et al. (2013, 2017) suggest scholars look at how strategic narratives are constructed, projected, and received, and in their description of strategic narratives they provide a spectrum of positions theorizing the role of communication in international relations. On one end are those who take a system and set of actors as a given, studying the interaction and persuasion among them; this position is taken by rationalist analysts providing thin accounts of communication. On the other end are those who study how identity is formed , usually by providing "thick" descriptions of the narratives that undergird those identities.

The usefulness of strategic narratives as a means to understand influence and persuasion in international affairs can be seen by its wide application in recent years. A significant body of research has applied the concept in a wide variety of geopolitical contexts (Schmitt, 2018; Coticchia, 2016; de Graaf, Dimitriu, & Ringsmose, 2015; Lemay-Hébert & Visoka, 2017; Irvin-Erickson, 2017; Roselle, 2017; Burton, 2018). This include considerations of soft power and public diplomacy (Roselle, Miskimmon, & O'Loughlin, 2014; Natarajan, 2014; Hartig, 2015; Faizullaev & Cornut, 2017), non-Western nations' challenges to world order (Miskimmon & O'Loughlin, 2017; van Noort, 2017), and ontological security and securitization (Eberle, 2017; Ejdus & Božović, 2017; Senn, 2017). Strategic narratives have also been applied to identity formation both nationally and transnationally (Heck, 2017; Szostek, 2017a, 2017b; Snyder, 1998; Schumacher, 2015; Berenskoetter, 2014; Roselle, 2017), with considerations to branding and geographical metaphors (Suslov, 2017; Szostek, 2017a), and contested orders of geo-economics (Garrett, 2018; Skalamera, 2018). Finally, strategic narratives have also been studied in the context of rhetorical strategies of persuasion within domestic and international political constituencies (Senn, 2017; Goddard & Krebs, 2015; Krebs, 2015; Chowdhury & Krebs, 2009; Snyder, 2015), including the role of persuasion in contemporary war and conflict (de Franco, 2012; Simpson, 2012), and justification of military engagement abroad (de Graaf et al., 2015; Ringsmose & Børgesen, 2011; Klarevas, 2002; Berinski, 2007).

Taken together, these studies largely share the perspective that human beings are essentially story-telling animals that come to understand their world and the events in them through narratives. These studies support the claim that narratives serve to define a political community, build up the identity of actors, shape understandings of the global order, justify policy orientations, and help mobilize public support. As such, narratives serve as essential elements in coming to understand and mobilize one's identity and, consequently, the identities of "outsiders," i.e., those outside of their political communities.

What is lacking, however, is a clearer description of the role media systems play in affecting the formation, projection, and reception of strategic narratives. This comes in part from concerns over who it is that creates narratives within a society and the societal transactions involved in that creation. As Miskimmon et al. (2013) note, in studying strategic narratives, questions of agency arise from who gives voice to the constructed narratives: are the actors governments, political leaders, media corporations, or non-state players? While many of the studies cited above analyze discourses within the media, they do so from the perspective of how political elites contest or disseminate their narratives through media systems. Furthermore, most of the scholarship from Miskimmon and colleagues overlook the central role of the media in affecting narratives, instead tending to rely on the content from official speeches or state documents (e.g., Miskimmon & O'Loughlin, 2017). While this is useful in understanding how government agents attempt to construct narratives, it diminishes how the media and the masses come to understand important issues and events through the discussion of media content. As Krebs (2015) argues, identification of dominant narratives must go beyond single sources such as official government pronouncements.

For this project, we are less concerned with who is producing the narrative than we are with what the final constructed narrative tells us about the shared societal meaning given to a particular event. While strategic narratives as a concept tends to imply agency from a specific actor, our study's use of regional media systems as the unit of analysis rather than individual political actors requires us to use the term more broadly to mean "narratives that have strategic importance and impact" rather than narratives that are clearly strategic in the sense of having agency and strategy, i.e., the work of a "strategist." Thus, within the continuum of Miskimmon et al. (2013, 2017) continuum, we are opting for a "thick account," in that we seek to analyze the narratives that are articulated by national media, with less interest into who in particular is responsible for that articulation.

Although it is evident that media ecologies, or the complex set of relations between various types and channels of media, are important elements to take under consideration, scholarship so far provides few comparative examples examining how strategic narratives, especially those involving the nature and legitimacy of the global order, are being contested around the world. Our perspective builds from the work of Miskimmon et al. (2013, 2017) on strategic narratives by answering their call for analyzing "the role of media in contributing to the meaning of events," as well as providing insight into how "events come to possess narrativity for audiences" (321) by focusing on how narratives on US democracy, including the legitimacy regarding the general process, as well as characterizations about candidates and their policies, are received and reconceptualized within foreign media systems.

To do so, we argue for the analysis of collective narratives within national and regional media ecologies, which Miskimmon et al. (2013) argue can be identified even when issues are in the midst of domestic contestation. Our approach is supported by Steele's (2012) argument that the outcomes of intrasocial debates result in narratives closely approximating the identity commitment a state will pursue in international relations. While media outlets are not entirely political actors in and of themselves, Arsenault et al. (2017) argue that mainstream media can function as actors by giving voice to certain narratives, both as a conduit and as a filter. This is likely to be even more true with the selection of our cases of Chinese, Middle Eastern, and Russian media, in that all three have closer state-media relationships.

Therefore, close analysis of national and regional media can help us determine to some extent the formation, and more importantly the resonance of strategic narratives within a political community. As Miskimmon et al. (2017) note, media ecologies are one system of discourse with enduring rules and roles that result in stable forms of news and political information that inform their audiences of visions of world order and provides the raw materials from which political leaders can craft strategic narratives. Previous research examining strategic narratives within national media ecologies has uncovered a clear analysis of Russian and Chinese intentions to contest in the arena of strategic narratives within their media ecologies (Hinck, Manly, Kluver, & Norris, 2016; Hinck, Kluver, & Cooley, 2018; Hinck, Manly, Kluver, & Norris, 2018).

Indeed, as the literature on comparative media systems demonstrates, there are significant variations between different media systems around the world influenced by their differing cultural, social, and/or political contexts. Again though, as Hallin and Mancini's (2004) seminal work demonstrates, this is dominated largely by studies on Western democratic systems, although their 2011 book does attempt to provide greater understanding of non-Western media systems (Hallin & Mancini, 2011). While the focus of our project is not on developing a new typology of non-Western comparative media systems, our focus on Russian, Chinese, and Arabic media requires a consideration of their state-media systems and level of political pluralism, especially given that all three regions rank low on Reporters Without Boarders' World Freedom Press Index, with Russia ranking 148 in the world, China 176, and Arabic-speaking nations such as Iraq 160, Jordan 132, Syria 177, and Lebanon 100 (Reporters Without Borders, 2018). In Chapter 2 we go into detail contextualizing these regional media ecologies and their state-media relations. It is important for us to mention here that, even though these systems are heavily controlled, it does not mean that the resultant narratives are entirely absent of shared interaction with the citizens of these nations. Indeed, for these narratives to be persuasive, they must be credible and not appear as pure propaganda. As such, they hinge on the public's acceptance of them (Schumacher, 2015), with elites and masses forming mutually constitutive interactions within the discursive terrain in which they manifest themselves (Liao, 2017). Strategic narratives, then, can be persuasive resources for more authoritarian systems to legitimate their rule, as well as insulate themselves from attacks arising from abroad. These elements reflect notions of soft power, which the next section discusses.

Strategic Narratives as Soft Power

Strategic narratives can be understood as a more effective concept and tool in explaining how soft power functions. The international relations scholar Joseph Nye (1990, 2004) has argued that an important element of a nation's "soft power," or its ability to attract other nations and citizens of other nations, rests in perceptions of the nation's political values and processes. Nye conceives of soft power as a different type of influence from coercive power, which is usually exemplified by military or economic strength. For Nye, the extent to which one's political values are positively perceived by foreign nationals is directly attributable to the nation's ability to persuade, entice, or otherwise cajole foreign nations, and their citizens, to support larger political or cultural goals. Political values are not the only element of soft power, of course, but to Nye, they are a critical element in impacting foreign attitudes. Other elements that are important for soft power, according to Nye, are a nation's culture and its policies. Here we further argue that media has a direct role in projecting a nation's soft power to domestic audiences through constructed narratives.

The concept of soft power has not gone unchallenged, of course, for its vagueness, the difficulty in quantifying it, and its overly simplistic use of a few indicators to capture something as difficult as geopolitical influence. Nevertheless, it remains a helpful construct for thinking about opinion formation of foreign audiences, and how sometimes abstract ideals and values can influence a nation's ability to engage foreign audiences. Although the Chinese have probably invested the most in soft power initiatives, other nations (such as India and South Korea) are, either directly or indirectly, seeking to increase their own geopolitical influence through enhancing soft power, normally in the form of cultural diplomacy.

Clearly, the concept is attractive to policy-makers, who see in as not just a description of how nations relate to one another, but often as a prescription for enhancing national prestige, and use it as a rhetorical justification domestically to pursue further investment in communication infrastructure (Hayden, 2012). Regardless, academic analysis has tended to shy away from attempts to systematically measure soft power.

In fact, while soft power has become one of the most used terms in international relations, the vagueness of the concept has discouraged systematic attempts to measure what actual soft power entails. When it is unclear what soft power is, it is hard to design measures to capture it. In recent years, a number of public diplomacy scholars have sought to better contextualize and define the concept, as well as provide metrics for measuring it (Banks, 2011; Hayden, 2012, Pahlavi, 2007). Moreover, as Pamment (2014) argues, when soft power is the focus of examination, it is typically on the policy goals and strategies for soft power, rather than its actual effects or manifestations. The number of academic efforts to evaluate soft power fall far behind the number of studies that explore the concept from a perspective that emphasizes policy goals or campaign activities. But, more to our purpose here, soft power metrics typically focus on what nations can do (and are doing) to influence their reputation, rather than on how events (and their responses to those events) might impact the nation's reputation, and hence, power of attraction.

For instance, in mid-2017, the Portland Group, a communications consulting firm, released the third edition of a "soft power index," which ranks thirty nations according to their soft power. In these rankings, the US slipped from first place the previous year to third, almost exclusively because of the "America first" rhetoric of Donald Trump, and the perceived shift to nationalist and isolationist political sentiments in the US. Although a number of factors in the analysis remained constant, and thus would not change the overall soft power ranking of the US, the one element that changed dramatically was a fall in global public opinion of the US and its political values. During the same time, the UK fell as well, because of global sentiment after the national referendum to leave the European Union, a move that seemed to also undermine the UK's commitment to global engagement (McClory, 2017). The author of the report explicitly linked the isolationist and nationalist stances of the US election and the Brexit referendum with dramatic falls in public opinion surveys of the reputations of the two nations, while France (which in an election had recently rejected a populist and nationalist candidate for President, Marine Le Pen) rose to first. While the methodology and the findings might be called into question on a number of levels, what the analysis does reveal is that the US presidential election and its aftermath took a clear toll on global perceptions of the US. There is undoubtedly some linkage between global perceptions of a nation's political values and institutions and its influence on that global audience.

Recently, Roselle et al. (2014) have called for the reconceptualization of soft power as a form of strategic narrative. They argue that the understanding that Nye was trying to advance was "hijacked" by efforts to create policy-specific tools and metrics, and that what Nye was actually trying to advance was an understanding of geopolitical influence shaped more by images of a nation. Those images come largely from what they call "strategic narratives," which are narratives that explain the world to audiences. The concept of strategic narratives becomes a more useful conceptual tool to help understand how attraction occurs in international relations, as well as how soft power resources become transferred into attempts to influence others through narratives. Roselle et al. (2014) provides an example of this in that, while state actors might attempt to augment their soft power resources by producing a documentary on some issue, that documentary, however, still needs to be aired and watched by audiences for it to have an effect. This example showcases the need to focus on how soft power resources are converted or made of use, not just built up by the home nation. Thus, soft power abroad is necessarily tied to how populations of foreign nations process and reconstruct messages through the shared understanding of the society. As such, conversion strategies are "critical variables that do not receive enough attention" (73). As Szostek (2017a) states, "The framework of strategic narrative thus offers a theoretical account of the relationship between communication and international influence that is more transparent and coherent than soft power" (575), and also shows how communication in international affairs is often a matter of contestation, not just soft or benign attraction.

According to Roselle et al. (2014), the idea of strategic narratives helps showcase how soft power resources are packaged and projected to define and attract other nations' notions of identity, political and cultural values, and notions of what is possible in conceptualizing visions of world order. Specifically, as a form of soft power, strategic narratives can be a power resource by a) creating compelling narratives as people are drawn to certain actors, events, and explanations that describe the history of a country, or its specific policies; b) processes to understand how power resources work broadly; and c) uses of narrative strategically in its manifestation of itself through narrative contestation in complex media ecologies. In understanding international influence from the perspective of strategic narrative construction, projection, and reception, rather than soft power, one can better understand how political actors attract, or make less attractive, their policies and interests more broadly, and how these narrative constructions are contested.

Similarly, Szostek (2017a) critiques Nye's conceptualization of soft power by explaining how different kinds of attractive power are often conflated, arguing in support of the use of strategic narrative instead. Attraction can occur naturally, from shared priorities and values resulting in subjects changing their priorities and values. However, this also occurs with attempts to make those of other actors unattractive. Citing Price (2015), Szostek (2017a) explains that "soft power can be 'surprisingly aggressive' and perceived among the elites and wider societies of target states as hostile, debilitating intrusion which threatens established societal norms" (574). Likewise, Roselle et al. (2014) explain that attraction is more than persuasion through rational argument in that it includes affect or feeling (Nye, 2004), with Mattern (2005a, 2005b) adding that attraction can be coercive, including the use of language to rhetorically trap others, by pointing to contradictions undermining their sense of identity and thereby restricting their action. Attraction can also be a fulfillment of needs based on values when they address individual and collective desires and needs; these values, once articulated and claimed, can also constrain future behavior. Thus, in the context of the 2016 US presidential election, narratives can serve to both define and augment US values and policies, as well as undermine more authoritarian, or less democratic, governments. However, if the narratives told about the US election are more critical, we can expect them to have the opposite effect as well.

When looking at the contestation of strategic narratives, we can better understand the complexities of political actors' offensive and defensive strategies of identity construction and resistance implicating the attractiveness of specific policies and conceptualizations of world order and power. Feklyunina (2016) provides a model to understand narratives as a means of soft power based on how widely narratives of collective identity projected by the former are accepted or resisted in the latter and how much influence the receptive audiences have over policy-making. However, Szostek (2017a) argues that this model places too much emphasis on the reception of narratives and over emphasizes the extent to which compatible narratives of collective identity being shared interests actually occurs. Drawing from the literature on nation branding and strategic narratives, Szostek (2017a) argues that political actors can use media to positively form identities, as well as employ defensive measures involving state-led attacks on the identities of critical other states via official pronouncements and mass media.

Strategic narratives then become a competitive projection of state identities and are not exclusively a matter of benign attraction, as the soft power framework implies they might be.

We should expect foreign nations to draw upon their own national identity discourse to resist, reinterpret, and ultimately reconstruct the narratives of US democracy and its benefits, as well as national identity constructions to reaffirm the commitment of that state's collective identity. As Szostek (2017a) explains, while identity is an important understanding of a shared collective self, no self can be understood in isolation resulting in narrative characterization of others as well. The strategic narrative framework allows both these aspects of state identity communication to be studied together, and thus aids holistic analysis of whether attempts to secure desired identities are succeeding (588). Thus, one must pay attention to both internal and external audiences of strategic narratives, or in the case of state actors' strategic narratives, domestic and external audiences.

However, there are limitations to this as well in that overly antagonistic definitions of other countries' identities threatens to undermine the purpose of strategic narratives as a form of international influence. As in the case of Russia, its strategic narrative and branding rhetoric emphasizes its prestige and power by characterizing the West as foolish, criminal, and immoral, making it successful on the domestic front, but not the international one (Szostek, 2017a). Such narratives also run the risk of losing domestic effectiveness, if they are allowed to drift too far from the collectively shared reality of the society or are in such contrast to other items of exposure from which the population forms its reality on a given event as to become altogether ignored. This is because successful narratives rely upon "the degree to which an external strategic narrative resonates with local political myths" (Schmitt, 2018, 2) in that a strategic narrative's reception and acceptance within a political community is contingent upon its ability to appeal to the values, interests, and prejudices of its target audiences. The legitimacy or credibility of these narratives is therefore extremely important, especially in authoritarian, non-organic news media systems. As Hartig (2015) found in his strategic narrative analysis of China's Confucius Institutes, the effectiveness of their strategic narratives is limited in that foreign audiences question whether they are hearing about the true versus "correct" image of China. The use of strategic narratives as a means to bolster one's soft power can be a double-edged sword in that those constructing narratives must decide how to balance their domestically oriented narratives with their external ones.

Thus, from the framework of strategic narratives, comparisons of national and regional news media reporting of the US presidential election tell us not just about perceptions of the US, they also tell us important stories about perceptions of the global order, and how other nations interpret their role in that order. This perspective is very helpful for understanding how "soft power" might be conceptualized in more concrete terms in that people's understandings of a nation, and their attraction to the culture, history, or values of that nation, are largely shaped and reflected in the constructed narratives that manifest in their media systems, whether of friendship, rivalry, or outright hostility. But, contrary to the hopes of policy-makers, most of the time it is exceedingly difficult, if not impossible, for a nation to firmly control the narrative that is told about it around the world. Rather, the narratives that matter are told by trusted voices from one's own culture and language, and the narratives that policy-makers and diplomats try to tell to foreign audiences are easily undermined by the local translators, usually in the form of the local press. In describing and commenting upon the US presidential election, national level media reveals underlying assumptions and narratives about that nation, and its role vis-à-vis the US, and its role in the global order. In reflecting upon the events happening in the US, national media outlets describe a reality that has to, in some sense, reflect the sensibilities and shared understandings of its audience. All media, in that sense, are reflective, in that they reveal underlying fears, assumptions, expectations, and even worldviews, as they seek to describe something external to that nation.

Theoretically, then, our project seeks to deepen our understanding, from a comparative methodology, of how "events," such as the US presidential election, provide the raw material for global contestations of the global order. We seek to show how these media outlets interpret the same raw material, to lead to competing narratives to those which are presented in "international media," such as the BBC and CNN. Although our analysis doesn't allow us to explore in depth the role of governmental policy in defining those strategic narratives, it does allow us to see how events are interpreted within dominant, regional strategic narratives, serving to reinforce rather than challenge them.

Plan for the Volume

It is in this context of a global contest for soft power, by telling stories (or strategic narratives) about the world, that we have examined global media responses to the US presidential election of 2016. We sought to understand how the narratives about the election that circulate among important global audiences might impact US standing in the world, as well as global understandings and contestation of democracy more generally. More specifically, we wanted to see how the candidates, the US democratic process itself, and the outcome of the election were "made sense of" by global media outlets and their audiences, and what lessons they took from the election in coming to define their own ideas about democratic governance and US leadership. The narratives that spread globally about the 2016 US election contained elements of all three narrative levels identified by Roselle et al. (2014). At the international system level, narratives about the election touched on the role of the US in the global order, relations between the US (the dominant superpower) and other nations, the values that would drive the global system moving forward, and ultimately, the global leadership role of the US. At the national level, these same narratives provided explanations about changing US values, culture and policies, potential US relations with one's own nation, and the future of the US itself. In doing so, they also came to define their own national identities in comparison to the US. Finally, at the issue level, these narratives informed global audiences about the character of the future US president, potential US policy responses to trade, immigration, defense, and human rights, as well as about the policies of other nations towards future engagement with the US and its global interests.

These responses to the election tell us not just about perceptions of the US, they also tell us important stories about the nations themselves that are telling the stories. In describing and commenting upon the US election, global media additionally reveal underlying assumptions and narratives about that nation, and its role vis-à-vis the US, and its role in the global order. In reflecting upon the events happening in the US, media outlets describe a reality that has to, in some sense, reflect the sensibilities of its audience. All media, in that sense, are reflective, in that they reveal underlying fears, assumptions, expectations, and even worldviews, as they seek to describe something external to that nation. In this project, we hoped to not just understand the perceptions of the US and its political processes, but also how those processes are explained, and how those explanations might uncover deeper narratives about place in the global system. The presidential election, in many ways, was the predefining event regarding the incoming administration and the US's soft power. The ways in which audiences around the world viewed the US's political processes, institutions, and values, will undoubtedly affect the ability of the US to further build goodwill around the world.

To uncover these narratives about the US and its role in the world, we developed a common methodological framework and similar data sources from three regions of the world. Each region was chosen because each sees itself in some ways as a rival or competitor to the US, or in some cases, a victim of US policy. While there would undoubtedly be much to learn from the many nations and regions we excluded (including most of Africa, Latin America, Western Europe, and countless other regions), we chose to focus our attention on the regions that are, in some ways, the most problematic to the US and its foreign policy.

In Chapter 2, we explain the overall methodological approach to the volume, including a discussion of the data sets, the mechanism we used for harvesting the data, the coding schemes we used to analyze them, and the ways in which we sought to guarantee the value of comparative analysis. All of the data for this project were drawn from a media harvesting system developed by BBN Raytheon and deployed at Texas A&M University. The researchers behind this project were primarily located at Texas A&M University and at Mississippi State University, although a number of other research assistants also worked on the project.

The chapters following all report on an individual region or country and provide the data results and observations for each. Many comparative studies end up comparing vastly different sets of data, but for this project, we sought to compare like data sets from different countries, using conceptual categories that could be easily compared with one another. Although the concerns and issues of Russia and China are very different, we sought to, as much as possible, include context-specific awareness of the country, its political and media environment, and past and current tensions with the US that might impact upon the narratives that were produced about the election. Each chapter thus begins with a brief overview of the country/region and its specific relations with the US that might impact coverage, then provides a quantitative overview of our findings, followed by a discussion of the key findings of that team. Chapter 3 reports on the findings from China, Chapter 4 from the Arab world, and Chapter 5 from Russia. These are provided not in order of importance, either politically or strategically, but merely in an order that helps us to clearly delineate the different concerns of each nation.

Chapter 6 provides an overall synthesis of the research findings, reflects upon the meaning of the US presidential election in comparative perspective, and discusses their implications for strategic narratives. We also discuss issues that arose during the course of this project that might impact our ability to generalize beyond the nations that we have observed, and we conclude with observations regarding how these narratives about the US and its political process are likely to impact the ability of the US to provide global leadership in the future. Whether desirable or not, there is little doubt that the US is a global leader, in finance, in military might, in cultural power, and in political priorities. We hope to provide specific insights into how that leadership is viewed, judged, enhanced, or undermined by global coverage of one of the premier political spectacles of the world, the US presidential election, and how our shared future might be impacted by that coverage.

Conclusion

We have argued in this chapter that the stories that circulate within nations, particularly those that are widely disseminated by major media outlets, form the foundational understanding of other nations on the part of the citizenry. We are by no means suggesting that citizens blindly follow the narratives that are articulated by media, whether state-run or private, but rather that the media do typically provide the narrative building blocks for geopolitical worldviews. When citizens don't have in-depth, personal knowledge of other nations, then they almost always rely upon the narrative elements provided to them by mass media. These narratives might emerge from popular media (movies and television shows), but the political narratives that take root are typically those provided by news media, whether through broadcast, web-based media, or print. This is true, not just of how US citizens view Mexico, Canada, China, or France, but also of how the citizens of those nations view the US.

Thus, an essential element of understanding how citizens of other nations view the US is to understand how the US political system, its processes and values, and the outcomes, are portrayed in news media around the world. When those narratives portray menacing or incompetent political figures, ill-intentioned policies or actions, or even system-wide breakdowns, it can dramatically impact the sense of security, goodwill, or comfort with other nations.

References

Aalberg, T., Papathanassopoulos, S., Soroka, S., Curran, J., Hayashi, K., Iyengar, S., & Tiffen, R. (2013). International TV news, foreign affairs interest and public knowledge: A comparative study of foreign news coverage and public opinion in 11 countries. *Journalism Studies*, 14(3), 387–406.

Arquilla, J., & Ronfeldt, D. (1999). The advent of netwar: Analytic background. *Studies in Conflict and Terrorism*, 22(3), 193–206.

Arsenault, A., Hong, S., & Price, M. (2017). Strategic narratives of the Arab Spring and after. In A. Miskimmon, B. O'Loughlin, & L. Roselle (Eds.), *Forging the world: Strategic narratives and international relations* (pp. 190–217). Ann Arbor, MI: University of Michigan Press.

Banks, R. (2011). *A resource guide to public diplomacy evaluation.* Los Angeles, CA: Figueroa Press.

Berenskoetter, F. (2014). Parameters of a national biography. *European Journal of International Relations,* 20(1), 262–288.

Berinski, A. J. (2007). Assuming the costs of war: Events, elites, and American public support for military conflict. *The Journal of Politics,* 69(4), 975–997.

Boudana, S., & Segev, E. (2017). The bias of provocation narratives in international news. *The International Journal of Press/Politics,* 22(3), 314–332.

Burke, K. (1969). *A grammar of motives.* Los Angeles: University of California Press.

Burton, J. (2018). NATO's "global partners" in Asia: Shifting strategic narratives. *Asian Security,* 14(1), 8–23.

Castells, M. (2008). The new public sphere: Global civil society, communication networks, and global governance. *The Annals of the American Academy of Political and Social Science,* 616(1), 78–93.

Chowdhury, A., & Krebs, R. R. (2009). Making and mobilizing moderates: Rhetorical strategy, political networks, and counterterrorism. *Security Studies,* 18(3), 371–399.

Coticchia, F. (2016). A controversial warplane: Narratives, counternarratives, and the Italian debate on the F-35. *Alternatives,* 41(4), 194–213.

CNN (2016, May 9). Why the US election is interesting and why it matters to the world at large. Retrieved from http://cnnpressroom.blogs.cnn.com/2016/05/09/new-research-shows-widespread-international-interest-in-us-election-with-cnn-as-1-news-destination/.

Curran, J., Esser, F., Hallin, D. C., Hayashi, K., & Lee, C. C. (2015). International news and global integration: A five-nation reappraisal. *Journalism Studies,* 18(2), 118–134.

de Franco, C. (2012). *Media power and the transformation of war.* Basingstoke: Palgrave MacMillan.

de Graaf, B., Dimitriu, G., & Ringsmose, J. (Eds.). (2015). *Strategic narratives, public opinion and war: Winning domestic support for the Afghan War.* New York: Routledge.

de Vreese, C. H., & Boomgaarden, H. (2006). News, political knowledge and participation: The differential effects of news media exposure on political knowledge and participation. *Acta Politica,* 41(4), 317–341.

Eberle, J. (2017). Narrative, desire, ontological security, transgression: Fantasy as a factor in international politics. *Journal of International Relations and Development,* 1–26.

Ejdus, F., & Božović, M. (2017). Grammar, context and power: Securitization of the 2010 Belgrade Pride Parade. *Southeast European and Black Sea Studies,* 17(1), 17–34.

Faizullaev, A., & Cornut, J. (2017). Narrative practice in international politics and diplomacy: the case of the Crimean crisis. *Journal of International Relations and Development,* 20(3), 578–604.

Farnsworth, S. J., Lichter, S. R., & Schatz, R. (2013). *The global president: International media and the US government.* Lanham, MD: Rowman & Littlefield.

Feklyunina, V. (2016). Soft power and identity: Russia, Ukraine and the "Russian world(s)". *European Journal of International Relations,* 22(4), 773–796.

Fisher, W. F. (1984). Narration as a human communication paradigm: The case of public moral argument. *Communication Monographs,* 51(1), 1–22.

Fisher, W. F. (1989). *Human reason as narration: Toward a philosophy of reason, value, and action.* Columbia, SC: University of South Carolina Press.

Flew, T., Iosifidis, P., & Steemers, J., (2016). *Global media and national policies: The return of the state.* London, UK: Palgrave MacMillan.

Freedman, L. (2006). *The transformation in strategic affairs.* London, UK: Routledge.

Garrett, C. S. (2018). Constructing narratives of global order: The Obama presidency, TPP, TTIP, and the contested politics of geoeconomics. *Atlantic Studies Global Currents,* 1–21.

Gerbner, G., & Marvanyi, G. (1977). The many worlds of the world's press. *Journal of Communication*, 27(1), 52–66.

Gill, B., & Huang, Y. (2006). Sources and limits of Chinese "soft power". *Survival*, 48(2), 17–36.

Goddard, S. E., & Krebs, R. R. (2015). Rhetoric, legitimation, and grand strategy. *Security Studies*, 24(1), 5–36.

Golan, G. (2006). Inter-media agenda setting and global news coverage: Assessing the influence of the New York Times on three network television evening news programs. *Journalism Studies*, 7(2), 323–333.

Hallin, D. C., & Mancini, P. (2004). *Comparing media systems: Three models of media and politics*. Cambridge, UK: Cambridge University Press.

Hallin, D. C., & Mancini, P. (Eds.). (2011). *Comparing media systems beyond the Western world*. Cambridge, UK: Cambridge University Press.

Hartig, F. (2015). Communicating China to the world: Confucius Institutes and China's strategic narratives. *Politics*, 35(3–4), 245–258.

Hayden, C. (2012) *The rhetoric of soft power: Public diplomacy in global context*. Lanham, MD: Lexington Books.

Heck, A. (2017). Images, visions and narrative identity formation of ISIS. *Global Discourse*, 7(2–3), 244–259.

Hinck, R. S., Kluver, R., & Cooley, S. (2018). Russia re-envisions the world: Strategic narratives in Russian broadcast and news media during 2015. *Russian Journal of Communication*, 10(1), 21–37.

Hinck, R. S., Manly, J., Kluver, R., & Norris, W. (2016). Interpreting and shaping geopolitics in Chinese media: The discourse of the "'New style of great power relations'". *Asian Journal of Communication*, 26(5), 427–445.

Hinck, R. S., Manly, J., Kluver, R., & Norris, W. (2018). Geopolitical dimensions of "The China Dream": Exploring strategic narratives of the Chinese Communist Party. *China Media Research*, 14(3), 99–110.

Irvin-Erickson, D. (2017). Genocide discourses: American and Russian strategic narratives of conflict in Iraq and Ukraine. *Politics & Governance*, 5(3), 130–145.

Kariel, H., & Rosenvall, L. A. (1995). *Places in the news: A study of news flows*. Ottawa, ON: Carleton University Press.

Klarevas, L. (2002). The "essential domino" of military operations: American public opinion and the use of force. *International Studies Perspectives*, 3(4), 417–437.

Kluver, R., Campbell, H. A., & Balfour, S. (2013). Language and the boundaries of research: Media monitoring technologies in international media research. *Journal of Broadcasting & Electronic Media*, 57(1), 4–19.

Krebs, R. R. (2015). *Narrative and the making of US national security*. Cambridge, UK: Cambridge University Press.

Lemay-Hébert, N., & Visoka, G. (2017). Normal peace: A new strategic narrative of intervention. *Politics and Governance*, 5(3), 146–156.

Liao, N. (2017). The power of strategic narratives: The communicative dynamics of Chinese nationalism and foreign relations. In A. Miskimmon, B. O'Loughlin, & L. Roselle (Eds.), *Forging the world: Strategic narratives and international relations* (pp.110–133). Ann Arbor, MI: University of Michigan Press.

Mattern, J. B. (2005a). Why soft power isn't so soft: Representational force and the sociolinguistic construction of attraction in world politics. *Millennium*, 33(3), 583–612.

Mattern, J. B. (2005b). *Ordering international politics: Identity, crisis and representational force*. New York: Routledge.

McClory, J. (2017). The Soft Power 30. The Portland Group. Retrieved from http://softp ower30.portland-communications.com/.

Miskimmon, A., & O'Loughlin, B. (2017). Russia's narratives of global order: Great power legacies in a polycentric world. *Politics and Governance*, 5(3), 111–120.

Miskimmon, A., O'Loughlin, B., & Roselle, L. (2013). *Strategic narratives: Communication power and the new world order*. New York: Routledge.

Miskimmon, A., O'Loughlin, B., & Roselle, L. (Eds.). (2017). *Forging the world: Strategic narratives and international relations*. Ann Arbor, MI: University of Michigan Press.

Mody, B. (2010). *The geopolitics of representation in foreign news: Explaining Darfur*. Lanham, MD: Lexington Books.

Natarajan, K. (2014). Digital public diplomacy and a strategic narrative for India. *Strategic Analysis*, 38(1), 91–106.

Nossek, H., & Kunelius, R. (2012). News flows, global journalism and climate summits. In E. Eide & R. Kunelius (Eds.), *Media meets climate: The global challenge for journalism* (pp. 67–86). Göteborg, Sweden: Nordicom.

Nye, J. (1990). Soft power. *Foreign Policy*, 80, 153–171.

Nye, J. (2004). *Soft power: The means to success in world politics*. New York: Public Affairs.

Pahlavi, P. C. (2007). Evaluating public diplomacy programmes. *Hague Journal of Diplomacy*, 2, 255–281.

Pamment, J. (2014). Articulating influence: Toward a research agenda for interpreting the evaluation of soft power, public diplomacy, and nation brands. *Public Relations Review*, 40(1), 50–59.

Papathanassopoulos, S., Coen, S., Curran, J., Aalberg, T., Rowe, D., Jones, P., & Tiffen, R. (2013). Online threat, but television is still dominant: A comparative study of 11 nations' news consumption. *Journalism Practice*, 7(6), 690–704.

Powers, S., & Gilboa, E. (2007). The public diplomacy of Al Jazeera. In P. Seib (Eds.), *New media and the new Middle East* (pp. 53–80). New York: Palgrave Macmillan.

Price, M. E. (2015). *Free expression, globalism, and the new strategic communication*. Cambridge, UK: Cambridge University Press.

Reporters Without Borders. *2018 World Press Freedom Index*. Retrieved from https://rsf. org/en/ranking

Ringsmose, J., & Børgesen, B. K. (2011). Shaping public attitudes towards the deployment of military power: NATO, Afghanistan and the use of strategic narratives. *European Security*, 20(4), 505–528.

Roselle, L. (2017). Strategic narratives and alliances: The cases of intervention in Libya (2011) and economic sanctions against Russia (2014). *Politics and Governance*, 5(3), 99–110.

Roselle, L., Miskimmon, A., & O'Loughlin, B. (2014). Strategic narrative: A new means to understand soft power. *Media, War & Conflict*, 7(1), 70–84.

Saari, S. (2014). Russia's post-Orange revolution strategies to increase its influence in former Soviet republics: Public diplomacy *po russkii*. *Europe-Asia Studies*, 66(1), 50–66.

Schmitt, O. (2018). When are strategic narratives effective? The shaping of political discourse through the interaction between political myths and strategic narratives. *Contemporary Security Policy*, 1–25.

Schumacher, T. (2015). Uncertainty at the EU's borders: Narratives of EU external relations in the revised European Neighbourhood Policy towards the southern borderlands. *European Security*, 24(3), 381–401.

Senn, M. (2017). The art of constructing (in)security: Probing rhetorical strategies of securitisation. *Journal of International Relations and Development*, 20(3), 605–630.

Simpson, E. (2012). *War from the ground up*. London: Hurst & Company.

Skalamera, M. (2018). Understanding Russia's energy turn to China: Domestic narratives and national identity priorities. *Post-Soviet Affairs*, 34(1), 55–77.

Snyder, J. (2015). Dueling security stories: Wilson and lodge talk strategy. *Security Studies*, 24(1), 171–197.

Snyder, T. (1998). The Polish–Lithuanian commonwealth since 1989: National narratives in relations among Poland, Lithuania, Belarus and Ukraine. *Nationalism and Ethnic Politics*, 4(3), 1–32.

Soldatov, A., & Borogan, I. (2015). *The red web: The struggle between Russia's digital dictators and the new online revolutionaries*. New York: Public Affairs.

Steele, B. J. (2012). *Defacing power*. Ann Arbor, MI: University of Michigan Press.

Suslov, M. (2017). The production of *Novorossiya*: A territorial brand in public debates. *Europe-Asia Studies*, 69(2), 202–221.

Szostek, J. (2017a). Defense and promotion of desired state identity in Russia's strategic narrative. *Geopolitics*, 22(3), 571–593.

Szostek, J. (2017b). The power and limits of Russia's strategic narrative in Ukraine: The role of linkage. *Perspectives on Politics*, 15(2), 379–395.

van Noort, C. (2017). Study of strategic narratives: The case of BRICS. *Politics & Governance*, 5(3), 121–129.

Wu, H. D. (2000). Systematic determinants of international news coverage. *Journal of Communication*, 50(2), 113–130.

2

RESEARCH DESIGN

Measuring Narratives Within Local Media Ecologies

Introduction

Elections, and US presidential elections in particular, are important political and cultural moments reflective of democratic values purported to be shared globally. Like many US citizens, international audiences come to witness the campaigning and discussion of issues primarily through media. Indeed, as Strömbäck and Kaid (2008) argue in their comparison of international election news coverage, mass media has become the main channel for political information, often serving as the locus of negotiation between a country's citizenry and the institutions involved in government and opinion formation. Consequently, depictions of "reality" are conveyed through the mass media thereby impacting how people perceive reality. Thus, media provides more than just information; it reveals the values and culture of political communities impacting how we make sense of our world and politics. Because news media marks an important cultural site where members ritualistically come to view the world in a particular way at a specific time (i.e., Carey, 2009) and with recent scholarship noting that globalization has led not to a homogenization of values but rather a strengthening of local, national, and regional media in reporting on international news (Flew, Iosifidis, & Steemers, 2016), it is imperative today to explore how other nations come to view and understand global electoral events like the US presidential election.

Unfortunately, data-driven research looking into global media tends to focus on Western-language news, underplaying the importance of non-Western language news reporting of global events (Kluver, Campbell, & Balfour, 2013). One reason for this arises from Western academics' lack of foreign language ability. As noted in Chapter 1, this is increasingly problematic, as rising control of localized media systems by nations across the globe results in an increased ability to package and apply narrative interpretation to news content in culturally unique ways. For Western scholars to overcome this issue, access to foreign media is a critical step. Utilizing the Media Monitoring System (M3S), an open source platform that automatically captures, transcribes, and translates foreign media, this project analyzed foreign media reporting of the 2016 US presidential campaign within Chinese, Russian, and Arabic language news.

Analysis of the 2016 US presidential election provides scholars with a unique site for study and comparison of global news media in a few key ways. US presidential elections are important global media events in that they receive considerable coverage across the world (Curran, Esser, Hallin, Hayashi, & Lee, 2015), with US policy effecting not only individual country's domestic politics and policies, but also the world at large. Furthermore, US foreign policy discourse traditionally places the US as the flag-bearer of democratic values and Western liberal democracy with its presidential elections being the model of democratic governance.

One hallmark of US presidential campaigns are presidential debates. Other countries have incorporated this democratic practice into their own elections and even modeled their debate formats after that of the US (Hinck, Hinck, Hinck, Ghanem, & Dailey, 2015). Consequently, US elections serve an important resource for American soft power implicating it in both advantageous and disadvantageous ways. New communication technologies, the increase in non-Western media outlets, and the advent of a global network society has resulted in foreign publics having greater exposure and knowledge of US campaigns making news reporting an important means by which countries can bolster soft power resources and formulate images of distant countries affecting foreign policy and public opinion towards those nations (Adoni & Mane, 1984; Peng, 2004; Castells, 2008). Furthermore, with US elections typically including three nationally televised debates allowing for domestic and foreign media coverage of the election to be extended before election day with significant commentary placed before and after each debate regarding who won, what the candidates must do given their current polling status, as well as providing audiences with visual "tests" of how the candidates perform under pressure. All of this helps ensure the newsworthiness of US presidential elections and provides insight into what type of president those candidates may become and what policy directions they might pursue.

This project aimed at understanding how various foreign localized media systems presented the US presidential election to their citizens; what narratives were used to present the US and its democratic processes; how various national interests were aligned with certain candidates; the attributes of the candidates most focused on; and the legitimacy of the US process. In doing so, those narratives told by foreign media also reveal and draw upon their own cultural, social, and political narratives and myths to connect the US election to their own experience in meaningful and coherent ways. Our analysis, then, aimed to accomplish two principal things: first, to show us how various foreign localized media system present the US and Western democracy; second, to show how these media systems see their own governmental system in relation to the US and the global order.

Selection of Cases

Three cases were selected for comparative analysis. Researchers examined national and regional media reporting from Russia and China, as well as Arabic language news outlets. These three areas were chosen because they, singularly and collectively, represent perhaps the most important sources of contestation of dominant American political values. There are some similarities between these cases, in that, generally speaking, they have tight state–media relationships with heavy government influence and censorship, as well as more authoritarian governmental systems relative to the US. As such, all three of these national/regional media systems are ranked as having little freedom of the press by Reporters Without Borders' World Freedom Press Index, with Russia ranking 148 in the world, China 176, and Arabic-speaking nations such as Iraq 160, Jordan 132, Syria 177, and Lebanon 100 (Reporters Without Borders, 2018).

Indeed, these nations are distinct from Western media ecologies in their close state–media relationships. Since the founding of the People's Republic of China (PRC), Chinese leaders have sought to control and define how their citizens understand their social realities in an effort to support and mobilize the Chinese public backing of Chinese Communist Party (CCP) policies (Link & Qiang, 2013), and today, control of the media is as important as ever in China. As Stockmann and Gallagher (2011) note, "the Chinese media serve as a bridge connecting Chinese citizens to the state, a bridge that is even more important as other key institutions of social control and influence have weakened" (442). Modern versions of this include self-censorship, news reporting and framing techniques, ideotainment, as well as China's propaganda department's instruction on news reporting resulting in conformity among media workers through their exercising of self-censorship to avoid trouble (Lee, He, & Huang, 2007). As a consequence of Chinese media's recent marketization, CCP influence in the media now goes beyond functioning as a "mouthpiece" for communist policy by providing more compelling messages in accord with state censorship demands, while satisfying Chinese news consumers' interest in real-life stories and problems (Stockmann & Gallagher, 2011). As Shen and Guo (2013) argue, Chinese media helps legitimize CCP governance through its monopoly of power over framing key issues in the media, helping to consolidate national identity and Party ideology.

Online, Chinese media influence tactics include controlling and monitoring systems such as firewalls, shutting down publications or websites, and jailing dissident journalists, bloggers, and activists (Xu, 2014). While carefully controlling who can speak and on what topics, the Chinese government pursues "authoritarian deliberation" (He, 2006), with the Chinese government experimenting with democratic institutions designed to provide feedback and information from its citizenry in promotion of state policy (Fishkin, He, Luskin, & Siu, 2010; Leib & He, 2006; Jiang, 2008; He & Warren, 2011; He, 2014; Stockmann & Luo, 2017). As Lorentzen (2014) argues, Chinese censorship takes a form of strategic censorship in that it permits some watchdog journalism in order to improve regime power and governance. Chinese authorities also utilize cultural myths in narrative forms such as, most recently, the China Dream (Hinck, Kluver, Norris, & Manly, 2018) and the New Style of Great Power Relations (Hinck, Manly, Kluver, & Norris, 2016).

Likewise, historically Russia too has enjoyed a close state–media relationship. While social reforms in the 1860s followed by more capitalist economic programs supported the growth of daily newspapers in major urban areas, even then the core feature of journalism in Russia was the practice of censorship. Pre-publication censorship started in 1804 in imperial Russia and with the later rise of communism the Party implemented censorship practices designed to suppress political resistance and shut down dissident voices. During communist rule, journalism was viewed as a transmission of information from political leaders to its citizens. This model was characterized as top-down control focusing on high-circulation, surveillance of content production and control of news flow, planned financing from state-Party resources, with heavy investment in communication infrastructure, and a lack of attention to audience needs or advertising. With the fall of communism, media ownership opened up and became a major force in Russian politics, leading politicians to exert greater influence and reassert control over state television broadcast in particular (Vartanova, 2012)

Today, a central aim in Russian state media control has been the creation of a single, controlled information space for citizens (Schenk, 2012). Russian media scholar Sarah Oates (2007) argues that virtually all Russian national TV channels are either directly or indirectly controlled by the state, and the major newspapers mainly reflect the views of the regime as they are heavily subsidized through the government. To further consolidate its control over the media, the Russian state has cracked down on civil society and independent media, with Human Rights Watch (2015) noting that the Kremlin was: "intensifying its crackdown on civil society, media, and the Internet, as it sought to control the narrative about developments in Ukraine, including Russia's occupation of Crimea and its support to insurgents in eastern Ukraine." Additionally, the Russian Parliament and authorities have adopted laws and engaged in practices to increase anti-Western hysteria, arrested political activists, shut down independent online media, stifled free expression, and encouraged sentiment against the LGBT (lesbian, gay, bisexual, and transsexual) community (Human Rights Watch, 2015).

In terms of messaging strategies, Paul and Matthews (2016) argue that state-led Russian communication practices reflect a "firehose of falsehood" strategy whereby Russian media utilizes high numbers of communication channels, such as the Internet, social media, journalism, and other media outlets to disseminate partial truths or outright fictions in order to entertain, confuse, and overwhelm audiences. Internally, President Putin has been found to brand himself through various stage-managed events by offering images of himself as a political brand emphasizing different personality characteristics for different target audiences (Hill & Gaddy, 2015). Russian media has also drawn on soft power concepts by positioning its reputation as a critical component of its media diplomacy by emphasizing its traditional values, prestige, and status (Skalamera, 2018; Krickovic & Weber, 2016; Lo, 2015; Hinck, Kluver, & Cooley, 2018; Cooley & Stokes, 2018).

Describing the Arab media landscape is more difficult, given the plurality of nations. And yet, this regional system is still based around a shared or mutually comprehensible language implicating consumer choice. Kraidy (2011) argues in support of treating pan-Arab media systems as a site for comparative media analysis, and openly contests the "universal applicability of the nation-state" as the unit of analysis in comparative media. Accordingly, Kraidy explains that this system, covering twenty-two nation-states, has formed a distinct transnational, pan-Arab system. This began in 1990 with Arab national broadcasting systems focusing on development and propaganda, and national unity becoming overshadowed by a pan-Arab satellite television industry.

Before its liberalization, pan-Arab media was a fragmented network of national media characterized by a high degree of political parallelism. But with the adoption of satellite technology in the 1990s, Arab media became an integrated transnational system which penetrates national terrestrial mediascapes (Kraidy & Khalil 2009). This interdependent pan-Arab market of private, state-owned, and mixed media is neither authoritarian nor mobilizing (Rugh, 2018), nor even liberal, because it is inconsistently monitored by the government and highly driven by commercial competition on a national, regional, and global scale. It transcends national and, in some aspects, regional borders to form an expanded market that also caters to diasporas around the world with a number of outlets still headquartered abroad.

With regards to state interference, Kraidy (2011) notes that the political and media systems in the region vary widely: whereas Saudi Arabia possesses more of a clerico-political authoritarianism with a quiescent media, Kuwait has a more "feisty press and robust legislature" (178); likewise, whereas Lebanon has a more fragmented polity with a pluralist media system, this contrasts greatly with Syria's one-party state and monolithic press. To understand this range of relations, Kraidy suggests examining the "opposite poles of the sociopolitical spectrum," these being Saudi Arabia and Lebanon. While both Lebanese and Saudi media are privately owned, both media systems reflect the mood of the society as a deliberate form of government media policy. Whereas Saudi influence is stronger, especially since the state launched vast efforts to modernise its media sector and with the Minister of Culture and Information now overseeing this modernization, Lebanon's state influence has declined as it has taken over networks such as Tele-Liban. Nevertheless, multiple laws in Lebanon still constrain how Lebanese media can report on issues (Kraidy, 2011).

While grouping together the Arabic media is problematic in that each country has had its own historical and cultural upbringing, these nations do share to a great extent a common heritage (and worldview) defined largely by the boundaries of language and religion. It is also true that identifying a common Chinese or Russian identity can be difficult to pin down in that China has over 1.4 billion people and Russia is so geographically dispersed that it covers eleven time-zones. Indeed, China, although one nation, contains much of the linguistic, cultural, and religious diversity of the Arab world. Thus, these regions are important voices challenging US policy, and grouping them becomes conceptually necessary to draw differences, and is commonly done in academic research and government policy formation.

While two of the case studies (the Chinese and Russian) national media are more or less contained within the borders of single nation-states, the third case (the Arabic) transcends multiple nation-states. This enables us to make both a like comparison between the Chinese and Russian cases, while the Arabic case marks a different case structured around the variable of regional versus national media. Furthermore, while all three cases have controlled media systems in common (with some exceptions in the Arabic world), we recognize that each has a unique media ecology. In selecting the news outlets for each dataset we purposefully tried to include a range of political views and slants, including conservative and liberal outlets, government and non-government outlets, as well as more economically oriented outlets and popular ones. While this might make close comparative analysis more challenging, we believe the payoff is worth it in capturing a more nuanced and accurate representation of how each national media grouping came to understand and report upon the US presidential election.

Finally, one more comment should be made about our inclusion of all three of these datasets, and that speaks to the issue of contestation. It is common in international relations policy, as well as academic literature, to speak of "contestation" as a battle between the Western-led liberal order and "the rest," implicitly assuming that the contest is a bi-polar one. But the world is far more complex than that, and our study attempts to illustrate this by showing three different reactions to the US election. Russian media is "contesting" Chinese media and Arabic media, just as it is contesting US and UK media. Our study attempts to capture these multiple contestations, just as it attempts to show how each of these reacts to and contests Western media coverage.

Identification of Websites and Articles

According to Krebs (2015), when identifying dominant narratives, researchers must utilize multiple sources beyond official government pronouncements, because that narrative may not be shared by other sources or because other narratives may retain a legitimate standing. Furthermore, when looking at news sources, researchers need to be sure that their news sources cover a wide variety of constituents as well as political leanings over the entire period of analysis to make valid comparisons. For this project, data collection for each case was generated by using the M3S to capture foreign language news reports the week prior to and that immediately following the three 2016 US presidential debates on September 26, October 9, and October 19, respectively, as well as the week leading up to the US election on November 8 and the week after. Initial selection of news sources for each language group occurred by soliciting Chinese, Russian, and Arabic subject matter experts. These sources were then checked for authority, popularity, and variety of viewpoints to provide a holistic understanding of how each language group reported on the US election. News sources selected for analysis ranged from government and privately managed news organizations, as well as industry and trade, to provide a range of political and topical slants. Over 62 different news sources were analyzed from three geo-linguistic regions, including Chinese, Russian, and Arabic. These three datasets were the basis for both case-specific and comparative analysis.

For the data collection, researchers used the M3S system which creates a searchable database of sources selected for analysis. After incorporating the selected news sources into the M3S, researchers were able to search for news articles pertinent to the US presidential election by entering key terms. To create a manageable corpus of articles relevant to the election, researchers began testing out combinations of search terms across each language grouping to identify both the quantity and quality (relevance) of the articles. For the Arabic and Chinese news sources, the search term "Presidential Debate" was used to select articles for analysis prior to the elections and "US Presidential Election" was the search term used to select articles the week prior to and that following the election. After initial testing and further probing of the articles generated by these search two terms, they proved most applicable in producing a large number of relevant articles barring duplication of content. For the collection of Russian news articles, four search terms were used: "Donald Trump," "Hillary Clinton," "Republican Party," and "Democratic Party." While these terms varied from those used for the other language groups, they generated a clearer and more consistent corpus of articles for analysis of the Republican and Democratic Party national conventions, as well as the debates and weeks leading up to and following the US election. After the exclusion of duplicate and irrelevant articles 1,578 articles were collected for analysis.

Mixed Method Design and Operationalization of "Strategic Narratives"

To uncover the media narratives of the US presidential election, researchers employed a mixed methods design. After the identification of sources, search terms, and articles for investigation, the data was analyzed both quantitatively and qualitatively to reveal how each foreign language group reported upon the US election. This approach has been similarly applied to studies of strategic narratives in the international relations literature (e.g., Krebs, 2015; Coticchia, 2016; Tsygankov, 2017). In doing so, the quantitative content analysis aided the qualitative narrative analysis by helping identify how discursive codes take narrative forms (Krebs, 2015). Our narrative analysis was operationalized by following

TABLE 2.1 News Sources Selected for Analysis

Arabic Sources	Chinese Sources	Russian Sources
Ad-Dustour	Caixin	Arguments and Facts
Al Ahram	Cankao Xiaoxi	EJ
Al Alam	China Elections	Gazetta Russian
Al Arabiya	Chinese Communist Party	Grani
Al Hayat	Enlightenment Daily	InoPressa
Al Jazeera	Global Times	Izvestia
Al Manar	Ifeng news	Kasparov
Al Riyadh	Jingji Cankao Bao	Kommersant
Al Sabaah	Ministry of Foreign Affairs	Komsomolskaya Pravda
Al Wehda Thawra	News 163	Moskovskij Komsomolets
SANA Arabic	Phoenix Info News	NEWSru
Al Mustaqbal★	qingdao news	Newtimes
Al Qabas★	QQ News	Novaya Gazeta
Al Rai Media★	Remin Ribao	Rossiya24
Al Wasat News★	Sina	Slon
alghad★	Sohu News	Chastny Korrespondent
al-Shuruq★	Southern Weekly	
Al-Wafd★	Tiexue	
Al-Watan Kuwait★	Xinhua	
Lebanese Broadcasting Corporation★	Zhongguo Qingnian Bao	
Lebanon Files★		
MTV★		
Tishreen★		

Source: Table created by authors.

Note: ★Sources added during week prior and following US presidential election only.

Miskimmon, O'Loughlin, & Roselle's (2013) definition of narratives as possessing "actors, an action, a goal or intention, a scene, and an instrument" (5). Researchers then mapped these narrative articulations onto Miskimmon et al.'s (2013) typology of narrative forms which fall on three levels: a) international system narratives describing how the world is structured; b) national narratives describing the story of the state, including its values and goals; and c) issue narratives describing why a certain policy is needed. It is important to note, however, that, while these narratives take shape within these three levels, they nevertheless overlap. As Roselle, Miskimmon, and O'Loughlin (2014) state, "strategic narratives at one level will be strengthened by resonance with narratives at other levels" (101). Our

TABLE 2.2 Articles Selected for Analysis

(a) Arabic Data Collected

	D1W1	D1W2	D2W1	D2W2	D3W1	D3W2	PRE-E	POS-E	Total
Ad-Dustour	2	6	2	3	1	0	0	1	15
Al Ahram	0	6	3	7	2	4	5	13	40
Al Alam	0	0	0	0	0	0	0	6	6
Al Arabiya	0	0	5	2	4	4	22	8	45
Al Hayat	0	7	6	6	4	3	2	1	29
Al Jazeera	1	6	3	9	2	7	3	4	35
Al Manar	1	5	0	1	0	1	4	9	21
Al Riyadh	2	5	1	2	0	3	7	2	22
Al Sabaah	4	1	1	0	0	2	0	0	8
Al Wehda Thawra	0	1	2	3	0	2	1	5	14
SANA Arabic	0	0	0	0	0	0	1	3	4
Al Mustaqbal★	na	na	na	na	na	na	na	5	5
Al Qabas★	na	na	na	na	na	na	na	4	4
Al Rai Media★	na	na	na	na	na	na	na	2	2
Al Wasat News★	na	na	na	na	na	na	na	2	2
alghad★	na	na	na	na	na	na	na	1	1
al-Shuruq★	na	na	na	na	na	na	na	6	6
Al-Wafd★	na	na	na	na	na	na	na	5	5
Al-Watan Kuwait★	na	na	na	na	na	na	na	4	4
Lebanese Broadcasting Corporation★	na	na	na	na	na	na	na	2	2
Lebanon Files★	na	na	na	na	na	na	na	1	1

(a) Arabic Data Collected

	D1W1	D1W2	D2W1	D2W2	D3W1	D3W2	PRE-E	POS-E	Total
MTV★	na	na	na	na	na	na	na	1	1
Tishreen★	na	na	na	na	na	na	na	3	3
Total	10	37	23	33	13	26	45	88	275

(b) Chinese Data Collected

	D1W1	D1W2	D2W1	D2W2	D3W1	D3W2	PRE-E	POS-E	Total
Caixin	3	8	0	6	0	6	9	12	44
Cankao Xiaoxi	3	13	3	16	4	11	21	26	97
China Elections	0	1	1	6	1	0	1	9	19
Chinese Communist Party	0	0	1	0	0	0	1	0	2
Enlightenment Daily	1	0	0	2	1	2	4	5	15
Global Times	0	10	1	21	4	15	27	62	140
Ifeng news	0	2	0	0	0	6	7	9	24
Jingji Cankao Bao	0	0	0	0	0	1	2	5	8
Ministry of Foreign Affairs	0	0	0	0	0	1	0	3	4
News 163	0	3	0	1	0	3	3	12	22
Phoenix Info News	0	0	0	0	0	7	25	0	32
qingdao news	0	0	0	0	0	2	7	2	11
QQ News	1	3	1	0	0	0	3	10	18
Remin Ribao	0	0	0	0	0	1	6	13	20
Sina	4	1	2	3	2	2	14	30	58
Sohu News	2	3	2	2	2	2	7	17	37
Southern Weekly	0	3	1	1	0	0	10	6	21
Tiexue	2	7	2	1	2	1	19	92	126
Xinhua	4	5	5	4	7	4	16	13	58

Zhongguo Qingnian Bao	2	2	0	0	0	0	0	7	14	25
Total	22	61	19	63	23	64	189	340	781	

(c) Russian Data Collected

	D1W1	D1W2	D2W1	D2W2	D3W1	D3W2	PRE-E	POS-E	Total
Arguments and Facts	5	7	4	9	5	2	9	6	47
EJ	3	5	3	0	0	0	0	5	16
Gazetta Russian	10	9	4	11	11	3	12	10	70
Grani	1	1	2	0	3	0	1	9	17
InoPressa	5	3	3	9	5	0	5	6	36
Izvestia	1	4	5	11	8	5	15	11	60
Kasparov	1	4	2	1	3	1	3	17	32
Kommersant	7	8	4	15	5	4	9	8	60
Komsomolskaya Pravda	3	0	1	0	0	0	0	0	4
Moskovskij Komsomolets	8	5	6	8	7	1	7	7	49
NEWSru	4	3	2	0	4	3	3	8	27
Newtimes	2	0	0	3	0	0	1	6	12
Novaya Gazeta	0	0	2	1	5	0	0	0	8
Rossiya24	7	9	2	0	9	7	4	7	45
Slon	6	9	4	7	5	3	2	2	38
Chastny Korrespondent	0	0	0	0	0	0	0	1	1
Total	63	67	44	75	70	29	71	103	522

Source: Tables created by authors.

Notes: *Sources added during week prior and following US presidential election only; na, not applicable.

analysis then focuses on how these three levels mutually reinforce each other in constructing their depiction of the 2016 US election.

Indeed, given that this study examined the strategic narratives regarding the 2016 US presidential election within Chinese, Russian, and Arabic media, the lines between these three levels of narrative analysis was at times blurred, with each region emphasizing and constructing issue level narratives in unique ways in contributing to their narrative construction of national and international narratives. We then sought to organize and explain how these three levels of strategic narratives worked in ways that best reflected the narrative themes that emerged. For instance, while many of the issue level narratives in all three cases worked to support national narratives depicting the US in negative ways, they diverged when depicting their own national identities. For example, although Chinese national level narratives were described primarily through a juxtapositioning of US national narratives, Russian narratives were found to be more concerned with international ones where US interests and identities were justified as supporting the decline in the US-led international order.

Before getting into the coder training, it is important to distinguish how narrative analysis is distinct from framing or discourse analysis. According to Miskimmon et al. (2013), narratives are different from discourse and frames through their inclusion of a temporal dimension and sense of movement. Accordingly, discourses "do not feature a causal transformation that takes actors from one status quo to another, as narratives do," while frames, as analytical units, "lack the temporal and causal features narratives necessarily possess" (7). However, in both instances, narratives include and draw upon discourses and frames by plotting elements of both into these narratives. Similarly, Coticchia (2016) argues that frames are more tactical in nature, providing only snapshots of events to serve the short-term purposes of elites. The idea of narrative, on the other hand, helps us go beyond the concept of framing in that narratives, through their inclusion of temporality, are strategic in that they focus on deeper, long-term sense-making of events. Thus, while frames may serve as the bricks helping to compose a narrative, narratives help shape our understanding of the world, not merely reflecting it in the case of frames, by tying in questions of identity, as well as latent social values and cultural myths. Likewise, narratives draw upon discourse because discourses are the "raw material of communication—bodies of knowledge about science, law, history, theology" (Miskimmon et al., 2013, 7).

Data Analysis and Coder Training

For the quantitative analysis, at least three coders for each set of data were trained to answer 25 common questions related to the research problem on what and how issues, the candidates, and the US election process was reported by Chinese, Russian, and Arabic media. In addition, each team was afforded additional region-specific questions for analysis. Within each coding group at least one coder possessed native language expertise, and in some cases, such as the Chinese coding team, all coders were native speakers. The coding categories included elements of the news story structure (i.e., foreign or US sources cited, editorial or news articles), US election process (i.e., explanation of debate and election process, process portrayed as legitimate or democratic), candidate and party portrayal (i.e., Clinton or Trump positively or negatively portrayed, Democratic or Republican Party unified/disunified), and implications of policy and election outcome for the region (i.e., Trump election good for the region, specific policy implications such as Iranian nuclear deal or US policy in the South China Sea). Not all questions held similar relevancy within each language grouping, and thus additional qualitative analysis of articles deemed especially relevant was afforded by each team and conducted independently by each language grouping to tease out further implications from the quantitative data.

For the quantitative phase of analysis, coders went through extensive training occurring in three phases. First, a codebook was developed dictating common coding procedures across each language group with definitions for each question asked. Coders met prior to reading the news articles to read over these question definitions and were provided with an opportunity to ask for clarification. Coders were then provided with a small sample selection of articles to be coded together to familiarize themselves with the coding procedures and question categories after which further edits to the coding book were made, including the listing of examples for difficult coding questions. The second phase included the initial assignment of 30–40 articles for each coder to code separately. After initial analysis of average pairwise percent agreement among the three-person coding teams, each coding team came together to go over differences in their coding and worked out additional examples and clarification of coding categories which were then added to the common codebook. Coding categories where average pairwise percent agreement was below 70 percent were further discussed, with up to seven articles selected based upon their high-level of disagreement. These were subsequently recoded together and discussed whereby differences were worked out. Finally, the third phase included the selection of a minimum 10 percent of articles for the final intercoder reliability tests. News articles were randomly selected from the corpus of data, representative of both news sources and publication date, which were then independently coded.

TABLE 2.3 Summary of Intercoder Reliability

	Total Stories Collected	Number of Intercoder Articles Analyzed	Percentage of Total Stories Collected	Number of Coders	Average Pairwise % Agreement Across All Questions
Arabic	275.0	35.0	12.7	3.0	84.1
Chinese	781.0	91.0	11.7	3.0	87.6
Russian	522.0	44.0	8.4	2.0	86.7

Source: Table created by authors.

Intercoder reliability tests were conducted by average pairwise percent agreement. This was primarily because this study is exploratory in nature, being the first of its kind to analyze native language news articles in understanding how three geo-linguistic regions reported upon the US presidential election. Although pairwise percent agreement is a more liberal measure of intercoder reliability, complications arising from using foreign language media, translation accuracy, and natural language ability makes the use of more sophisticated intercoder reliability tests difficult and poses a limitation to the study. Nevertheless, our use of three coders aids in providing further insurance of internal coder reliability, and our reliability tests were similar to those of Krebs (2015) who relied upon percent agreement between two coders.

For the qualitative analysis, regional experts in China, Russia, and Arabic media conducted grounded thematic analysis (Strauss & Corbin, 2015) rather than a Critical Discourse Analysis for the reasons mentioned above distinguishing narrative and discourse analysis. Coders began by reading through the qualitative data before rereading through it again and marking initial coding categories and themes before reading through the material and developing larger thematic categories identifying the narratives present. Coders met intermittingly to discuss their initial codes and work out disagreement among them, as well as determine how these narratives mapped onto Miskimmon et al.'s (2013) concepts of issue level, national level, and international level narratives.

Most of the translated material presented in this volume was machine generated using the MMS system. When those translations were too difficult to understand in English, we have improved the translations by the use of native speakers. In many cases, however, when the intent was clear, we have left the machine-generated translations intact so as not to fundamentally change the meaning of the quoted material.

References

Adoni, H., & Mane, S. (1984). Media and the social construction of reality: Toward an integration of theory and research. *Communication Research*, 11(3), 323–340.

Carey, J. W. (2009). *Communication as culture, revised edition: Essays on media and society.* New York: Routledge.

Castells, M. (2008). The new public sphere: Global civil society, communication networks, and global governance. *The Annals of the American Academy of Political and Social Science*, 616(1), 78–93.

Cooley, S. C., & Stokes, E. C. (2018). Manufacturing resilience: An analysis of broadcast and Web-based news presentations of the 2014–2015 Russian economic downturn. *Global Media and Communication*, 14(1), 123–139.

Coticchia, F. (2016). A controversial warplane: Narratives, counternarratives, and the Italian debate on the F-35. *Alternatives*, 41(4), 194–213.

Curran, J., Esser, F., Hallin, D. C., Hayashi, K., & Lee, C. C. (2015). International news and global integration: A five-nation reappraisal. *Journalism Studies*, 18(2), 118–134.

Fishkin, J. S., He, B., Luskin, R. C., & Siu, A. (2010). Deliberative democracy in an unlikely place: Deliberative polling in China. *British Journal of Political Science*, 40(2), 435–448.

Flew, T., Iosifidis, P., & Steemers, J. (2016). *Global media and national policies: The return of the state*. London, UK: Palgrave Macmillan.

He, B. (2006). Western theories of deliberative democracy and the Chinese practice of complex deliberative governance. In E. Leib & B. He (Eds.), *The search for deliberative democracy in China* (pp. 133–148). New York: Palgrave Macmillan.

He, B. (2014). Deliberative culture and politics: The persistence of authoritarian deliberation in China. *Political Theory*, 42(1), 58–81.

He, B., & Warren, M. E. (2011). Authoritarian deliberation: The deliberative turn in Chinese political development. *Perspectives on Politics*, 9(2), 269–289.

Hill, F., & Gaddy, C. G. (2015). *Mr. Putin: Operative in the Kremlin*. Washington, DC: Brookings Institution Press.

Hinck, E. A., Hinck, S. S., Hinck, R. S., Ghanem, S. I., & Dailey, W. O. (2015). Cultural differences in political debate: Comparing face threats in US, Great Britain, and Egyptian campaign debates. In F. H. van Eemeren & B. Garssen (Eds.), *Argumentation in context* (pp. 29–48). Amsterdam, The Netherlands: John Benjamins Publishing.

Hinck, R. S., Manly, J. N., Kluver, R. A., & Norris, W. J. (2016). Interpreting and shaping geopolitics in Chinese media: the discourse of the "New style of great power relations". *Asian Journal of Communication*, 26(5), 427–445.

Hinck, R. S., Kluver, R., Norris, W., & Manly, J. (2018). Geopolitical dimensions of "The China Dream": Exploring strategic narratives of the Chinese Communist Party. *China Media Research*, 14(3), 99–110.

Hinck, R. S., Kluver, R., & Cooley, S. (2018). Russia re-envisions the world: Strategic narratives in Russian broadcast and news media during 2015. *Russian Journal of Communication*, 10(1), 21–37.

Human Rights Watch (2015). *World report 2015: Russia*. Retrieved from https://www. hrw.org/world-report/2015/country-chapters/russia.

Jiang, M. (2008). Authoritarian deliberation: Public deliberation in China. New Media and the Social Reform (pp. 273–290). *Proceedings of the 2008 Global Communication Forum, Shanghai, China, 21–22 June, 2008*. Shanghai: School of Media and Design, Shanghai Jiao Tong University.

Kluver, R., Campbell, H. A., & Balfour, S. (2013). Language and the boundaries of research: Media monitoring technologies in international media research. *Journal of Broadcasting & Electronic Media*, 57(1), 4–19.

Kraidy, M. (2011). The rise of transnational media systems. In D. C. Hallin, & P. Mancini (Eds.), *Comparing media systems beyond the Western world* (pp. 177–200). Cambridge, UK: Cambridge University Press.

Kraidy, M. & Khalil, J. (2009). *Arab television industries*. New York: Palgrave Macmillan.

Krebs, R. R. (2015). How dominant narratives rise and fall: Military conflict, politics, and the Cold War consensus. *International Organization*, 69(4), 809–845.

Krickovic, A., & Weber, Y. (2016). To harass and wait out. *Russia in Global Affairs*, 14(2), 54–64.

Lee, C. C., He, Z., & Huang, Y. (2007). Party-market corporatism, clientelism, and media in Shanghai. *Harvard International Journal of Press/Politics*, 12(3), 21–42.

Leib, E., & He, B. (Eds.). (2006). *The search for deliberative democracy in China*. New York: Palgrave Macmillan.

Link, P., & Qiang, X. (2013). From grass-mud equestrians to rights-conscious citizens: Language and thought on the Chinese internet. In P. Link, R. P. Madsen, & P. G. Pickowicz (Eds.), *Restless China* (pp. 83–106). Lanham, MA: Rowman & Littlefield.

Lo, B. (2015). *Russia and the new world disorder.* Washington, DC: Brookings Institution Press.

Lorentzen, P. (2014). China's strategic censorship. *American Journal of Political Science*, 58(2), 402–414.

Miskimmon, A., O'Loughlin, B., & Roselle, L. (2013). *Strategic narratives: Communication power and the new world order.* New York: Routledge.

Oates, S. (2007). The neo-Soviet model of the media. *Europe-Asia Studies*, 59(8), 1279–1297.

Paul, C., & Matthews, M. (2016). The Russian "Firehose of Falsehood" propaganda model: Why it might work and options to counter it. RAND Corporation. Retrieved from https://www.rand.org/content/dam/rand/pubs/perspectives/PE100/PE198/RAND_PE198.pdf.

Peng, Z. (2004). Representation of China: An across time analysis of coverage in the *New York Times* and *Los Angeles Times*. *Asian Journal of Communication*, 14(1), 53–67.

Reporters Without Borders (2018). *World Press Freedom Index.* Retrieved from https://rsf.org/en/ranking.

Roselle, L., Miskimmon, A., & O'Loughlin, B. (2014). Strategic narrative: A new means to understand soft power. *Media, War & Conflict*, 7(1), 70–84.

Rugh, W. (2018, February 15). Challenges for US public diplomacy in the age of Trump. *Arab Media & Society.* Retrieved from https://www.arabmediasociety.com/challenges-for-u-s-public-diplomacy-in-the-age-of-trump/.

Schenk, C. (2012). Nationalism in the Russian media: content analysis of newspaper coverage surrounding conflict in Stavropol, 24 May–7 June 2007. *Nationalities Papers*, 40(5), 783–805.

Shen, F., & Guo, Z. S. (2013). The last refuge of media persuasion: News use, national pride and political trust in China. *Asian Journal of Communication*, 23(2), 135–151.

Skalamera, M. (2018). Understanding Russia's energy turn to China: Domestic narratives and national identity priorities. *Post-Soviet Affairs*, 34(1), 55–77.

Stockmann, D., & Gallagher, M. E. (2011). Remote control: How the media sustain authoritarian rule in China. *Comparative Political Studies*, 44(4), 436–467.

Stockmann, D., & Luo, T. (2017). Which social media facilitate online public opinion in China? *Problems of Post-Communism*, 64(3–4),189–202.

Strauss, A., & Corbin, J. (2015). *Basics of qualitative research: Techniques and procedures for developing grounded theory* (4th ed.). Los Angeles, CA: Sage Publications.

Strömbäck, J., & Kaid, L. L. (Eds.). (2008). *The handbook of election news coverage around the world.* New York: Routledge.

Tsygankov, A. P. (2017). The dark double: The American media perception of Russia as a neo-Soviet autocracy, 2008–2014. *Politics*, 37(1), 19–35.

Vartanova, E. (2012). The Russian media model in the context of post-Soviet dynamics. In D. C. Hallin & P. Mancini (Eds.), *Comparing media systems beyond the Western world* (pp. 177–200). Cambridge, UK: Cambridge University Press.

Xu, B. (2014, September 25). Media censorship in China. Council on Foreign Relations. Retrieved from https://www.cfr.org/backgrounder/media-censorship-china.

3

ILLEGITIMACY OF US DEMOCRACY AND DECLINING US INFLUENCE

Juxtaposing Chinese Success Among US Failures within Chinese Media Coverage of the US Election

Introduction

The US–China bilateral relationship is one of the most consequential for the twenty-first century. China's continued economic growth and subsequent global reach implicates US interests abroad in myriad ways (Shambaugh, 2013). While cooperative or conflictual relations is not a foregone conclusion, unfortunately, US presidential elections tend to highlight areas of tension rather than cooperation (Carpenter, 2012; Dwyer, 2015). US officials up for election frequently engage in China bashing, crying foul most often over questions of unfair trade practices and human rights with more recent aspersions arising over future consequences of China's military might and US policy in the Asia Pacific. While many of these hard stances wane once officials reach office, their campaign rhetoric nevertheless sets the tone, informs, and results in more enduring expectations among domestic and foreign audiences regarding the future of US–China relations, a topic increasingly impactful for Asian Pacific countries, US allies, and friendly nations in the region (i.e., Japan, the Philippines, Taiwan).

US elections are especially important for US–China relations in that they mark potential changes in US leadership and personnel, an issue of importance given Chinese leaders' preference for stability and predictability not only on policy, but also in knowing their interlocutors. Further complications arise from US interests in seeing a more democratic Chinese government. The perception by Chinese officials that the US ultimately wishes to undermine its more authoritarian government remains a sticking point in the overall US–China relationship (Sutter, 2013; Wang & Lieberthal, 2012). Additionally, the US touts its economic and political system as exemplars for continued Chinese reforms and US democratic values are showcased during presidential campaigns.

However, these lessons are not directly communicated to foreign audiences, but rather mediated, in part, through the lens of national and regional news media. Indeed, there is a long history of both US and Chinese officials and publics viewing the "other" through "images" or "narratives" of either country, as well as their bilateral relations (Shambaugh, 1993; Spence, 1998; Isaacs, 2015; Jespersen, 1999; Mackerras, 1989; Tucker, 2013; Goh, 2005). Thus, US presidential elections are a particularly fertile site whereby both US and Chinese leaders draw upon these understandings of each other, with US candidates articulating their US–China policy and Chinese officials publicly commenting on such positions within their media system.

As this chapter will show, Chinese media reporting of the 2016 US presidential election demonstrates a strong interest in the election, but focused less on substantive policy issues and tending to grant more coverage towards scandals plaguing both of the two major candidates for the US presidency. The 2016 presidential campaign was thus reported to Chinese audiences as less of an example of democratic values in practice and more like a soap opera or rendition of House of Cards, highlighting the failings of US democratic governance, while offering the opportunity to juxtapose these narratives with those of effective Chinese governance and resurgent strength vis-à-vis the US. Taken together, Chinese media narratives of the 2016 US presidential election showcases a decline in US soft power, challenging its moral and practical authority in articulating effective governance models, while legitimizing the Chinese leaderships' policies in modernizing and governing China.

Narratives and Images of US–China Relations: Cyclical Friction and Global Order

The US and Chinese publics have long had a fascination with the other, dating back at least to the eighteenth century (Isaacs, 2015). More modern representations of China within the US have been argued to follow a cyclical pattern of polarization resultant of changes in US–China relations and Western political interests in China (Jespersen, 1999; Mackerras, 1989). This pattern has been summarized as periods including an Age of Hostility (1949–1972), after the founding of the People's Republic of China and turn to communist rule and alignment with the Soviet Union, an Age of Admiration (1972–1977), with Nixon's opening to China and cooperation against the Soviet Union, an Age of Disenchantment (1977–1980), whereby progress stalled on cooperative relations, and an Age of Benevolence (1980–1989), with the advent of normalized relations. Following the Tiananmen Square crisis, the pattern continued, with US opinion returning to a period of Disenchantment (1989–2001) (Isaacs, 2015; Mosher, 1990; Cao, 2012). Currently, Cao (2012) argues we are in the Age of Uncertainty (2001–present) distinguished by the expanding human contacts and access to information about China which complicate and challenge previous characterizations.

Similarly, Tucker (2013) argues that modern US–China relations can be broken into four decades: The first decade occurred from 1969–1979 when the US and China underwent rapprochement and a normalization of relations. The second decade from 1980–1989 marked the honeymoon phase of US–China relations ended by the Tiananmen Square Crisis. The third decade is from 1989–2001, a period of disarray following the aftermath of the Tiananmen Square Crisis and dissolution of the Soviet Union. The fourth decade is from 2001 until the present. This final decade is a period of mixed opportunities and challenges as the US and China cooperate against the global war on terror and deal with China's rising military and economic strength.

These narratives and images of each other are important in that they affect policy decisions regarding the possibility of conflictual or cooperative relations. For instance, Goh (2005) traced internal policy debates within the US executive branch demonstrating how the relabeling of China as a "Red menace" to that of a "Tacit ally" provided support for Nixon's opening. More recently, Garrison (2005) looked at how group decision processes shaped emerging policy definitions by framing US–China relations within the "national interest" from the Nixon to George W. Bush administration demonstrating how complex foreign policy situations lead to differing definitions of political problems to prevail over others. Other examples include attempts by US leaders to encourage China to become a "responsible stakeholder" in world affairs (Zoellick, 2005). From the Chinese side, narratives of the US, such as it being a "beautiful imperialist" (Shambaugh, 1993) or criticism from Chinese leaders complaining that the US perpetuates a "China Threat Theory" (Deng, 2006; Broomfield, 2003) both implicate how Chinese come to understand the ways in which the US exercises its power and the potential challenges it has on China's growing influence. As the Pew Research Center has found, Chinese have a mixed view of the US, with half the population holding favorable views of the US and half the population seeing the US as trying to contain it (Wike & Stokes, 2016). More recently, China's attempt to describe US–China relations as falling under a "New Style of Great Power Relations" (Hinck, Manly, Kluver, & Norris, 2016) can be understood as encouraging the US to treat China as an equal. Importantly, with US presidential elections comes the possibility of redefining issues of importance to US–China relations within new administrations.

Contributions of US Elections Towards Contentious US–China Relations

US elections pose an interesting dilemma for Chinese officials. Dating back to the initial stages of rapprochement between the US and China during Nixon's time in office, Chinese officials developed significant momentum on a number of important issues between the two countries; most notably including the political status of Taiwan, US–China cooperation against the Soviet Union, and formal normalization of relations. However, with the Watergate scandal and the subsequent diminished powers of the executive branch, Chinese leaders were taught an important lesson of US electoral politics: namely, the complications posed by Congress and the difficulty of ensuring consistency in policy-making across presidential administrations (Kissinger, 2011; Vogel, 2013). The impact of US electoral politics in US–China relations was perhaps most heightened during the 1990s with the threat of China's Most Favored Nation status constantly jeopardized during the Clinton administration with concerns over China's human rights policies and pressure from congressmen and their constituents threatening Chinese interests (Sutter, 2013). Beyond issues of trade, US ties to Taiwan, including future arms sales to the country, remain a recurring thorn in the bilateral relationship.

Since the 2000s, China's perceived currency manipulation vis-a-vis the US dollar had been the "hot-button" issue within US domestic politics (Ramirez, 2013). The topic is easy fodder during election season, with congressional leaders and presidential candidates frequently stirring domestic support by threatening to label China a currency manipulator to bolster working-class support. They claim that China's artificially low yuan makes US products less competitive with Chinese, costing US workers their jobs. Likewise, on the foreign policy front, voter concerns regarding China's rise and military growth combine with feelings of US global decline, providing another point to stir American emotions against China. Meanwhile, US elites worry over the future of the Asia Pacific and the need to shore up support from allies in the region to combat China's rise. Thus, continued support for Taiwan's safety, territorial claims in the South China Sea, North Korea's nuclear aspirations, and regional trade pacts such as the TransPacific Partnership were all key issues faced by the Obama Administration and policy issues during the 2016 US presidential campaign.

Recent Developments of US–China Relations

Since the George W. Bush administration, the US decided upon a policy of engagement with China on primarily economic issues and, to a lesser extent, security issues (Wilder, 2009). The US position was to welcome China to the global community, albeit arguing for China to take a more "responsible stakeholder" position whereby it shared in shoring up international norms established by the US (Zoellick, 2005). The Obama administration doubled down on these efforts, instituting the Strategic and Economic Dialogues as a forum by which the leaders and government officials in both nations could work together and come to understand their interlocutors' policy positions and worldviews in order to expand areas of cooperation. While US–China relations during the Obama administration were relatively cooperative, with US–China cooperation on a number of key issues such as Iran and North Korea's nuclear program and the global financial crisis, moments of friction did erupt, specifically over the continued US arms sales to Taiwan and truculent Chinese behavior in the South China Sea (Sutter, 2013).

Even after eight years of consistent policy making of constructive engagement during the Obama administration, key areas of tension between the two countries exist. Sutter (2013) summarizes four areas of Chinese concern and two categories of US disagreement. First, on the Chinese side, officials disagree with US policies arising from Chinese opposition to US support of Taiwan and other sensitive sovereignty issues in areas like Tibet, Xinjiang, and Chinese territorial disputes along its eastern and southern maritime borders. Second, Chinese oppose US efforts to change its political system. Third, the Chinese are weary of US attempts to play a strategic role on China's Asian periphery, viewing such actions as intended to contain its rise. Finally, Chinese are cautious and generally opposed to US leadership in world affairs. According to public opinion data from the Pew Research Center, Chinese citizens are most apprehensive of US power and influence, followed by global economic instability and global climate change (Wike & Stokes, 2016).

On the American side, US leaders tend to focus more on differences in economic issues including trade inequities such as the massive US–China trade deficit, Chinese currency manipulation, lax enforcement of intellectual property rights, and industrial espionage. On the security front, US officials disagree with the Chinese leadership over US interests in Taiwan, Chinese human rights practices, sovereignty questions over Taiwan, Tibet, Xinjiang and Hong Kong, maritime transit and sovereignty disputes in the South and East China Sea, Chinese deviation from US-backed global norms, and Chinese policy in Africa Africa, which is interpreted as undermining US interests of democracy and transparency (Sutter, 2013). While resolution for many of these issues is difficult, US presidential elections pose a unique juncture for reevaluation and changes in course of US–China policy.

Context of the 2016 US Presidential Election and US–China Relations

Chinese officials and citizens alike paid close attention to the 2016 US presidential campaign. Despite the debates being censored within the country, more than 118,000 Chinese were able to live steam the first debate on *Weibo*, China's version of Twitter (Meyers, 2016). Even student groups who normally volunteer to translate Chinese subtitles for American televisions shows worked together to translate campaign speeches and primary debates for Chinese audiences. One group, after uploading the translated video of the first Republican primary debate on August 6, 2015 to *Weibo* and other Chinese video-sharing sites, generated millions of views days after its release (Own, 2016). Despite lacking access to the actual debate performances, Chinese news outlets reported extensively on the campaigns providing commentary and analysis of the two major party candidates' policy stances on US–China relations, as well as their scandals.

Both Hillary Clinton and Donald Trump engaged in the typical China bashing that recurs during presidential elections. For instance, in June 2016, Donald

Trump laid out a seven-point plan to toughen US trade policy, taking aim at China. Only a few hours later, Hillary Clinton claimed Trump stole these ideas from her (Bradsher, 2016). Both candidates suggested taking further steps to pressure China to appreciate the value of its currency, with Donald Trump expressing his willingness to label China a currency manipulator. At campaign rallies, Trump repeatedly stated how Chinese imports are "killing us" and threatened to impose a 45 percent tax on Chinese imports if trade relations did not change (Irwin, 2016). On the Trans-Pacific Partnership (TPP), Donald Trump called the trade pact a disaster, while Hillary Clinton repeatedly stated her desire to renegotiate it, although she had played a crucial part in its initial ideation (Bradsher, 2016). Despite the economic saber rattling, US and Chinese scholars stated that Chinese policy-makers were skeptical of either candidates' willingness to follow through on such efforts. Hillary Clinton was viewed largely as a continuation of Obama-era policies, and thus less unlikely to change US policies given her support of Obama's free trade efforts (Bradsher, 2016; Rosenfeld, 2016; Dong, 2016). Donald Trump, was more of an unknown factor, praised for his pragmatism and pro-business outlook, but also overly bellicose, with Chinese audiences doubting his knowledgeability on the subject, irrational nature and "childish style of speaking," as well as possessing a "dubious record of success as a businessman" (Dong, 2016; Rosenfeld, 2016).

The two candidates separated themselves more so on foreign policy issues. Wang Dong, an associate professor at Peking University's School of International Studies, noted that with Donald Trump, Chinese were both excited and unsure (Dong, 2016). Donald Trump's criticism of US alliances with Japan and South Korea as not paying their fair share regarding US military support and military bases stationed in their countries was viewed optimistically by Chinese seeking the US to play a minimal role in the Asia Pacific. Likewise, Trump's focus on fighting terrorism in the Middle East, including more involvement in fighting the Islamic State, further suggested US military might would be directed elsewhere rather than China's backyard. According to US and Chinese experts, Chinese audiences tended to view Trump as more of a pragmatist, a positive characteristic in their eyes, as they believed this would remove any ideological red lines hindering the larger promotion of US–China relations, especially in terms of human rights policy (Dong, 2016; Rosenfeld, 2016).

Chinese audiences understood Hillary Clinton as more of a continuation of Obama-era policies, albeit with more hawkish foreign policy tendencies. As such, Chinese were hesitant about endorsing Hillary Clinton's policies, believing she would maintain the Obama administration's "Pivot to Asia," resulting in greater exertion of US power and influence into the region. If Hillary Clinton were elected, Chinese believed she would be tougher towards China, taking stronger stances on pressuring Chinese action on North Korean nuclear proliferation, supportive of anti-ballistic missiles in South Korea, pursuant of a more confrontational policy in the South China Sea, and greater encouragement of Taiwan to follow policies decoupling it from the Chinese mainland (Dong, 2016). Hillary Clinton's human rights policy was also viewed more negatively. Chinese have a long memory, and believed Hillary Clinton would lecture them on human rights abuses given her criticism of China in a speech she gave in Beijing back in 1995. Nevertheless, all of these were known factors. Thus, unlike Donald Trump, Hillary Clinton was seen as a consistent politician whose policies towards China could be anticipated, even predicted, and worked through successfully, although recognizing Clinton would take a tougher stance towards China than would Trump (Dong, 2016; Rosenfeld, 2016).

Taken together, Chinese associate professor Wang Dong summarized that Hillary Clinton was regarded as the "devil we know," while Donald Trump remained an unknown quantity with worrying levels of volatility and a celebritism (Dong, 2016). Nevertheless, China expert Kenneth scholar and expert Kenneth Lieberthal was quoted in a *CNBC* article as stating Chinese leaders were uncertain about what US–China relations would be like under either major party candidate (Rosenfeld, 2016). Despite Chinese leaders refraining from endorsing one candidate over the other, some Chinese netizens interestingly came out in support of Donald Trump, as well as satirizing him. For instance, Donald Trump received multiple online followings in China with internet groups such as the "Donald Trump Super Fans Club" and "God and Emperor Trump" (Rosenfeld, 2016). While some were inspired by his flamboyant, celebrity factor, others used his performances as satire, considering him a clown, funny, and unscrupulous. Regardless, Chinese came to understand the US presidential election as one full of strife, leading them to question whether the US could govern itself, and if not, how then could it lecture others about American democracy (Dong, 2016).

Quantitative Results

In order to better understand how the Chinese media reported upon the US presidential elections beyond the anecdotal and expert perspectives provided above, researchers as part of this project conducted a quantitative and qualitative analysis of 781 Chinese news articles collected from 20 different Chinese news sources chosen for their authority and popularity, private and government ownership, as well as political and topical slant. Three coders with Chinese language ability coded 30 separate questions regarding the content of the articles. Quantitative analysis of these articles demonstrated what topics and issues were most often covered, whether the candidates and major parties were positively or negatively portrayed, source content and type of articles—whether editorial or news, and general perceptions of US democracy. This section will overview the quantitative analysis of the Chinese articles with further exploration of key themes following in the qualitative section. For a more extended discussion of the research design and methodology, refer to Chapter 2.

In terms of article type and structure, 441 (56 percent) of the articles analyzed were news stories, with 261 (33 percent) being editorial in style. Sources cited within the articles were relatively balanced, with 317 (41 percent) of stories including US sources and 249 (32 percent) including foreign sources. In total 591 (76 percent) articles included explanations regarding how the presidential debates and US election process functioned, with 412 (53 percent) accurately explaining the process, while 179 (23 percent) were found to be inaccurate. When explaining the process, 753 (96 percent) of the articles remained neutral in their evaluation of the process. Out of the remaining four percent, no articles lauded the US electoral process, with 28 stories (3.6 percent) viewing it in a negative manner.

Hillary Clinton was mentioned in 655 (84 percent) of the articles, with 520 stories (67 percent) taking a neutral tone including both positive and negative aspects of her character and issues associated with her campaign. Only eight stories (1 percent) took a positive view, whereas 127 stories (16 percent) portrayed her negatively. Issues associated with Hillary Clinton included discussion of her health, her email scandal and the FBI investigation into it, paid speeches from Wall Street, the questionable dealings with the Clinton Foundation, her husband's sexual infidelities, and Benghazi. As such, the negative characterizations of her character coalesced into describing her as dishonest and corrupt.

Donald Trump was mentioned within 705 (93 percent) of the articles, 9 percent more frequently than Hillary Clinton. Like Clinton, a majority of articles, 529 stories (68 percent), discussed Trump in neutral ways, highlighting both positive and negative characteristics. However, Trump was portrayed slightly more negatively, with 164 (21 percent) of articles doing so, with only 12 (1.5 percent) taking a positive portrayal of his character and issues associated with his campaign. Issues associated with Donald Trump revolved less around serious policy discussion and included his scandals and personal character. Most frequently reported upon were his numerous instances of sexism ranging from calling a former Miss Universe pageant winner "Miss Piggy," to the recoding of his comments during a discussion with Billy Bush, among others. Additionally, Trump was criticized for his refusal to release his tax returns, connections to Russian, irrational speech, and depictions of him as a racist, isolationist, populist, silly, and inexperienced.

Donald Trump was viewed as a danger to China in only 16 out of the 781, making up only 2 percent of the total. Hillary Clinton on the other hand was viewed as a danger only in six (0.77 percent) of articles analyzed. Thus, while Trump was viewed as a riskier, potentially detrimental candidate in a few of the articles, neither candidate was consistently viewed as a significant threat to China throughout the campaign and among the corpus of texts analyzed. Likewise, 750 (96 percent) of the articles refrained from mentioning a "preferred" candidate, although within the 4 percent that did, Hillary Clinton was favored in 28 (3.6 percent) of the articles and Donald Trump only in three (.4 percent) of the articles. These two major party candidates dominated the Chinese news discourse, with only nine (1 percent) of the articles including references to third party candidates.

Discussions of political party were more muted compared to reporting of the individual candidates and their campaigns. Only 22 percent of articles directly referenced the two parties. Within this 22 percent both parties were never positively portrayed and instead articles took a neutral tone. The Democratic Party was viewed neutrally in 157 (20 percent) of the articles, while negatively in 11 (1.4 percent) of the articles and the Republican Party was viewed neutrally in 163 (21 percent) of the articles and negatively in 10 articles (1.3 percent). Dissensus within both parties was highlighted, with 173 (22 percent) of articles portraying disunity within the Democratic Party and 226 (29 percent) within the Republican Party. In the case of the Democratic Party, disunity arouse from Bernie Sanders supporters' lack of enthusiasm for Hillary Clinton. Dissension among the Republican Party was broader, with multiple influential Republican leaders criticizing Donald Trump.

In terms of the portrayal of US democracy, the quantitative findings were unclear. The vast majority of articles analyzed did not explicitly praise or blame the US system, making coding of the questions difficult. With regards to whether the articles reported on the US election as democratic, that is, representative of the "will of the people," only 31 stories (4 percent) within the total corpus clearly articulated a positive or negative evaluation; seven articles (0.9 percent) did find the US election reflecting the desires of the US populace, while 24 (3 percent) claimed it did not. With regards to whether the US election was viewed as legitimate, that is, correctly following US election procedures, coders were unable to identify any articles that clearly argued for or against the US election's legitimacy. This is most likely due to issues with the coding schema and coders, rather than a true reflection of how the Chinese media reported on the election. Indeed, closer qualitative analysis revealed some doubts regarding the legitimacy of the election, specifically claims by Donald Trump to only accept the results if they turned out in his favor, which will be discussed further in the next section. When reporting on whether democracy is desirable, again, a vast majority of articles analyzed failed to take a clear position. Only 27 articles (3.5 percent) provided a positive or negative evaluation, with all 27 viewing democracy as undesirable.

Four region-specific coding questions were asked for the Chinese data. These questions were about specific policy issues of relevance for US–China relations as a whole, and included prospects for US–China trade relations, conflict over the South China Sea, the political status of Taiwan, and concerns over human rights. Within the corpus of Chinese media articles, these policy issues were less discussed compared to the political candidates' personal characteristics and scandals. Only 59 articles (7.5 percent) included discussion with regards to the impact of Trump's election for US–China trade relations. Of those articles, 39 (5 percent) provided a mixed outlook, with 15 articles (2 percent) viewing Trump's election as negatively impacting US–China trade relations, and only five articles (0.6 percent) viewing Trump's election as leading towards more positive trade relations. Little discussion of US policy in the South China Sea occurred, with Trump's South China Sea policy discussed in only 15 articles (2 percent) providing a mixed or positive interpretation of his policy. Only 13 articles (1.66 percent) viewed Trump's policy as mixed, two (0.25 percent) as positive, and no articles portraying it negatively. The low number of articles discussing US policy in the South China Sea is most likely reflective of the little attention the issue received in the US campaign. Likewise, US policy towards Taiwan was minimal, with only one article discussing Trump's election as positively impacting US–China relations on the Taiwan issue, two articles viewing it negatively, and 12 (1.5 percent) providing a mixed outlook. Finally, with regards to Trump's election's impact of US–China policy on human rights, only five articles (0.64 percent) out of the 781 discussed the topic, with three articles (0.38 percent) viewing Trump's election as positively impacting US–China relations over human rights, no articles viewing it negatively, and two articles (0.26 percent) viewing it as mixed.

Qualitative Narrative Analysis of the 2016 US Presidential Election

The strategic narratives in Chinese media overwhelmingly focused on the US election process as a whole, with all of its scandals, plot twists, and sensational content. The focus then was less on the policies of the two major party candidates and more on the spectacle and lack of reasoned discussion that took place. These elements suggest that the US democratic system is an ineffective one, failing to produce social harmony. Historical allusions and political commentary situated the presidential election into a wider debate on governance models which placed in doubt the universality of democracy and functioned to support the Chinese system of more authoritarian rule. Finally, the little discussion there was of US–China policy related issues revolved around demonstrating Chinese strength, and thus ability to weather either candidates' confrontational policies regarding trade or territorial claims in the South China Sea.

Issue and National Level Narratives: Failures of US Democratic Values in Context

National level narratives focused on explaining and commenting on the US election process, as well as the candidates. The overall picture of the US election was not one of rational policy debate or qualified candidates, but rather full of strife and drama[1] more akin to House of Cards, a Soap opera,[2] or a sporting event,[3] rather than of thoughtful democratic governance. The bulk of the articles kept Chinese readers up to date with the most recent happenings of the campaign, including attacks made by the candidates and revelations of new or recurring scandals, but also provided in-depth and nuanced commentary on how the US political process unfolded. Thus, Chinese media coverage included descriptions of the debate format and voting procedures, as well as the candidates' credentials. A majority of the articles were neutral, or purely informational in their reporting with closer analysis revealing a considerable fascination regarding the US electoral system albeit lacking clear narrative evaluations; however, a smaller subsection of the articles did provide more narrative accounts of the process, raising doubts as to the efficacy of American democracy.

Informational Narratives: Neutrality of Information

Chinese citizens were presented with a considerable amount of information regarding the US election process. Indeed, as mentioned in the quantitative overview, over half of the articles analyzed described the election process, with the overwhelming majority of those being informational or neutral in content. These informational articles are the closest examples of positive reporting on the US election process. Chinese citizens learned how Americans can vote, including articles noting that "United States citizens aged 18 [and up]" were qualified to do so. Details regarding registration were provided, even listing both a website and deadline to do so. Even minutia regarding who else was on the ballot in various states, how absentee ballots worked, how to locate polling stations, and what identification documents were needed were all covered.[4] Perhaps less surprisingly, articles discussed the electoral college procedure, noting, "general elections are not directly [counted] into the presidential candidate of the votes, but through the Electoral College elect[ing] [the] president." The electoral college was described as preventing "irrational factors" and "controlled" by the "elite." Articles frequently mentioned how many electoral votes are needed, with fewer noting how many electoral votes each state had, and exceptions to the "winner take all" element of electoral votes; with examples provided such as the 2000 election where Gore won the popular vote and still lost the electoral college.[5]

Articles focusing on the debates explained the debate format, including information regarding the number of debates, their time and location, and, in some cases, going into details recounting the participants, as well as their moderators.[6] For instance, an article from *Caixin* reported that "The first presidential debate [on] September 26 will be held in New York Governor island of Hofstra University," going on to list the locations and dates of the other two debates, and further explaining that there is only one vice presidential debate at Longwood University in Virginia on October 4. Likewise, the Townhall style debate format was explained, including who asks the questions, how many questions, and the time candidates have to answer them[7] with details regarding historical reasons for the format, noting "It is the tradition of elected officials to hold from time to time citizens to participate in the meeting, on these occasions citizens directly question officials on the performance of government policy."[8]

Articles explained the rules governing who can participate in the debates. For instance, it was reported that the "Commission on Presidential Debates established standards" determining the threshold for participating, with candidates needing to poll with at least "15% in support." Thus, it was explained why only

Donald Trump and Hillary Clinton would be debating because "Gary Johnson and the Green Party candidate Jill Stein did not receive enough support ... according to the web site RealClearPolitics the average rate of Johnson [was] 8.4% Jill Stein was 3.2%." Articles even named each of the moderators for each debate, as well as their affiliations, with one article noting the moderators were "of the more diversified options, including two women, [the] first Asian American, and an open homosexual (*CCN* anchor, Anderson Cooper)."[9]

Further attention was given to the topics expected to be covered and time devoted to answering questions. For instance, "The first presidential debate will be for a period of time, about 15 minutes each, a total 90 minutes, during which no advertising [would occur]" and the "topics selected by the Chairman" were decided "at least a week" in advance.[10] General topics to be addressed were explained, including "America's direction, achieving prosperity, and securing America" with the Commander in Chief Forum focusing "on the United States national security, military action and veterans." Describing how the candidates were expected to answer the questions, articles explained that the moderator "at the beginning of each time [will ask] a question, each candidate [has] the time to answer two minutes later, a candidate can respond to each other's answer." Finally, articles even provided historical explanations regarding US presidential debate practice, with one citing the Commission on Presidential Debates' website stating the practice "dates back to 1858, [between] Lincoln and Douglas." The article continues to note who puts on the debates, stating that the Commission on Presidential Debates was "founded in 1987 ... to ensure that presidential debate [remains] as a permanent part [of US Presidential Elections]" and is a "non-profit, non-partisan organization" engaged in "debate research and education." According to the article, this institution was set up to "ensure ... the best possible information to the audience."[11]

While Chinese readers ostensibly became informed consumers regarding US debates and democratic election procedures, positive appraisals of the process were largely lacking. Instead, the details of the election process more likely served to explain the "rules" of the process like a sport. For instance, a common theme was the debates' large viewership.[12] As *Sohu News* reported, "it is expected that the debate on the TV viewers will be high, experts said the figure might be more than 100 million" noting this would be more than those tuning in to the 2015 Super Bowl. *Enlightenment Daily* compared the campaign to a "war situation" and *Global Times,* when recounting the Vice Presidential Debate, explained how "Kane 'strategically attacked' frequent[ly] interrupting and disrupt[ed] his opponent's speech." Other characterizations noted the "fierce competition," or the debates being "filled with gunpowder;" comparisons were even made to Roman gladiatorial matches and circuses.[13] In addition, the coverage included extensive commentary regarding "who won," as well as close tracking of the latest polls noting who was pulling ahead, what impact that had on the election, and how the candidates might come back. Thus, the election process was reported as a political contest, rather than a practice of democratic governance, despite the rich informational content of news reporting.

Negative Depictions of the US Process: Narratives of Illegitimacy

Whereas Chinese readers were provided with significant information on how US democracy worked, the absence of positive evaluations in combination with this information resulted in an unclear narrative outside of understanding it as a contest. However, when turning to commentary and reflection of the candidates' actual debate performances, a clear narrative questioning and even critique of the process emerged. For instance, numerous articles challenged the informational nature of the 2016 debates.[14] As *Xinhua* reported, while the first debate lasted "about 90 minutes, the two candidates for election basically [did] not [present] a new idea, but only briefly reiterate[d] their economic, security and diplomatic [stances], [instead spending] more time to attack each other." These attacks weren't on policy, but instead "the two sides engage[d] in more personal attack[s] on each other." Thus, the debates "lack[ed] substantive content of the policy environment" and "had become empty words;"[15] as an article from *Southern Weekly* put it, the debates were like "television soap operas, lo[sing] the serious policy issues"[16] and the persuasive purpose of the debates was questioned, whereby despite "US media claim[ing] that Hillary won the first debate in the election ... only a few Americans changed their mind after the debate."[17] Thus, the debates were not exemplars of US democracy, but instead, the "debates [are] increasingly dirty acts that undermine the virtues of democracy in the West."[18]

The visceral attacks within the 2016 debates were explained as standing out from other election years. As an article published by *Cankao Xiaoxi* noted, "at first glance [one] would imagine that this is a normal presidential debate, the two candidates competing, intense discussion in their respective [stances on] abortion and arms control policy, even on immigration rules [being] properly implemented." However, the article continued by noting how the debates degenerated into discussion of the candidates' various scandals, including Hillary's "attack" towards Trump and "the mystery ... [of his] relations between Russia" with Trump "answer[ing] back sarcastically" that she was a "puppet of Russia," and continuing to attack Hillary's email server scandal, her ties to the Clinton Foundation, and the "embarrassing" hacking incident disclosing her campaign's emails. This behavior proved "he [Trump] was not ... suitable to be 'President' [and] doomed [his] platform into confusion," as well demonstrating his failure to "exercise restraint" in the debates.[19] Indeed, this campaign was distinct as, "there is no need to worry about a week [without] such explosive materials," leading to "loss [of] the serious policy issues," and that "regardless who is bound to the White House...it will be an interesting election."[20]

Further evidence was given, questioning the extent to which people actually tuned in and listened. As *Xinhua* noted, the debates' "ratings are expected to create a new high," but that "a number of people watching fell asleep before the end of the debate. [After] half an hour, only about half of the people were [still watching]." Articles placed the high ratings of the debates in context, noting that "support of the two parties" is "the lowest in 10 years" and suggested that "many people [tuned in] out of curiosity" expecting "the debate will be ugly" with "fierce competition" or "filled with gunpowder."[21] Thus, the extent to which Americans were following the campaigns as a means to become informed was in doubt, with *Southern Weekly* comparing the process to the Roman Empire's use of circuses and free bread as an "enduring weapon" to keep the masses entertained: "In the Roman period ... there are two important means ... to attract voters" and maintain support: "people's hunger for bread and excitement ... The US presidential election this year, the world has witnessed a modern version of the 'bread and circus.'"[22] As *Global Times* put it, "citizens do not care about the many problems, but will focus on ... scandal."[23]

Disenchantment with the US process was highlighted. Part of this disenchantment fell to the candidates, but also the system in general. The candidates' scandals and voters' distrust of them were frequently cited. As the *Chinese Communist Party* reported, "the two presidential candidates are mired in disputes, enhancing the voters' dissatisfaction and uncertainty in the future.[24] Another article quoted one of the moderators in the Vice Presidential debate asking the candidates, "the chairpersons so sharp[ly] ask[ed] why 60% [of] voters did not trust the Democratic Party's presidential candidate Hillary [and] 67% voters why the Republican presidential candidate election [was a] risk?"[25] The article continues by noting that both candidates appear to be digging up dirt with negative campaign tactics dominating the discourse in "shameful" ways in place of substantive policy discussion. As an article from *News163* put it, the candidates were "injuring" each other, showing to voters "the true features of the candidates" suggesting that they must choose between two bad candidates, feeling ashamed of both, and that "of course no matter who will win, it would certainly be bad for the United States."[26] The choice between "two bad candidates" appeared in other articles as an indictment towards the political system, leaving US audience with two "status quo" candidates; thus, whereby "American people are [supposed] to receive guidance from the leader, however, they found that apart from maintaining the status quo, there is no alternative. They have lost hope."[27]

Even after the debates, reflection on where the election stood showcased continued dismay from voters and, thus, the failure of the process: "The US presidential election has entered the final stage, the two candidates competing for more and more intense, and the people of confusion and frustration has deepened." Polling data was cited to show that "in a recent opinion poll shows that of the registered voters as high as 60% dissatisfaction" with "Hillary Clinton the most unpopular candidate in 25 years."[28] Furthermore multiple articles picked up a quotation from a North Carolinian individual, who stated "No matter who is the president, it is the same [outcome]" and "no matter who wins the general election, the United States lost."[29]

Further questioning of the fairness or democratic nature of the US process included questions of elites and money in politics, corruption, and excessive lobbying. As an article noted, "the 2016 presidential election will spend more than 5 billion US dollars, becoming the most expensive election [in] history" with voters "dissatisfied with money politics."[30] Another article explained how lobbyists have undue influence, injecting cash into the election with political elites being the only ones capable of gaining their support.[31] The dominance of elites was described as creating a "new aristocracy," as well as an "oligarchy" whereby in "the political arena family color [is] increasingly strong." Thus, politics was a game played only by elites, not reflective of "representative democracy."[32] Furthermore, both Clinton and Trump were viewed as corrupt, and the election was frequently called a "farce."[33] The media was charged as biased,[34] and the extent to which the process was legitimate was further questioned with Trump's insistence of voter fraud, unwillingness to uphold the election outcomes, and suggestion that Clinton should be in jail,[35] as well as reports of militias taking up arms worrying that if Hillary is elected she will take their guns, causing the group to march on Washington.[36]

Taken together, these negative characterizations of the US election process coalesced into a narrative of US decline and failing democratic governance. One article commenting on the implication of the 2016 election in reference to the American Dream noted that "the United States social realities" reflect "increasing disparity," with the presidential candidates "turning a blind eye" to these realities. Furthermore, the weak US economy was attributed as leading to increased "political polarization, economic recession in the middle class and racial discrimination" with a "flood of guns ... further intensify[ing] social rift."[37] Polls were often cited in support of this, showing "a large number of [voters] dissatisfied with the national situation ... the Government and Congress ...followed by the Economic and migration, [and] unemployment." Even more explicitly, articles reported that "[t]he highlight of the ... shortcomings of the United States political election ... for many people dissatisfied with money politics and elections [and] for a procession [of] scandal"[38] Altogether, "increasing inequality and slowing productivity growth, [shows] the democratic system [has] become unbearable and capitalism has gradually lost its legitimacy." Thus, the 2016 election marked a "ten road junction" whereby "[f]or a long time, the United States ... election symbol[ized] the advantages of the system ... however, the meaning of [the] election [points] to the grim reality;" that reality being "no matter who is elected, restor[ing] social division of the United States is [an] extremely arduous tasks"[39] with which "political figures in the mission of good governance [did] not engage in the democratic election."[40]

National and International Narratives: China's Place in the World and US–China Relations

The international narratives described what role the US was to play in the global order with much greater detail placed on its implications for Chinese power. National and issue-specific narratives were drawn upon to compose these international narratives including what the future of US–China relations would look like, juxtaposing US decline with Chinese strength, and the implications for US moral leadership more broadly. The winner of the election was viewed as both possessing important consequences for China,[41] yet having limited impact on the larger relationship, stressing the continuity of the bilateral relationship regardless of who entered the White House.[42] Thus, while at times articles criticized the US, they nevertheless concluded that "no matter who the next president of the United States, China and the United States as two big countries to deal with the best choice is cooperation rather than confrontation."[43]

Narratives of US–China Relations

Overall, discussion of US–China relations within the campaign was reported as "declining in number" because "voters and candidates [wanted] to focus on issues of the United States and the people's internal affairs."[44] As *China Elections* reported, "The only reference to the diplomatic issues ... suggested that China is capable of hacking, and stressed that China should resolve the DPRK nuclear issue." Thus, "it is not difficult to see the intention of [the] ruthless pursuit of the Chinese diplomatic issues" with "the main [topic being] Chinese taking away jobs from Americans."[45] Indeed, direct mentioning of China during the debates was limited, and the issues discussed revolved primarily around economic and trade topics. The Chinese media picked up on this and reported, for example, how China was accused of causing unfairly low steel prices, with an article quoting Hillary Clinton as stating "I will appoint [a] Prosecutor to ensure that China will not be lowering [prices of] steel."[46] Likewise, Trump's preference for trade protectionism raised concerns over the potential for a trade war,[47] while also using China as a foil of the American economy whereby he stated, "We [the US] have no growth, China's gross national product to 7% is a national disaster, but we have GDP of only 1%" with the article noting that Trump was "commending" China as "strong" and the US economy was "weak."[48]

In general, both candidates were described as "not friendly" to China. As the *Global Times* noted,

> It was reported that the attitude toward China, the two candidates did not seem to [be] friendly. During the election, the number of criticisms on China [included] trade issues ... [taking] jobs away from the United States ... [and with] the South China Sea issue, a hardline stance of China.[49]

Experts interviewed explained that regarding the two candidates' China policies "the major difference lies in coherence." Hillary's policy would "strike a balance between the cooperation and friction" and wouldn't test relations between the two countries.[50] Trump on the other hand was noted as having "no real 'China policy'" outside an "overall position of protectionism" and "isolation." These elements of Trump's policy were described as incongruous with the past 60 years of American foreign policy, and thus, "If he is elected, he will not represent the continuity of the China policy and [in] practice what it means [is] that [he is] unpredictable."[51]

Regardless of Trump's unpredictable nature, he was reported as having a better impression in China than Clinton. As *News163* explained, "he is the long-term businessman, compared to Hillary more inclined to transactions, so [he is] easier to work with."[52] Another article noted that if Hillary won, "we [China] may face more from the strategic and geopolitical challenge." However, while Hillary was viewed as providing a "tough stand of China" including her support of Obama's pivot to Asia policy, she was also commended for her experience as Secretary of State and aiding in promoting cultural exchanges.[53] Even with Hillary's supposedly tougher stance towards China, it was nothing to worry about given Chinese economic and political strength, with a *Global Times* article concluding that if Hillary won, China will "unlikely [be] subverted" as China has "undergone many changes in the United States President."[54]

Despite the candidates' differing implications for US–China relations, articles reassured that the bilateral relationship would continue as previously established. As the *Global Times* reported, no matter "who is elected, there is not a real impact on China [policy]" because there are forces outside of who is elected that provide continuity in US–China relations.[55] Furthermore, regardless of "who is President of the United States, there are forces [that] cannot change the trend … [of] high degree of integration" and "[f]undamentally speaking, the United States and the two countries have maintained very good [relations which] cannot change … [because] too many interests involved" suggesting a "stable relationship."[56] Another reason for continuity in US–China relations came from praising of Chinese power: "China has now become the strength of the positive momentum in relations" and the "Chinese people have now have more confidence, not long ago In Washington between the United States took the initiative." The article then states that "[t]he South Sea is an example" of this renewed Chinese strength whereby the US attempted to leverage its influence through "the notorious Asia Pacific balance [Obama's pivot/rebalance to Asia policy]" but that this "tough policy toward China was broken" thanks to Chinese influence.[57]

This narrative of Chinese strength vis-à-vis the US continued in discussion of future US–China trade relations. Concerns over both candidates' desire to toughen US trade relations with China led the Chinese media to reassure its audience that the US ability to win an "extreme trade war has diminished," noting that both candidates attempts to do so is a "cheap show" that "should not be [taken] too seriously."[58] Furthermore, the US was portrayed as "dependent on exports to China" and needing to "increase its investment to boost the employment of the United States;" thus, the US economy is viewed as weak whereas the Chinese economy is strong. As the *Global Times* put it, while "China and the United States does not want to fight a trade war" if one does occur "we [China] may not be unarmed."[59]

While the US presidential candidates focused their discussions on US–China relations on trade issues, the Chinese media still forecasted the implications of both Trump and Clinton's election for foreign policy topics. The key foreign policy issue discussed by the Chinese media focused on regional security, specifically in the Asian Pacific, and whether "the United States may withdraw its forces in Asia in the short term." The Obama administration's pivot to Asia was the starting point for this discussion, and whether the US would continue the policy or not.

Obama-era policies were viewed as trying to "split" China by developing relations with Southeast Asian nations, with the suggestion that, whoever is elected president, this "strong policy will not disappear."[60] This build-up of forces in the region was noted as "causing a lot of confusion" and "[t]his ambiguity to the situation is unstable, and the United States on the contrary would likely to increase input in Asia."[61] Given this tenuous situation, an article stressed the need for both continuity in US–China relations, as well as the US adapting to Beijing's legitimate interests: "Washington will have to adjust their policies in future [and] should take into account the legitimate interests [of] Beijing, but also to prevent the reckless behavior of the new situation" specifically by "ceas[ing] more military assets, such as aircraft carriers and other equipment to the naval forces of the region" otherwise the two would be in a "fierce collision."[62] Within this context previous US policy was criticized as "coercive" but that recent Chinese strength had limited this,[63] and, reflective of the 2016 election discourse, specifically its focus on issues internal to the US, it was "hope[d] that the United States [will] shrink in its imperial ambitions [and focus] more effort to revitalize the economy and employment."[64]

Narratives of US Soft Power

US soft power, moral leadership, and the legitimacy of democratic governance was portrayed as dimensioning due to the 2016 election. The 2016 election was described as a "showcase of democracy in the United States, the world has witnessed a negative example" that included "lacking concern for policy" and instead "indulging" in political scandals, and undermining the image of women.[65] The "image" of the US and its democratic system was challenged as unable to provide "competent" leaders, representing the failure of "western great aspirations of democratic elections" and marking a "declining empire."[66] As another article by the *Global Times* sarcastically noted, the US's "great democratic institution" leaves "voters faced" with a "choice" between "only two evils" and thus, "love of the United States' political system … is very difficult to praise."[67]

Money in politics, specifically the role of lobbyists, was cited as corrupting the system, leading the authors of one article to conclude that: "There is no doubt that the US election system needs to enhance transparency and introduce a new code of ethics." While others noted the process was incorrigible, stating "we believe that democracy should be done." In this sense, the 2016 election reflected

US democracy as running "out of democratic myths." Indeed, the US system was deemed not as "achieving representative democracy, but [the] election [of] nobility" with "elites ... becoming the master of games" or "instruments of domination, either for the political elite to shirk its responsibility under the pretext of 'legitimacy' ... and to become masters of democracy." Again sarcastically, an article listed the democratic "achievements" as causing "the financial crisis and the global economic recessions" which served to "further highlight" the "inefficiency of Western democracy."[68]

Other articles called the election "poor advertising," although it was "the most entertaining election."[69] Students studying in Beijing asked whether they thought US democracy or the Chinese Communist Party would eventually "win" selected the CCP, explaining their "reasons for not standing for the US election" which included "the election exacerbated the different social groups, and tore cohesion and effectiveness, and I think that this system will get nowhere." Chinese media reported that "there is no bottom" to the election, with it "becoming a joke."[70]

All of this was put into further historical context, noting that when the Soviet Union collapsed and took up democracy, "Russian democracy [became] frustrated," with another article going into greater detail stating that the Soviet Union's adoption of democracy was its "first political failure" and a "grave mistake" as Gorbachev gave "into [the] democratic myth, falling into the Western political trap" which led to the "disintegration" and "whole failure of the Soviet Union."[71] China on the other hand, under the leadership of the CCP became "increasingly prosperous" making "China into a model" of effective governance. Further challenges to democracy included US operations in the Middle East and the Arab Spring as showcasing the "weakening [of] democratic election."[72] Likewise, Western democracy was critiqued for claiming it is "universally applicable" and for forcing its "exporting," all as a means to "cover [its] geopolitical interests."[73] This led to "another round of international competition [causing] political turmoil and terror" leading to "incitement [of] ethnic, cultural and religious conflicts" with "democracy," "freedom," and "human rights," all "political tool[s]" which "won the cold war," destroyed the socialist political system, and, as the 2016 election demonstrated, has proven ineffective to govern and simply a cover for elites to exercise political control.[74]

Conclusion

Whereas Washington proudly touts itself as a model for democratic governance, Chinese media reporting of the 2016 presidential election highlighted the hypocrisy of such claims. While the majority of articles analyzed in this study presented information regarding the "nuts and bolts" of US electoral politics, narrative accounts of the candidates, their policies, the electoral process, US-style democracy, and US–China relations revealed considerable doubt regarding the efficacy of democracy as a form of effective governance, implicating US soft power and moral leadership in important and detrimental ways. As story-telling beings, the narratives we employ to make sense of the myriad of information, events, and potential futures we face have a significant and enduring impact on the choices we make and the policies we advocate for. In this sense, the 2016 election was used to affirm Chinese strength and the leadership of its ruling party by highlighting the failure of US electoral politics.

As Roselle, Miskimmon, and O'Loughlin (2014) argue, strategic narratives operate on three levels: issue, national, and international. On the issue level, the Chinese media drew upon statements from Hillary Clinton and Donald Trump's debate performances and their campaigns, US polls, and commentary from US news outlets as to who the candidates were and where they stood on a variety of issues. The predominant issue, however, was the multitude of scandals both candidates faced, questioning their character. On the issue of US–China relations, Hillary and Trump were deemed "unfriendly" and likely to challenge China on trade issues. Hillary was viewed as more likely to test Chinese strength in the Asia-Pacific region, while Trump was portrayed as more isolationist and transactional, potentially shifting US focus away from the Pacific, either towards the Middle East or back at home. Either way, the most prevalent topics of concern showcased an American electorate more inwardly focused, reflective of US domestic problems.

On the national level, the US was viewed as facing numerous problems from insipid economic growth to political polarization and social disintegration. The American electorate was portrayed not as democratically engaged citizens but instead as clamoring for political drama. Neither candidate provided Americans with a "good" choice to lead the nation and the election process lent itself towards political entertainment rather than thoughtful policy analysis. The US democratic system was described as corrupt, favoring elites, and ineffective for dealing with the numerous problems facing America, all acute problems given American decline economically and socially.

On the international level, the issue and national level narratives coalesced into a story of US decline, a lack of moral leadership, and evidence of the failure of democratic politics as a model for the world. For Chinese, this international narrative helped embolden their sense of accomplishment. China was juxtaposed as gaining in strength and influence, as well as economically proficient with competent leadership directing the nation in these areas. The 2016 election helped debunk the "myth" of democratic governance, showcasing its inefficiency and using the US as an example of failed governance.

To better understand the strength of these narratives in impacting US soft power, one can turn to Fisher's (1984, 1989) criteria of narrative coherence and fidelity. In terms of coherence, one can see the issue, national, and international level narratives supporting a common image of US decline due to its democratic governance. The US is in decline because of its political system; the political system is flawed because the American populace craves entertainment, money has corrupted the system, elites have taken control of the process; the candidates' shortcomings are a product of this failed system, leading to personal attacks, political polarization, economic stagnation, and general discontentment. This narrative is strengthened because of the multitude of problems and criticisms of the candidates and issues, as well as the numerous outlets and polls echoing this sentiment. Indeed, the candidates' statements and debate performances provided an ongoing account of all these problems and the Chinese media needed only to cite the US media's own account and reporting of its own failings.

In terms of fidelity, it is useful to reflect on a typical Chinese citizen's worldview. Within Chinese political thought social cohesion and effective governance have been the primary concern for millennia. Political dynasties collapse when internal cohesion unravels combined with economic stagnation and increasing social strife; good governance is supposed to create social harmony and rulers govern through moral leadership. In this sense, the narrative of political polarization within the US and the candidates' corruption or lack of integrity clearly points to an inability for effective governance. Furthermore, turning to US–China relations in particular, the Chinese have long considered the US as a hypocritical and hegemonic power, while craving their own return to power. Thus, narratives of US decline and lack of moral leadership further play in to the desired or gratifying picture of US weakness and Chinese strength.

Regardless of whether the US is in decline or whether Western style democracy is the "best" form of governance, the Chinese media narratives of the 2016 US presidential election nevertheless serve as a cautionary tale. The ability of Washington to continue pressuring China for further democratic reforms will be more difficult, with Chinese leaders less likely to be persuaded of its benefits and Chinese citizens likewise believing in the deficiencies of the US system, and perhaps more aware of their own system's successes. On issues of US–China relations, the belief in US decline will likely embolden the Chinese leadership to continue its quest for political supremacy in the Asia-Pacific, while raising doubts regarding the US commitment to the region or its ability to continue its influence in the future. If soft power is anchored in the image of one's nation, following the 2016 US presidential election, the US's image has lost much of its attractiveness.

Notes

1 *Xinhua*. (2016, November 6). Data captured by Texas A&M's Media Monitoring System. Unpublished raw data.
2 *Southern Weekly*. (2016, October 9). Data captured by Texas A&M's Media Monitoring System. Unpublished raw data.
3 *Global Times*. (2016, November 8). Data captured by Texas A&M's Media Monitoring System. Unpublished raw data.
4 *Sohu News*. (2016, nd). Data captured by Texas A&M's Media Monitoring System. Unpublished raw data.
5 *Caixin*. (2016, November 8). Data captured by Texas A&M's Media Monitoring System. Unpublished raw data; *Ifeng News*. (2016, November 8). Data captured by Texas A&M's Media Monitoring System. Unpublished raw data; *News 163*. (2016, November 8). Data captured by Texas A&M's Media Monitoring System. Unpublished raw data.
6 *Enlightenment Daily*. (2016, September 23). Data captured by Texas A&M's Media Monitoring System. Unpublished raw data; *Caixin*. (2016, September 24). Data captured by Texas A&M's Media Monitoring System. Unpublished raw data.
7 *Southern Weekly*. (2016, October 13). Data captured by Texas A&M's Media Monitoring System. Unpublished raw data.

8 Ibid.

9 *Caixin*. (2016, September 24). Data captured by Texas A&M's Media Monitoring System. Unpublished raw data; *Enlightenment Daily*. (2016, September 23). Data captured by Texas A&M's Media Monitoring System. Unpublished raw data.

10 Ibid.

11 Ibid.

12 *Enlightenment Daily*. (2016, September 23). Data captured by Texas A&M's Media Monitoring System. Unpublished raw data; *Sohu News*. (2016, nd). Data captured by Texas A&M's Media Monitoring System. Unpublished raw data; *Global Times*. (2016, October 6). Data captured by Texas A&M's Media Monitoring System. Unpublished raw data.

13 *Southern Weekly*. (2016, October 13). Data captured by Texas A&M's Media Monitoring System. Unpublished raw data; *Xinhua*. (2016, September 28). Data captured by Texas A&M's Media Monitoring System. Unpublished raw data.

14 *Xinhua*. (2016, September 28). Data captured by Texas A&M's Media Monitoring System. Unpublished raw data; *Chinese Communist Party*. (2016, October 8). Data captured by Texas A&M's Media Monitoring System. Unpublished raw data; *Global Times*. (2016, November 8). Data captured by Texas A&M's Media Monitoring System. Unpublished raw data.

15 *Xinhua*. (2016, September 28). Data captured by Texas A&M's Media Monitoring System. Unpublished raw data.

16 *Southern Weekly*. (2016, October 9). Data captured by Texas A&M's Media Monitoring System. Unpublished raw data.

17 *News 163*. (2016, October 11). Data captured by Texas A&M's Media Monitoring System. Unpublished raw data.

18 *Tiexue*. (2016, November 60). Data captured by Texas A&M's Media Monitoring System. Unpublished raw data.

19 *Cankao Xiaoxi*. (2016, October 20). Data captured by Texas A&M's Media Monitoring System. Unpublished raw data.

20 *Southern Weekly*. (2016, October 9). Data captured by Texas A&M's Media Monitoring System. Unpublished raw data.

21 *Xinhua*. (2016, September 28). Data captured by Texas A&M's Media Monitoring System. Unpublished raw data.

22 *Southern Weekly*. (2016, October 13). Data captured by Texas A&M's Media Monitoring System. Unpublished raw data.

23 *Global Times*. (2016, November 8). Data captured by Texas A&M's Media Monitoring System. Unpublished raw data.

24 *Chinese Communist Party*. (2016, October 8). Data captured by Texas A&M's Media Monitoring System. Unpublished raw data.

25 *Southern Weekly*. (2016, October 9). Data captured by Texas A&M's Media Monitoring System. Unpublished raw data.

26 *News 163*. (2016, October 11). Data captured by Texas A&M's Media Monitoring System. Unpublished raw data.

27 *Global Times*. (2016, November 8). Data captured by Texas A&M's Media Monitoring System. Unpublished raw data.

28 *Chinese Communist Party*. (2016, October 8). Data captured by Texas A&M's Media Monitoring System. Unpublished raw data.

29 *Xinhua*. (2016, September 28). Data captured by Texas A&M's Media Monitoring System. Unpublished raw data.

30 *Chinese Communist Party*. (2016, October 8). Data captured by Texas A&M's Media Monitoring System. Unpublished raw data.

31 *Global Times*. (2016, November 8). Data captured by Texas A&M's Media Monitoring System. Unpublished raw data.

32 *Southern Weekly*. (2016, November 8). Data captured by Texas A&M's Media Monitoring System. Unpublished raw data.

33 *Global Times*. (2016, October 14). Data captured by Texas A&M's Media Monitoring System. Unpublished raw data; *Global Times*. (2016, November 8). Data captured by Texas A&M's Media Monitoring System. Unpublished raw data.

34 *Cankao Xiaoxi*. (2016, November 8). Data captured by Texas A&M's Media Monitoring System. Unpublished raw data.

35 *Sina*. (2016, October 17). Data captured by Texas A&M's Media Monitoring System. Unpublished raw data.

36 *Tiexue*. (2016, November 6). Data captured by Texas A&M's Media Monitoring System. Unpublished raw data.

37 Ibid.

38 *Chinese Communist Party*. (2016, October 8). Data captured by Texas A&M's Media Monitoring System. Unpublished raw data.

39 *Southern Weekly*. (2016, October 13). Data captured by Texas A&M's Media Monitoring System. Unpublished raw data.

40 *Chinese Communist Party*. (2016, October 8). Data captured by Texas A&M's Media Monitoring System. Unpublished raw data.

41 *Global Times*. (2016, November 8). Data captured by Texas A&M's Media Monitoring System. Unpublished raw data.

42 Ibid.

43 *News 163*. (2016, November 8). Data captured by Texas A&M's Media Monitoring System. Unpublished raw data.

44 *China elections*. (2016, October 11). Data captured by Texas A&M's Media Monitoring System. Unpublished raw data.

45 Ibid.

46 Ibid.

47 *Jingji Cankao Bao*. (2016, November 8). Data captured by Texas A&M's Media Monitoring System. Unpublished raw data.

48 *China elections*. (2016, October 11).

49 *Global Times*. (2016, November 8). Data captured by Texas A&M's Media Monitoring System. Unpublished raw data.

50 Ibid.

51 Ibid.

52 *News 163*. (2016, November 8). Data captured by Texas A&M's Media Monitoring System. Unpublished raw data.

53 Ibid.

54 *Global Times*. (2016, November 8). Data captured by Texas A&M's Media Monitoring System. Unpublished raw data.

55 Ibid.

56 Ibid.

57 Ibid.

58 Ibid.

59 Ibid.

60 *Global Times*. (2016, November 8). Data captured by Texas A&M's Media Monitoring System. Unpublished raw data.

61 Ibid.

62 Ibid.

63 Ibid.

64 Ibid.

65 Ibid.

66 Ibid.

67 *Global Times*. (2016, October 14). Data captured by Texas A&M's Media Monitoring System. Unpublished raw data.
68 *Global Times*. (2016, November 8). Data captured by Texas A&M's Media Monitoring System. Unpublished raw data.
69 *Tiexue*. (2016, November 6). Data captured by Texas A&M's Media Monitoring System. Unpublished raw data.
70 *Tiexue*. (2016, 11/6). Data captured by Texas A&M's Media Monitoring System. Unpublished raw data.
71 *Global Times*: Zhang Shuhua, the West to democracy has become a "bad" 10/14/2016.
72 *Tiexue*. (2016, November 6). Data captured by Texas A&M's Media Monitoring System. Unpublished raw data.
73 *Global Times*. (2016, October 14). Data captured by Texas A&M's Media Monitoring System. Unpublished raw data.
74 Ibid.

References

Bradsher, K. (2016, June 29). In trade stances toward China, Clinton and Trump both signal a chill. *New York Times*. Retrieved from https://www.nytimes.com/2016/06/30/business/international/hillary-clinton-donald-trump-trade-china.html.

Broomfield, E. V. (2003). Perceptions of danger: The China threat theory. *Journal of Contemporary China*, 12(35), 265–284.

Cao, Q. (2012). Modernity and media portrayals of China. *Journal of Asian Pacific Communication*, 22(1), 1–21.

Carpenter, T. G. (2012, October 11). China bashing: A US political tradition. Reuters. Retrieved from http://blogs.reuters.com/great-debate/2012/10/11/china-bashing-a-political-tradition/.

Deng, Y. (2006). Reputation and the security dilemma: China reacts to the China threat theory. In A. I. Johnston & R. S. Ross (Eds.), *New directions in the study of China's foreign policy* (pp. 186–214). Stanford, CA: Stanford University Press.

Dong, W. (2016, November 9). Watching the US presidential election from China. The Diplomat. Retrieved from http://thediplomat.com/2016/11/watching-the-us-presidential-election-from-china/.

Dwyer, P. (2015, August 28). Republicans' misguided China-bashing. Bloomberg. Retrieved from https://www.bloomberg.com/view/articles/2015-08-28/republicans-misguided-china-bashing.

Fisher, W. F. (1984). Narration as a human communication paradigm: The case of public moral argument. *Communication Monographs*, 51(1), 1–22.

Fisher, W. F. (1989). *Human Reason as narration: Toward a philosophy of reason, value, and action*. Columbia, SC: University of South Carolina Press.

Garrison, J. A. (2005). *Making China policy: From Nixon to GW Bush*. Boulder, CO: Lynne Rienner.

Goh, E. (2005). *Constructing the US rapprochement with China, 1961–1974: From "Red Menace" to "Tacit Ally"*. Cambridge, UK: Cambridge University Press.

Hinck, R. S., Manly, J. N., Kluver, R. A., & Norris, W. J. (2016). Interpreting and shaping geopolitics in Chinese media: The discourse of the "New style of great power relations". *Asian Journal of Communication*, 26(5), 427–445.

Irwin, N. (2016, March 17). What Donald Trump gets pretty much right, and completely wrong, about China. *New York Times*. Retrieved from https://www.nytimes.com/

2016/03/17/upshot/what-donald-trump-gets-pretty-much-right-and-completely-wrong-about-china.html.

Isaacs, H. R. (2015). *Scratches on our minds: American images of China and India*. New York: M.E. Sharpe, Inc.

Jespersen, T. C. (1999). *American images of China, 1931–1949*. Stanford, CA: Stanford University Press.

Kissinger, H., & Hormann, N. (2011). *On China*. New York: Penguin Press.

Mackerras, C. (1989). *Western images of China*. Oxford, UK: Oxford University Press.

Meyers, J. (2016, September 26). China tunes in to US presidential debate to witness "a drama of hurting each other". *Los Angeles Times*. Retrieved from https://www.nytimes.com/2016/01/04/world/asia/china-presidential-debates-trump-clinton.html.

Mosher, S. W. (1990). *China misperceived: American illusions and Chinese reality*. New York: Basic Books.

Own, G. (2016, January 3). Bringing US presidential debates to a Chinese audience. *New York Times*. Retrieved from: http://www.latimes.com/nation/politics/trailguide/la-na-trump-clinton-debate-updates-china-tunes-in-to-u-s-presidential-1474953609-htmlstory.html.

Ramirez, C. D. (2013). The political economy of "currency manipulation" bashing. *China Economic Review*, 27, 227–237.

Roselle, L., Miskimmon, A., & O'Loughlin, B. (2014). Strategic narrative: A new means to understand soft power. *Media, War & Conflict*, 7(1), 70–84.

Rosenfeld, E. (2016, July 7). Trump vs. Clinton: How China views the US elections. CNBC. Retrieved from http://www.cnbc.com/2016/07/07/trump-vs-clinton-how-china-views-the-us-elections.html.

Shambaugh, D. (1993). *Beautiful imperialist: China perceives America, 1972–1990*. Princeton, NJ: Princeton University Press.

Shambaugh, D. L. (2013). *China goes global: The partial power*. Oxford, UK: Oxford University Press.

Spence, J. D. (1998). *The Chan's great continent: The Chinese in Western minds*. New York: W.W. Norton.

Sutter, R. G. (2013). *US–Chinese relations: Perilous past, pragmatic present*. Lanham, MD: Rowman & Littlefield.

Tucker, N. (2013). The evolution of US–China relations. In D. Shambuagh (Eds.), *Tangled titans* (pp. 29–52). Lanham, MD: Rowman & Littlefield.

Vogel, E. (2013). *Deng Xiaoping and the transformation of China*. Cambridge, MA: Harvard University Press.

Wang, J., & Lieberthal, K. (2012). *Addressing US–China strategic distrust*. Washington, DC: Brookings Institution.

Wike, R., & Stokes, B. (2016, October 5). Chinese public sees more powerful role in world, names US as top threat. Pew Research Center: Global Attitudes & Trends. Retrieved from http://www.pewglobal.org/2016/10/05/chinese-public-sees-more-powerful-role-in-world-names-u-s-as-top-threat/.

Wilder, D. (2009). The US–China strategic and economic dialogue. *China Brief*, 9(10), 4–6. Retrieved from https://jamestown.org/wp-content/uploads/2009/05/cb_009_03.pdf?x87069.

Zoellick, R. (2005, September 21). Whither China: From membership to responsibility? Remarks to National Committee on US–China Relations. Retrieved from https://2001-2009.state.gov/s/d/former/zoellick/rem/53682.htm.

4

ARAB VIEWS OF THE US ELECTION

Culturally-Positive and Politically-Negative Depictions of US Democracy

Natalie Khazaal and Robert Hinck

Introduction

The US has a complicated relationship with the Middle East. Prior to 2001 and during the Cold War, the US sought to reduce Soviet influence by supporting anti-communist regimes and backing Israel against Soviet-sponsored Arab countries, while working to safeguard a stable flow of Gulf oil. Since 2001, however, the US' focus has been on fighting the war on terror and spreading democracy within the region to mixed results. Today, partnership with Arab nations is as important as before, and yet, Arab audiences, having watched past US presidential candidates explain their visions for the region, remain pessimistic about US intentions, albeit receptive to larger ideas of democracy.

Despite the considerable amount of resources poured into the region by the US, its relations remain fraught as few Arab nations hold positive images of the country. For instance, five Arab states ranked among the top 10 countries with the most negative perceptions of the US in 2014 (Stokes, 2014). This negative image of the US is important to consider in that it is harder for a state to exercise influence over international audiences who take negative attitudes about that state. Influence (or "soft power") depends on three basic resources: culture, political values, and foreign policies (Nye, 2004). More importantly, influence depends on how these resources are perceived by others (Lock, 2010). The role of international audiences, then, is not that of a receptacle but a participant (Mattern, 2007). As power is exercised in the context of relationships, international audiences condition a state's behavior. All this is based on expectations of how these audiences interpret a state's attractiveness (Lock, 2010). How then has the US engaged with Arab actors as international audiences, given that they have an important participatory role as evaluators of US attractiveness, and therefore influence? And how can narratives of the 2016 US presidential election in the Arab media be illuminated by exploring the role of Arab audiences?

This chapter examines coverage of the 2016 US presidential election within regional Arab media rather than a single Arab country because the unified, interdependent regional media shapes and reflects shared perceptions about Arabs and the US, despite social and political differences among Arab countries. Such narratives didn't appear in a vacuum but out of a dialogue with the West (Sabry, 2010), which had defined itself as modern and progressive against a backward Arab world (Said, 1979). If the US sees itself as a benevolent actor, a defender of democracy, and unbiased mediator, Arabs see it through a more ambivalent, culturally-positive/politically-negative narrative (Berger, 2014; Furia & Lucas, 2008; Charney & Yakatan, 2005). Arab public opinion polling during the 2016 US presidential election demonstrates this dual attitude. According to a poll conducted by the Arab Center, more than 70 percent of the interviewees held positive attitudes towards US citizens, while around 70 percent held negative attitudes towards US policy in the Arab world with these results being consistent with Arab attitudes towards the US since the 1940s and 1950s (ACW, 2016).

Arab Narratives of the US: Culturally-Positive but Politically-Negative

Arab narratives regarding the US are not solely negative. Indeed, a positive narrative exists, underscoring admiration for many aspects of the American political and social system like democracy, human rights, the rule of law, independent press and judiciary, strong economy, and technological progress (Rugh, 2018). Although this is not widely known, this positive narrative was the dominant one until around World War II, espoused even by Islamists. For example, the leader of the Muslim Brotherhood, Sayyid Qutb, praised the US after his visit in 1948: "All that requires power and muscle are where American genius shines. [...] For humanity to be able to benefit from American genius they must add great strength to the American strength" (Qutb, 2000, 26). In this early period, Arabs perceived the US as a benevolent force in comparison to the Ottoman Empire, which suppressed Arab nationalist identity, and later to Britain, France, and Russia, known for their imperialist aspirations and colonial practices. The positive image of US benevolence was primarily due to the contributions of US religious missions to the region's educational system and printing industry.

However, a second, more negative narrative emerged in the 1940s and 1950s and "profoundly complicate[d] the meaning of America for Arabs" (Makdisi, 2002, 539). This narrative was not an outcome of inherent blind hatred or a clash of civilizations (Berger, 2011; Makdisi, 2002). Instead, US policies and failure to consider Arabs' role in assessing those policies—in other words, to engage with Arab actors as key international audiences—generated images of a hypocritical, aggressive, and deaf US (Matar, 2016). The US understood itself as a benevolent advocate for democracy, yet it turned a blind eye on the repression of local opposition by authoritarian Arab regimes after they built a symbiotic relationship with the US government and oil companies. The US image in the Arab world further deteriorated with the devastating invasion of Iraq in 2003, the ensuing misguided democracy projects, as well as state-sponsored torture and unintended Muslim radicalization (Hinnebusch, 2007; Amine, Chao & Arnold, 2005; Charney & Yakatan, 2005; Robichaud & Goldbrenner, 2005). US diplomacy has traditionally been a device to tell the American story, given the asymmetrical US–Arab relationship (Matar, 2016; Yaqub, 2002). This has created perceptions of a deaf propagandist and triggered Arabs' identity defense mechanisms (Zaharna, 2010; Kurlantzick, 2007). For instance, the U.S. State Department's office for public diplomacy employed no American Muslims until 2008, after which Secretary of State Clinton also started "listening tours" in the Middle East to partially address Arab perceptions of US deafness.

Although all of these issues play a role in perceptions of the US, it is US policy on the Arab–Israeli conflict that is the strongest trigger for the negative US narrative. This issue is of primary political importance for Arabs because of the millions of Palestinian refugees who add to already tough economic and social problems in host Arab states and because of the common identity Palestinians share with other Arabs. The American public—unfamiliar with the details of this historical conflict—sees the creation of Israel exclusively as a way to correct the injustice of the Holocaust. Consequently, the US has articulated its own role in the conflict as an honest broker (Makdisi, 2014; Patrick, 2011; see also McAlister, 2005). By contrast, Arabs see staunch US support for Israel, despite the latter's discrimination against Palestinians, as wrong, and argue that it makes Arabs pay for the "grave moral wrong" of European anti-Semitism (Patrick, 2011). The Palestinian issue, then, has crystalized American conceptions of Arabs, Arab conceptions of Americans, and Arab–American conceptions of their place in these relations. Of course, such narratives overlook the complexity of internal Israeli politics, as well as the exploitation of the Palestinian issue by authoritarian regimes and the Islamist opposition for their own survival. Yet, Arabs find this issue so vital for negotiating their place in the global community that even Islamist and secular groups with diametrically opposing views on US democracy share a negative US narrative when it comes to Palestine (Makdisi, 2002, 554). According to the previously cited poll conducted by the Arab Center during the 2016 US elections, a just solution to the Palestinian cause ranked among the top three issues for Arabs, together with US non-intervention in the Arab world and combatting ISIS (ACW, 2016).

This negative narrative has not prevented a number of Arab states from seeking the US as an ally. However, developments in US–Arab relations since 9/11 have pushed even those states to search for alternatives. George W. Bush alienated former US allies in the Arab world because he intervened too much (Freeman, 2009). By contrast, Barak Obama intervened too little (Zogby, 2017), but this very reserve divided Arab regimes and their people in new ways. Arab authoritarian regimes fear that the US would forsake them overnight like when it sided with the Egyptian people against their dictator Mubarak (Khatib, 2017). US inaction against Assad's use of chemical weapons, on the other hand, has left the Syrian people despondent. Further, US failure to grow a moderate opposition to Assad's regime, despite spending half a billion dollars has convinced Gulf states that the US is a weak protector now (Tomlinson, 2015). A US isolationist mood, triggered by public outcry against involvement in Iraq and Afghanistan and the infusion of domestic shale oil into the US economy, has further pushed Gulf states to start acting more independently (Khatib, 2017).

To many Arabs, then, the current world order headed by the US was in serious trouble heading into the 2016 election campaign. Global competitors for influence, such as Iran, Turkey, Russia, China, and others reemerged, causing Arab societies to seriously deliberate their alignment with the US. In the new competitive environment, Iranian influence in particular has increased dramatically, luring Arab states and actors such as Iraq, Lebanon, and the Palestinians away from reliance on the US (Freeman, 2009). At the same time, states like Saudi Arabia, who feel threatened, try to challenge Iranian influence in the Arab world indirectly.

US Elections and Arab Perceptions

While the 2016 US presidential election garnered the attention of Arab audiences, it was not the first election to do so. Arab cynicism of US presidential candidates reaches at least back to the 2004 George Bush–John Kerry election. During this time, leading Saudi commentator and editor of *Arab News Dailey*, Khaled al-Maeena, claimed that both Bush and Kerry could do little to help the Middle East solve its problems (Pejman, 2004). Likewise, Egyptian journalist and deputy head of Cairo's Al-Ahram Center for Political and Strategic Studies, Al-Sayed Saeed, opined that Middle Easterners had low expectations for both candidates as neither were felt to truly reflect their interests. He went on to state (Pejman, 2004):

> While Arab public opinion has no particular preference in the present U.S. elections, different Arab governments have different preferences. But the dominant theory in the Arab street is the theory of "no difference." [In other words,] the two are [generally] seen to be anti-Arab, anti-Islamic, and the two are seen to be absolutely aligned to Israel.

Both commentators felt that ultimately it was Arabs themselves that would have to "take care of their own and not have their fate decided by reaction to what is happening outside" (Pejman, 2004).

The pessimism continued in the 2008 and 2012 elections. While candidate Obama at first garnered positive reactions from Arab audiences who viewed him as someone that could bring positive change to US policy in the Middle East, these feelings declined as Obama entered the presidential election and distanced himself from Middle Eastern and Muslim issues. *Al-Jazeera*, citing a Pew survey, reported that there was little enthusiasm for either candidate. As Arab audiences gained more information about the candidates' policies towards the Middle East they again began to see Obama's views on the Middle East as not radically different from McCain's or Bush's (Bayoumi, 2008). During the 2012 election, disenchantment over Obama's Middle Eastern policies grew as he was unable to deliver many of the promises he made in 2008 (Arab American Institute, 2012). This led Sobhi Ghandour, writing for the Arabic-language newspaper *Al Bayan*, to conclude that: "Reality and experiences have confirmed that there are American goals, interests and institutions that are fortified against the impact of changes in the American political scene and internal voting races" (Arab American Institute, 2012).

Turning to the 2016 election, both candidates' campaigns did little to change the persistent negative narrative on US policy, and in fact confounded Arabs. While Hillary Clinton appeared to endorse the majority of Obama's policies, Trump sent mixed signals to the Arab world. On one hand, his demands that Saudi Arabia pay for US protection scared Gulf states. On the other, his anti-Iranian rhetoric gave some Gulf states hopes that they could again serve as an important US ally in containing Iran, whose encroachment in the Arab world concerned them (Khatib, 2017). While Trump's anti-Muslim rhetoric alienated Arab publics, his militant statements against ISIS resonated with them. Many were relieved that Trump was unconcerned with nation-building and regime change, which has been a thorn in US–Arab relations since George W. Bush (Aqqad, 2018). But others saw him as an ignorant demagogue who would threaten American institutions and cause much harm internationally because he considered himself unrestrained by the traditions of US political doctrine (Aqqad, 2018). Despite the positive response to some of the mixed messages, Trump was seen as the worse choice. According to a poll conducted by the Arab Center (ACW, 2016) roughly 78 percent of Moroccans preferred Clinton as the next US president with only 20% who preferred Trump. The difference in Egypt and Iraq was only about three-fold, but the average difference for the Arab world showed a six-fold disparity in the positive associations with each candidate in favor of Clinton. The results also showed that six times more Arabs predicted that Clinton, not Trump, would have a positive impact on US policy in the Arab world (ACW, 2016).

Given this political environment, we would have two sets of expectations for Arab media's coverage of the 2016 US presidential election. First, Arab media's engagement with questions of democracy should be filtered through the ambivalent culturally-positive and politically-negative views of the US. We would expect the media to reflect Arab resentment about being ignored when it came to evaluating US policy in the Middle East. Second, given the complexity in negotiating modernity, politics, and culture among Arab governments and non-state actors, there should also be some diversity in the narrative constructions of the election and the two candidates.

Media Environment: Regional Diversity and International Competition

Whereas Russian and Chinese media are regulated by the laws of a single state and characterized by a high level of government control or influence, the Arab media environment differs in significant ways. First, Arab media constitutes a diverse regional system, not a national one like in the Russian and Chinese cases. Before its liberalization, it was a fragmented network of national media characterized by strong links between media organizations and political actors (Hallin & Mancini, 2004). However, with the adoption of satellite technology in the 1990s, Arab media became an integrated transnational system which penetrates national terrestrial markets (Kraidy & Khalil, 2009, 146–152). In some respects, it transcends even regional borders to form an expanded market that also caters to diasporas around the world, with a number of outlets still headquartered abroad. This pan-Arab market of private, state-owned, and mixed media is neither authoritarian nor liberal because it is inconsistently monitored by Arab governments and highly driven by commercial competition on a national, regional, and global scale.[1] The liberalization of broadcasting and the press in the 1990s led to debates on the issue of journalistic ethics (Hafez, 2008, 148). The outcome of this conversation was the establishment of current corporate ethics in Arab media that demonstrate support for objectivity and accuracy (Hafez, 2008, 154; Hafez, 2002).

The second key characteristic of Arab media is that it has become an international battleground for the attention of Arab audiences. The spectacular rise of regional Arab media in the 1990s led to a decrease in Arab dependence on Western information media (such as BBC Arabic radio or the Voice of America) and therefore to greater difficulty in passing on Western narratives.[2] The attacks on 9/11 in particular sparked US fears of losing the war for the "hearts and minds" of Arab audiences to stereotyped portrayals of the US in Arab media. Contrary to such fears, Arab reporting on international issues is far from the infantilized, government-manipulated coverage imagined in the West (Guaaybess, 2008, 201). As a result of its new corporate ethics, it is a negotiation of objective reporting and an "Arab perspective," or Arab community orientation (Ramaprasad & Hamdy, 2006). The Arab perspective's focus on the Palestinian issue (Bekhait, 1998) and on debates around an authentic Arab modernity, or multiple modernities, have often rendered it a challenger to dominant Western narratives.

The mediation of an Arab regional counter-narrative to Western perspectives sparked renewed global competition over influence in the region. As a result, global and regional players created state-backed outlets in Arabic language such as the US *Radio Sawa* (2002) and *al-Hurra TV* (2004), *Germany's DW Arabia* and *DW Arabia 2 TV* (2002), Iran's *al-Alam TV* (2003) and *al-Kawthar TV* (2006), *France 24 Arabic TV* (2007), Russia's *RT Rusiya al-Yawm TV* (2007), *BBC Arabic TV* (2008), and China's *CCTV Arabic* (2009). In an attempt to have a global reach, *al-Jazeera* launched *al-Jazeera English* (2006) and the short-lived US-based *al-Jazeera America*, which lasted from 2013 until 2016.

In sum, based on the diversification of Arab media, we should expect that its portrayals of the 2016 US presidential election would reflect diverse opinions rather than a single view. Yet, most of the coverage should focus on neutral, or balanced representation, given the developments in journalistic ethics, ownership, and competition.

Quantitative Results

To understand how Arabic language media reported on the 2016 US presidential election, researchers conducted a quantitative and qualitative analysis of 275 Arabic language news articles. The data was collected from 23 different Arabic language news sources chosen for their authority, popularity, political slant, as well as geographical location. Researchers were careful to select state, regional, and pan-Arab sources to better reflect the opinions of the region as a whole rather than one country in particular. The collection of data from 11 major sources during the weeks covering the presidential debates was substantively boosted with additional data. We included 12 more sources when Arab coverage of the elections increased dramatically—during the week leading up to and that directly following the presidential election. Three coders (one heritage speaker and two with some Arabic language ability) coded 30 separate questions regarding the content of the articles. Quantitative analysis of these articles demonstrated what topics were most often covered, whether the candidates and major parties were positively or negatively portrayed, source content and type of articles (editorial or news), and general perceptions of US democracy. This section will overview the quantitative analysis of the Arabic language articles with further exploration of key themes following in the qualitative section. For a more extended discussion of the research design and methodology, refer to Chapter 2.

With regards to the type of articles analyzed, 88 percent were news stories, 8.4 percent were editorials, and 3.6 percent were mixed or unclear in their orientation. Perhaps not surprisingly, Arab media relied heavily upon US sources to provide information on the election, with 52 percent of articles citing English language sources and only 24.5 percent citing foreign-language sources other than English. Slightly under a quarter of the stories included descriptions of the US election or presidential debate process, with 23.7 percent accurately explaining the process, and only 0.4 percent inaccurately doing so. When explaining the process, 87.6 percent of the stories took a neutral or purely informative tone, whereas 11 percent portrayed the process negatively, and only 1.5 percent portrayed it positively.

Hillary Clinton was mentioned in roughly 82 percent of the articles. She was most often neutrally described balancing both positive and negative characterizations of herself, policies, and campaign in 54 percent of the articles, positively portrayed in 13.9 percent, and negatively portrayed in 14.2 percent. Positive characterizations of Clinton came by articles reporting on her experience and intelligence, a more hawkish approach to Russian relations, superiority to Donald Trump, and her symbolic value as the first woman to win the US presidential nomination. She was also frequently mentioned as a continuation of Obama-era policies, which were praised and criticized. More negative issues and characterizations faced by her campaign most frequently included her e-mail scandal, the FBI investigation, and the Wikileaks' leaking of Democratic National Party e-mails, as well as her husband's infidelities. Recurring, yet less frequently mentioned issues included her handling of Middle East policy—especially Benghazi, her speaking honoraria from Wall Street executives, other signs of corruption, as well as her health and stamina. Clinton and her policies were rarely perceived as a threat to the region with, only 4.4 percent of articles raising serious concerns.

Trump was mentioned in 95.3 percent of the articles. Like Clinton, articles primarily balanced both positive and negative characterizations of his persona, policies, and campaign, doing so 51.8 percent of the time. However, unlike with Clinton, 40.9 percent of stories reported negatively on him, with only 2.6 percent focusing on positive attributes. Negative characterizations of Trump's character and policies were most frequently commentary on his numerous sexist remarks and additional "un-presidential" behavior such as his temperament, anger, undisciplined nature, lack of leadership qualities, and apparent racism towards Mexican and Middle Eastern immigrants. He was further criticized for not revealing his tax returns, ties with Russia, poor debate performances, and policy towards Middle Eastern refugees. Unlike with Clinton, Trump and his policies were portrayed as dangerous to the region, with 24.8 percent of the articles raising serious concerns about those policies.

The two major party candidates dominated reporting on the US presidential election, with only 3.6 percent of the articles analyzed including any references to third party candidates Gary Johnson and Jill Stein. While 80.2 percent of articles did not clearly suggest a preferred candidate for the Middle East, Clinton was nevertheless a 20-to-1 favorite compared to Trump. Nineteen percent of articles favored her, whereas only 0.7 percent favored Trump. After Trump's victory, a majority of articles refrained from directly commenting on whether the outcome was positive or negative for the Middle East. However, 16 articles remarked directly and none of them viewed his election as positive for the region, 4 percent suggested that it was negative, and 1.8 percent provided a mixed outlook.

The Republican and Democratic Parties were discussed far less frequently than their respective candidates. In only 19.3 percent of the stories was the Democratic Party mentioned, most often taking a neutral tone within 17.2 percent of the stories, a negative tone in 0.7 percent of the stories, and a positive tone in 1.5 percent. The Republican Party was mentioned in 28.4 percent of the articles, more frequently than the Democrats. None of the articles ascribed strictly positive attributes to the Republican Party, while 11.3 percent portrayed the party negatively, and 17.1 percent took a balanced or neutral stance. Questions of party unity within the Democratic Party appeared not to be of major concern. Although only 2.9 percent of the articles suggested the Democratic Party was unified, even fewer, 0.7 percent, raised questions of disunity. However, a larger number of articles focused on dissent within the Republican ranks, with 14.2 percent of articles reporting on disunity within the Party and only 0.7 percent suggesting Republicans were unifying around Trump.

We also examined coverage on whether the coverage suggested that the US election was "democratic," that is, representative of the "will of the people." This data set showed that 9.1 percent of the articles affirmed that the election reflected the desire of the US public, while 5.1 percent claimed it did not. However, a majority of articles, 85.8 percent, remained neutral or did not include discussion of the issue. In terms of the legitimacy of the US election, that is, whether the process correctly followed US election procedures, 5.8 percent of the articles overtly claimed it was illegitimate balanced with 5.1 percent affirming its legitimacy and 2.9 percent posing a mixed evaluation. Concerns over the legitimacy of the elections primarily took one of two forms: either criticism over the Electoral College trumping the popular vote, or questions of the role of corporations funding campaigns (campaign finance) and corruption in determining the outcome. Overall, the coverage suggested that US-style democracy is not worthy of emulation, with no articles positively describing it and 6.9 percent arguing against it. When reporting on whether democracy is desirable, again, the vast majority of articles analyzed failed to take a clear position. Only 3.5 percent of articles provided a positive or negative evaluation, with all 3.5 percent viewing democracy as undesirable.

The research team also asked four additional, region-specific coding questions for the Arabic data. These questions included specific US policy issues of relevance for the region including the candidate's plans for dealing with the conflict in Syria, combatting ISIS, the Iranian nuclear deal, and the Palestinian–Israeli conflict. Unfortunately, a majority of the articles tended not to focus on the candidates' policies on these topics. Out of the corpus of articles analyzed, 0.7 percent viewed Trump's Syria plan as positive for the region, with 2.9 percent viewing it as negative, and 3.65 percent as mixed, or composing both positive and negative elements. Similarly, Trump's plan for combatting ISIS was viewed primarily negatively, with no articles positively commenting on it, 2.9 percent viewing it negatively, and 1.1 percent being mixed. The implications regarding Trump's plan to renegotiate or renege on the Iranian nuclear agreement for the Middle East were unclear. No articles deemed it solely negatively or positively, while 5.1 percent of the articles described it as mixed. Finally, few articles suggested that a Trump presidency would contribute to an Arab–Israeli conflict resolution. Only 0.7 percent of all articles believed Trump would positively affect the conflict, 1.1 percent believed he would negatively contribute to it, and 1.1 percent posed a mixed evaluation.

Qualitative Narrative Analysis of the 2016 US Presidential Election

The strategic narratives in the Arab news coverage tackled the potential implications of each candidate's victory on Arab countries and issues. Not only did Arab regional media have to assess American influence but it also had to contend with the reality of US vested economic interests and military presence on Arab soil. Therefore, we see comparatively in-depth analysis of the candidates' positions extrapolating what US policy in the region might look like under a Clinton or a Trump presidency. In doing so, the Arab sources came to portray the election, on the whole, as a media event with candidates who were ignorant of the region and who represented a continuation of ineffective US policies. Nevertheless, democracy was held in a positive light, even though the 2016 US presidential election was a poor exemplar of democratic processes. Pessimism about US actions in the region, US connections to Israel, the future of Palestinian–Israeli relations, and foreign nations' operations in Syria all contributed to negative national and international level narratives of US policies. These portrayals contributed to calls for advocating for Arab interests given the failure of the US-led international order to genuinely benefit the Middle East.

Issue and National Level Narratives

Arab media described the election as a media event, rather than rational deliberation of ideas. Narratives of the candidates' character demonstrated overall neutral-to-positive views of Clinton and negative views of Trump as dangerous and immoral. Two important issue narratives garnered wider exposition: first, US support of Israel and its implications for the Palestinian–Israeli conflict, showcasing further Arab disillusionment with US policies and actions; and, second, US actions and policy regarding regional leadership tied to the conflict in Syria. Issue level narratives coalesced to inform Arab audiences of a self-interested US out of touch with Arab interests with waning influence in the region.

The Elections as a Media Event

Arab media provided ample but mostly unoriginal information about the elections. Television channels and the Arab press informed Arab publics of day-to-day developments in the Clinton and Trump campaigns, election polls, and procedure, e.g., what is an electoral college, how debates work, etc. Overall, unique, local analysis was rare. Instead, Arab media relied heavily on regular digests of campaign and election analysis gathered from international media, including US, UK, French, Israeli, Chinese, and Russian, such as the *Arizona Republic, CNN, New York Times, Washington Post, Agence France-Presse, Sunday Telegraph, Guardian, Financial Times*, and the Chinese newspaper *Global Times*. Arab media also frequently quoted prominent individuals, e.g., journalist and writer Robert Fisk, the President of the

European Commission Jean-Claude Juncker, actor Robert De Niro, and many others. The narrative construction of the election was signaled by Arab media's choice of sources and the selection of data from each source. In this way, Arab media appeared overall informed and unbiased.

The primary dependence on US sources betrayed high confidence in them but also reflected the problems of news coverage with which the American industry itself was coming to grips. For instance, Arab sources reported that the unprecedented US media coverage helped Trump's campaign by gifting him free coverage worth millions of dollars, even though he attacked the media viciously. Ultimately, the Arab sources concluded that US media served its own financial interests by turning the political event into a media event with huge financial profits. Ironically, attention to the election in Arab media was similarly heightened, thereby likewise transforming the coverage of the election into a media event, which even the Miss Lebanon beauty pageant could not avoid discussing.

Similarly to US coverage, Arab media described the election as unusual and problematic. Outside of logistics coverage, reports depicted it as entertainment based in conflict, e.g., boxing match, horse race, drama, theater, cultural war. The election was dramatic, teeming with "threats and scandals, [...] leaks and rumors, [...] conspiracies" and chaos.[3] It was also petty; for example, some reports noted Trump's complaint about his microphone or refusing to shake Clinton's hand before the debate. Seeing the election as conflict-based entertainment led some sources to conclude that the US may fail a serious test for democracy.

Issue Level Analysis of Clinton and Trump

Issue narratives regarding the candidates were mixed. Positive narratives in the overall neutral Clinton coverage extolled her symbolic value (being the first woman to win a US presidential nomination) and her superiority over Trump as she was seen as smart, witty, and prepared for the presidency. For instance, many Arab sources included Clinton's successful retorts to Trump, e.g., "Donald, you live in your own world," "You supported the invasion of Iraq, Donald."[4]

By contrast, the negative Trump coverage was sixteen-fold greater than his positive portrayal. In addition to the regular and more dispersed themes that he was dangerous, dishonest, unqualified, unable to control himself, and petty, narrative clusters of two events took over Arab media coverage as soon as each event was first reported. The first cluster, "sexual predator Trump," described Trump's repeated sexual harassment and obscene statements. If his abusive sexual behavior and vulgar talk were scandalous and shocking for American publics, they were unthinkable not just in Arab political space, but in Arab pubic life in general. Consequently, Arab sources ran sanitized reports of the Access Hollywood tape cutting Trump's words short at the end. Instead, they detailed his acts using more matter-of-fact language, which emphasized rather than diminished from framing his behavior as unthinkable: his repeated, non-consensual groping of women "under the underwear" and kissing them directly on the mouth.[5] Arab sources described him as an octopus and a "women's curse,"[6] reporting that his behavior was creepy even during the presidential debates when he was pacing back and forth behind Clinton "like a horror movie villain who slowly approaches his prey."[7] The second cluster, "banana-republic dictator Trump," exploded in Arab sources when the US media reported on Trump's contempt for US institutions and democracy and his baseless accusations of a forged election (see below).

Palestinian–Israeli Conflict and Arab Disillusionment

Arab media's pre-election coverage of the candidates' agenda for solving the Palestinian–Israeli conflict was meager, despite the importance of the issue for the region. The candidates' comments deepened the disillusionment of the Arab publics who are already full of rational cynicism about unwavering pro-Israel bias and disregard for the Palestinian people among US presidents. As al-Ahram reported, "no new US administration deviates from the clear and consistent policy to support Israel, defend it with all kinds of advanced weapons, and boost its economy, such that the competition [among presidential candidates] is about how to support Israel" rather than whether to support it.[8] Before the elections, Trump's strong anti-Muslim sentiments, his promises to move the US embassy from Tel Aviv to Jerusalem, and his discounting of Israeli settlements as an impediment to the peace process increased negative Arab coverage of his agenda on the Palestinian issue. The media also channeled an alternative, more tolerant opinion making light of his speech due to his inexperience in politics and ignorance about the Middle East.

Once he won, however, a number of Arab sources sounded an alarm about Palestinians' fate. One reason was the reported jubilation of the Israeli press, which saw Trump's victory as an Israeli victory. According to Arab sources, although the majority of Israelis supported Clinton, most Israeli papers and right-wing parties favored Trump. The Israeli government was reportedly overjoyed as well. Netanyahu praised Trump as a true friend of Israel,[9] although the Israeli government had been convinced that no matter who won, it would have a representative in the White House. The second reason for alarm was that the Israeli government interpreted Trump's victory as a license to scrap the two-state solution and destroy the idea of a Palestinian state, as the reports stated. Reflection on this possibility showcased Arab distress that the Israelis are planning the move of the US embassy, reminding readers that the status of Jerusalem is one of the most complex issues in the Palestinian–Israeli conflict. Minister of Justice Ayelet Shaked reportedly called on Trump to fulfill his campaign promise to transfer the embassy, "in a departure from the policy of successive US administrations," as al-Jazeera reminded its audiences.[10] What comes into focus in these media narratives is the emphasis on Israeli ministers' claims that the Trump win is a license for settlement expansion in Jerusalem and the West Bank and the end of the Palestinian state. According to several reports, the Minister of Infrastructure, Yuval Steinitz, had admitted in an interview on Israeli public radio that his ministry intended to carry out extensive settlement work in the West Bank.[11] According to another report, Education Minister and leader of the Jewish Home party Naftali Bennett announced that "the idea of a Palestinian state ended" with Trump's election.[12] Perceptions of a deaf US administration and Israeli manipulation of US policy reared their head quickly, despite the lack of pre-election analysis on this Arab issue, as this example demonstrates: "Israeli ministers and Knesset members say that they must seize the opportunity now for the eradication of the two-state solution [...] the time has come to bring Israeli sovereignty over the entire West Bank."[13]

Issue-level narratives of the Palestinian–Israeli struggle had a remarkable fidelity to the key aspect of the politically-negative US perceptions among Arab publics. Trump's disregard for developing a meaningful platform on solving the conflict, his pro-Israel statements and Islamophobic rants provided Arab media with coherent evidence of synergy between US and Israeli policy. They became the building blocks of a negative issue and national level narratives.

Syria

Despite extensive regular coverage of the Syrian conflict in Arab media, only a small percentage of the Arabic sample reported on the discussion of the conflict by the presidential campaigns. The war in Syria became a major international battle after the US, Russia, Iran, and Turkey joined in. In 2014, the US began airstrikes against ISIS and the Assad regime, while Russian airstrikes the following year targeted mainly the anti-Assad Free Syrian Army and to a lesser extent ISIS.

As the Syrian cluster in the Arabic sample shows, Clinton received harsher coverage on Syria compared to the region's overall preference for her. Clinton's image as an Obama-era continuation allowed the media to transfer onto her Arab bitterness over Obama's non-involvement in Syria. Yet, the media also depicted Clinton as a serious politician with a concrete platform to end the conflict such as no-fly zones and safe areas for civilians, as well as pledges to keep US ground troops out and to investigate Russia's war crimes in support of Assad.[14]

The reception of Trump's plan to handle the Syrian conflict was more polarizing. Arab sources noted that he lacked anything general or concrete. At one point, Trump was losing even the US electorate on account of his hateful speech and lack of concrete program for domestic and foreign issues such as ISIS and Syria, according to *al-Ahram*.[15] Instead of creating a platform, he dedicated himself to smear tactics and personal attacks. Among the top ones reported were his declaration that Assad was tougher and smarter than Clinton and Obama,[16] his unfounded accusation that Clinton and Obama founded ISIS, and his conviction that toppling Assad would be worse than keeping him.[17] He also accused Clinton of being responsible for Aleppo and of supporting the Syrian opposition without knowing who they were.[18] Both Trump and his running mate accused Clinton of being weak and ineffective in facing Russia in Syria, pointed out *al-Sabah*.[19] Ironically, Trump's platform on Syria enacted solely through lambasting Clinton and Obama struck a cord with some Arabs in a region used to criticizing US policies.

Trump's animosity towards Syrian refugees also received regular mention. At the time of the election, the Syrian conflict had contributed greatly to the worst refugee crisis since World War II. Arab coverage noted that the candidates' discussions of the crisis regularly turned into US homeland security narratives instead of humanizing the refugees and discussing their predicament. As one article published in *al-Sabah* noted, "Trump used last week's attacks on New York and New Jersey to return to his favorite topic, immigration, in particular the admission of Syrian refugees."[20] The article explained how Trump's son maliciously compared Syrian refugees to Skittles candy in a mispunctuated Tweet, "If I had a bowl of skittles and I told you just three would kill you. [*sic*] Would you take a handful? That's our Syrian refugee problem."[21]

At the same time, though, some Arab sources also interpreted Trump's departure from US doctrine as opening new possibilities. That was the attitude regarding his widely reported aspirations for a warm relationship with Putin. The sources surmised that a relationship of this kind might help solve the conflict in Syria, as in this example from Lebanon—a country with 1.5 million Syrian refugees (Funk & Parkes, 2016): "Trump's victory could be good for Syria, which may create understandings with the Russians, because his relationship with the Russian president is good, contrary to the relationship between the Russian president and Hillary Clinton."[22] Several days before the election, the official Syrian news agency *SANA* and the Syrian government daily, *al-Thawra*, printed an interview with Assad claiming no preference for either Clinton or Trump on the basis that both would be bad for Syria.[23] On Nov 10, *al-Thawra* similarly reported that Syrians do not count on Trump but on the Syrian army.[24] *Al-Arabiya* contradicted these reports, however, describing the Assad regime's jubilance and optimism with Trump's election.[25] Eventually on November 15, *al-Thawra* admitted its preference for Trump. It also adopted the Russian government's frame of an affectionate Trump–Putin relationship as a solution to the ongoing Syrian crisis, despite the fact that Obama was still president:

> Russian President Vladimir Putin discussed during a telephone conversation yesterday with US President-elect Donald Trump ways of settling the crisis in Syria and the need to unite their efforts in the fight against terrorism. The Kremlin said in a statement that Putin conveyed to Trump Moscow's readiness to build a dialogue based on partnership with the new American administration, equality, mutual respect, and non-interference in internal affairs. He extended again his congratulations to Trump for his win in the US presidential election and wished him good luck in the implementation of his election platform [...] they agreed to hold phone conversations and meet in person in the future.[26]

Al-Thawra reported too on Trump's "doubts about the nature of the so-called 'armed Syrian opposition,' backed by [Obama's] Washington, warning that its members may be loyal to ISIS."[27] The article's implicit accusation of Obama and Clinton brought out in stark relief its depiction of an affectionate Trump-Putin relationship and a conceivable Trump-Russia-Assad alliance.

The issue level narratives, then, regarding US policy towards Syria appeared mixed. While Trump's plans remained largely inchoate, his election opened the possibility for a new direction through a reevaluation of US–Russia relationships. Nevertheless, cynicism and pessimism ruled as Arab audiences still remembered past promises made by US presidents and their failure to deliver significant change. Issue level narratives constructed a negative portrayal of US policies in the region: the two candidates' platforms appeared uninformed, providing further credence to depictions of anti-Arab bias in the US government. US power and influence in the region were seen as ineffective, requiring cooperation with nations such as Russia.

Regional and International Level Narratives

Unlike the national and issue level narratives that appeared unified in their portrayal of anti-Arab bias, the regional and international level narratives were more ambiguous. On one hand, they described a US unconcerned and ignorant of Arab plight. They also depicted a waning US influence in the region and a political and economic international order under contestation by increasingly important nations other than the US. On the other hand, democracy was viewed as a positive form of government. There were in fact no arguments against democracy in general; its negative portrayal coalesced around US inability to enact it. Arab media also placed the election and its implications within a global context recognizing how Chinese and Russian media critiqued it as a means to tarnish US reputation. Finally, within these international level narrative constructions is evidence of an incipient pan-Arab identity arising out of concern for protecting their common interests. The rationale for this identification and cooperation, unfortunately for the US, arose out of a view of the US-led international order as uncaring and unhelpful to Arab interests.

Arab Lives Matter

A cluster of regional and international level narratives presented the Arab world as a political victim of an unjust order headed by the US. This cluster did not portray the Arab region as a rival to the US for dominance in the global order like Russia or China. It aimed at demonstrating to Arab publics that the presidential candidates were ignorant of the region, unconcerned with Arab suffering, and that their policies would hurt the Arab countries.

The candidates' ignorance of the region was a common element in the coverage. Sources labeled both Clinton's and Trump's statements on the Middle East "absurd and useless chatter,"[28] while others called them "old clichés" deficient in substance.[29] A number of reports indicated that the two candidates either mentioned the region to whip up anti-Arab support from pro-Israeli voters at home or to outbid each other in militarism, as this report noted:

> ISIS, then ISIS, then ISIS, then Iran; here the debate returns to its usual narrow topic about another invasion of the region or deserting it to its fate. No one discusses reform. No one speaks about resolving the conflict (peacefully or by any other means that may lead to a political solution).[30]

The most glaring solecism was Libertarian candidate Gary Johnson's widely reported gaffe. Johnson stated he had never heard of Aleppo and couldn't name any leader of a foreign state. The Arab sources concluded that the candidates' superficial remarks were a reflection of the American institutions' naiveté about the Middle East.

In addition to the displeasure at dwarfing Arab issues, there were also frequent comments on how this self-serving, inward-focused rhetoric left the US oblivious to the tremendous suffering in the region. The above quotation continues, neither candidate "cares about the millions of displaced persons"; just "who of the two can hit ISIS more [...] All the Arab viewer can deduce from this heated debate is that American politicians of all stripes still have no idea that they really do not know the region." Critical Western sources, like prominent journalist and writer Robert Fisk, were sometimes cited to give such comments greater credibility. First, one source disclosed how Fisk ridiculed Trump who had said that the Middle East was in "total destruction," then, it noted:

> Fisk asked what destruction Trump was talking about: "Is this the destruction of hospitals in East Aleppo? Or the destruction of human rights in Egypt? Or the destruction left by the bombing of the Doctors Without Borders Hospital in Afghanistan?" Or the destruction of Palestine, whose name, he said, was not mentioned by either of the candidates who plan to assume the presidency of America.[31]

The case put forward in the coverage was that US policies were intentionally malicious. For instance, Trump was quoted justifying looting Iraq's oil, harboring regrets around US failure to take it all in 2003, and refusing to consider Israeli settlements in the Palestinian territories an obstacle to peace. Trump symbolized an America that "acts like a child that throws its old toy off the window to get a new, more entertaining one."[32] According to the Arab sources, such a narcissistic, impulsive expression of America's interests "contributed to increased tension and instability, as well as to the escalation of the threat of terrorism, which made the Arab region the world's inferno."[33]

The themes concerning an unjust global order had a high degree of narrative fidelity to the politically-negative frame of the US as an aggressive, deaf hegemon. They also invoked and reinforced a sense of the tragic injustice Arabs suffer under the current global order by coherently explaining why its dominant players do not recognize that Arab lives matter. As a result, these strategic narratives aimed at connecting to a long-standing Arab sense of a need for global advocacy on behalf of Arabs and against Islamophobia.

US–Arab Relations: Rational Cynicism of the Candidates' Policies

In addition to discussing the candidates' short-sighted bluster and the unjust order it perpetuated, Arab media also discussed the implications of each candidate's victory for US–Arab relations and the region, even with Clinton's and Trump's limited commentary. As mentioned above, despite a general preference for Clinton over Trump, both candidates' policies were grouped together to illustrate uninformed and problematic decades-long US policies in the region. The Arab sources often emphasized that the similarities among Bush, Obama, Clinton, and Trump were more than their differences (seen to be in form only) when it came to the Arab region. Multiple sources concluded that it did not matter who would win the election since all "US administrations were moving from failure to failure, leaving behind a lot of destruction and casualties."[34] As one headline pointing to the US track record in the region described it: "Clinton or Trump: Who will destroy the region more?"[35]

Despite the moral equivalency implied in the rational cynicism about either candidate's policies, economic and political fears of a Trump administration were prevalent, given his remarks about looting Iraq's oil and greenlighting Israeli settlements. These fears were further reflected in Arab reporting on Trump's electoral victory. At that time, the Arab media reported a split attitude towards his victory and the development of US–Arab relations. Pessimists predicted that his presidency would be disastrous for the region. Some of their fears revolved around economic issues such as taxes. Stoked by his campaign slogans, they warned that he would impose a *jizya* tax on the Arab states for protection guided by purely material interests and desire for personal gain. The term *jizya* carries the connotation of punishment, tribute, or reward. It also draws a historical parallel to the *jizya* head tax levied on certain religious minorities for protection or as exemption from military service, occasionally done under humiliating circumstances (Dagli, 2013). Although the historical *jizya* was abolished by the nineteenth and early twentieth centuries, according to a number of reports, ISIS and the Taliban were extracting it from minorities (Caris, 2014). In this context, the "pay-for-protection" narrative reflected Trump's image as a global danger, and that of his presidency as a "warning to the Middle East, a headache for the leaders of Europe, damage to the status of industrial Asia, reduction in assistance to Africa, and a volatile relationship with Latin America."[36] His pledge to impose tariffs on imports to the US also warned pessimists of his potentially catastrophic economic impact, including in the region, as the Hezbollah outlet *al-Manar* noted, quoting Thilo Brodtmann, Executive Director of the German Engineering Federation: "If the world's largest economy chooses to go with protectionism, it would affect the rest of the world."[37]

By comparison, "optimists" in Arab sources remained unperturbed by Trump's election for two reasons. First, they pointed out that earlier US presidents were no better for the Arab world, reflecting the regional cynicism towards US policy. Some even believed that Trump might do the world some good after all because he would expose the true face of US policy. More optimistically, some trusted Trump's professions of a warm relationship with Russia, surmising that such a relationship might help solve the conflict in Syria. A few sources even struck an upbeat tone, discussing possibilities for new economic ventures during a Trump administration.[38] Second, the more optimistic accounts within Arab media attempted to rationalize Trump's campaign slogans. While Trump's routine of making Islamophobic statements and economic threats to Arab states triggered a fair amount of anxiety in the Arab world, immediately after the election Arab media responded to audiences' fears by imparting that campaigns are freak shows and the promises candidates make on the campaign trail should not be taken seriously. An article posted in the Lebanese daily *al-Anbaa* rationalized Trump's campaign slogans as empty rhetoric that would not guide subsequent policy and mused that president Trump would be different from candidate Trump.[39] This source also apparently hoped that Trump would form a team to study the issues since he never developed a detailed foreign policy platform:

> [...] it is hard to predict from now Trump's performance as a president since his positions as a candidate in his stump speech won't remain the same after he takes office on January 20 [...] Trump the candidate will be different from Trump the president, especially since despite his positions, he did not put forward a comprehensive program on foreign policy. One is supposed to wait for him to put together a working group to study all the issues, after which we'll have a clear picture how he'll deal with them.[40]

Taken together, both the pessimistic and the slightly optimistic accounts of the candidates' policies demonstrated a clear overall cynicism towards US policies, which set the stage for a reevaluation of US–Arab relations and an open discussion of regional leaders.

Reevaluation of US–Arab Relations and Regional Leadership Rivalry

The overall cynicism towards the candidates' policies led the Arab press to make the case for the reevaluation of US–Arab relations. Some sources concluded that the Arab nations should turn to themselves in articulating Arab interests to escape the unequal relationship with the US and its waning influence in the region. One article from the Egyptian daily *al-Ahram* for instance stated:

Most importantly, Arab states shouldn't remain reactive, waiting to see the new administration's policies; they shouldn't be afraid of the risk, regardless of what these policies might be. Instead, they should cultivate clear and specific Arab policies that maximize Arab interests, and are based on balance and independence from the US.[41]

This narrative of the loss of faith in US leadership in the region was likewise conveyed in discussions of the candidates' policies regarding Syria. The Syrian conflict had caused the biggest refugee crisis and after the US, Russia, Iran, and Turkey joined in, it became a major international battle. Before the elections, Arab media reports on the candidates' agenda about Syria and ISIS were limited but critical of the lack of substantive understanding of the Middle East. In a climate of mounting disillusionment, a major Arab source began wondering why some Syrians bet on Trump when others saw his anti-Muslim rhetoric as a gift to ISIS and al-Qaeda.[42] In the US, the clashes between the two presidential campaigns pitted the US against Russia; in fact, the debates focused mostly on the establishment of no-fly zones and accusing Russia of perpetrating war crimes in Syria. By comparison, Arab perceptions that the US and Russia are less opponents than bedfellows were widespread. Both countries provoked Arab resentment: Syrians felt that Obama did not keep his promises to protect them from Assad's chemical weapons and ISIS, while the Russians came to fight the opposition rather than ISIS as they had promised.

The strategic narrative presented to Arab audiences regarding Syria was, of course, that the US was changing coalition commitments. It was supposed to fight ISIS and Assad on behalf of the Syrian people, and yet, Trump was ingratiating himself with Putin and his sidekick Assad. But nowhere were the long-term repercussions of such changes on the Arab world and its US allies clearer than in narratives about waning US clout and a fierce international rivalry over influence in the region. For instance, Qatar, which has had a tumultuous relationship with Trump because it declined to give a loan to his son-in-law,[43] painted a picture of a dwindling US role in a region under the influence of multiple superpowers. According to one *al-Jazeera* piece, Robert Fisk mocked Trump for failing to grasp Iran's achieved superpower status in the region after Trump blamed its imminent rise to such status on Clinton and Obama. Similarly, *al-Ahram* expressed irritation towards the two presidential candidates for not acknowledging the extent of Iranian influence, as well as resentment towards the US for "letting" Iran "take over" the region:

Both candidates' warning that Iran was turning into a regional power hostile to 'US friends' was completely naïve. How can Hillary Clinton say that? [...] During this administration, Iran has dominated entire Arab countries, and the daily conflict between Sunnis and Shiites has contributed to bringing other countries to the brink. [...] Today [Trump] is in fact the Republican Party nominee [...] What did the Republican Party offer Arabs in the face of Iran last time its candidate, George W. Bush, took over the presidency? Did America, for example, succeed in overthrowing the regime, which constantly dreams of exporting a sectarian revolution to the Arab world? [...] Has America at least tried to build-up its 'friends' so they can face Iran's heinous expansionist vision? Quite the opposite. Bush, and with him the Republican party of course, decided to invade Iraq [...] Today, after America deserted it in complete destruction, Iraq has become a backyard for Iran's Supreme Leader [...] The US can no longer market itself as a country that does not abandon its friends.[44]

The article went on to blame the US for letting Iran take control of Assad's regime, Hezbollah in Lebanon, and the hardline Shi'ite parties in Iraq, "once an Arab state," as it remarked. It even added Egypt to the list where Iran lay in wait "like a predator" for the first opportunity. Ultimately, most Arab media in the sample communicated to their audiences this strategic narrative: "the balance of power is upset in favor of the Russia–Syria–Iran alliance,"[45] and if Arab states continue to support the US and its unchanged policy, they may end on the losing side.

By contrast, some Gulf states' strategic narratives showcased to Arab audiences a united US–Arab front against a menacing but imperiled Iran. For instance, the Kuwaiti daily *al-Watan* published an article with the headline "Trump forms a coalition with the Gulf," which misled the readers that there was no such coalition under the current Obama administration.[46] The first paragraph featured an indirect quotation from Trump's Middle East affairs adviser Walid Phares in a *BBC* interview. Phares claimed that "the future US government led by Trump will establish a coalition with the Gulf states, Egypt, and Jordan against terrorism. Barak Obama," he went on, "opposed this coalition during his presidential term to ensure the success of the nuclear deal with Tehran, which allowed militias loyal to Iran to have the largest presence in Iraq."[47] Only in a half sentence in the last paragraph did the article reveal that the *BBC* reporter contradicted Phares on the grounds that such coalition exists under Obama. The remaining paragraph quoted Phares directly, hedging the question and reiterating his earlier statement. Yet even in that quote Iran looked like a powerful rival for regional dominance, if not a hegemon.

In this way, the national and international level narratives depicted a disconcerting global order where the US was losing its hegemonic power, while the region was the target of the appetites of new rising powers. A main component of this order, the democratic form of government, was also being challenged.

Democracy Under Attack: The Limits of US Power

According to Arab sources, external and internal developments had flung US democracy into crisis. Externally, the sources argued, this crisis was precipitated by an attack from US competitors. Internally, it resulted from the system's failure to produce quality candidates, which doubled as a failure to give people voice and reflect their desires. Overall, the sources suspected that the American people had lost confidence in democratic procedures. However, the sources did not conclude that democracy was an inherently bad system, and at times extolled its values. Such positive narratives of democracy in Arab media stem from the older, culturally-positive frame of the US. They also connect to a more recent Arab advocacy for human rights, and therefore regional identity, that has been most visible since the 2011 Arab uprisings and the region-wide struggle against authoritarian regimes. The call for democratically elected governments was one of the leading calls in the uprisings and continues to resonate in the region, despite counter-revolutions like that in Egypt. Arab media accordingly was sensitive to the wave towards democratization ushered in by the Arab people and did not particularly seek to undermine US institutions and democratic processes like the coverage in Russia and China.

This context helps us understand why the more analytical Arab coverage talked of an attack on US democracy, and not of its demise. According to Arab narratives, three factors were attacking US democracy: Trump, a sector of the American citizenry, and foreign powers. The reports presented the danger Trump posed out of ignorance of and disrespect for the tradition of "peaceful transition of power." His accusations that the electoral system was rigged against him, especially before the vote took place, filled much of the election coverage at one point. The Arab sources carefully explained that fair elections were one of the pillars of US democracy, and that recognition of defeat was what distinguished democracies from dictatorships. Most coverage emphasized that Trump's claims lacked any evidence and his efforts to incite his supporters to rebel against the results undermined democracy. Some sources even channeled a level of sarcasm. For instance, the Egyptian daily al-Ahram quoted president Obama: "There is no way to forge the elections in a country of this size. I wonder if Trump has been to any ballot boxes."[48] Even the Saudi news channel al-Arabiya (before Muhammad Bin Salman arrested its owners in the 2017 purge and the Saudi government took control of 60 percent of the channel's holding company) commented that Trump's accusations were reminiscent of the practices of "Third World" dictators painfully familiar to an Arab region striving to rid itself of these very practices, but utterly "bizarre for a healthy democracy."[49]

In a climate of mounting disillusionment, many Arabs were apprehensive of Trump's apparent cozying up to authoritarian-style rulers like Turkey's Erdogan, Egypt's Sisi (the only Arab leader he met as candidate), and most importantly Assad, whom he vowed to leave in power. Even if issues like free speech, minority rights, and immigration may have seemed internal US affairs to some Arabs according to the media, to others, they were intertwined in a complicated global world that inevitably affected Arab states as well. Sacrificing basic freedoms over security under a strongman was too big of a concession for that group.

The attack on US democracy by US citizens got less coverage than Trump. One report claimed that a quarter of Americans born after 1980 believed that democracy was a bad form of government.[50] Other reports tracked the erosion of democratic values reflected in Trump supporters' rebellion against the political elite to a sense of retreat in American influence in the wake of war, terrorism, and globalization.[51] As mentioned before, constructing the elections as entertainment based on conflict between two camps led *al-Jazeera* to conclude that the US may fail a serious test for democracy, fulfilling Lincoln's prediction of a house divided: "The essence of US democracy is cooperation. Whatever happens on Tuesday (election day) is unlikely to live up to that," given the divisive political environment.[52]

As for foreign powers, according to the Arab sources, Russia tarnished the reputation of the US electoral system by mounting a fierce public relations campaign and forging documents on election eve.[53] China bashed the US over corruption and impotence, despite being the strongest and oldest democracy in the world, as the Syrian government daily *al-Thawra* quoted:

> These unusual events show not only the predicament of the American political establishment but also directly the corrupt practice of the American political system [...] [T]he US has been boasting for a long time about its very lively elections, even used this to criticize the big majority of developing countries while it itself lacks the most basic features of a vital democracy.[54]

Therefore, it "has no right to teach others lessons on democracy."[55] In sum, the dominant Arab media narrative of democracy, albeit slightly negative of the US, was that of an overall valuable model under concerted attack rather than a failing, corrupt, or inherently inadequate model. A minority negative narrative was primarily based on citations from Chinese and Russian sources (e.g., in the Syrian government outlet *al-Thawra*), possibly signaling its minority status, on one hand, and, on the other, the multi-polarization of geo-political rhetoric. Strategic narratives on democracy invoked the centuries-old, culturally-positive depiction of the US as a champion of democracy, human rights, the rule of law, and independent institutions. However, they lacked the same narrative coherence characteristic of politically-negative depictions of the US. The main reason might be a sense of bewilderment if the US was trying to abandon democracy as the Arab world was struggling to enter it, and what that portends for Arab prospects.[56] One of the articles captured this sentiment by quoting UK journalist Gideon Rachman that Trump's conduct during the election was not just embarrassing for the US, but damaged the prestige of democracy everywhere.[57]

Conclusion

This chapter set out to explore news items from the Arab region for strategic narratives related to the 2016 US presidential election on three levels: international, national, and local issues. We also added the regional level for the Arab case because of its unique media system and geo-political identity. The analysis looked at narratives about the US, the Arab world, and US–Arab relations. We expected the political environment of an unequal historical relationship between the US and the Arab world to have an impact on the media narratives. The past and current tensions with the US revealed a dual culturally-positive / politically-negative narrative through which most Arabs see the US. In particular, we expected the culturally-positive narrative, which depicts the US historically as an advocate for democracy and human rights, to influence media narratives about the value of democracy in the global order. Further, the 2011 Arab pro-democratic uprisings and their aftermath should have activated the importance of this narrative. On the other hand, we also expected historical Arab perceptions of an aggressive, hypocritical, and deaf US to color Arab media narratives about the presidential candidates' platforms on Middle East policy as a whole and on some of the major Arab issues. The negative narrative, in particular, was significant because it demonstrated the power of international audiences, in this case, the Arab publics whose perceptions of the US and its policies determined US attractiveness and influence in the region. In addition, the system of regional Arab media was expected to shape these strategic narratives as stories leaning towards accuracy and impartiality due to the media's uneven regulation by the authorities, corporate journalistic ethics, and commercial logic.

On the whole, our findings confirmed these expectations; yet, they also revealed an unexpected consequence regarding the actual US influence with Arab publics compared to that extrapolated on the basis of resources alone. First, negative narratives of the presidential candidates on the international, regional, national, and specific issues levels in Arab media coverage exhibited a high degree of narrative fidelity and coherence with the historical negative perceptions of US policy. Second, strategic narratives on the value of democracy and the US-led global order that promotes it lacked the high degree of fidelity and coherence with positive historical Arab attitudes towards the US. We postulate that the main reason boils down to the attack on democracy by Trump's authoritarian tendencies and Islamophobic rhetoric, and to a lesser extent to some US citizens' disenchantment with democracy due to economic strain, non-democratic forces like the electoral college, and unlimited corporate campaign funding.

The negative strategic narratives on US policy in the Arab world did not undermine the US image much lower than its already low level, despite their widespread use in the media. Rather, they seemed to confirm Arabs' rational cynicism on US–Arab relations. On the other hand, the assault on the positive narratives on US democracy and human rights led to a different result at a time when the Arab world is collectively struggling to move towards democracy. The assault seemed to undermine the US image and therefore overall US influence in the region. Furthermore, even in cases when the media registered Arab support for Trump, e.g., stemming from hopes that his affectionate relationship with Putin might end the Syrian war, such evaluation did not advance the US image. On the contrary, it coincided with Arab reinterpretations of the US as a new addition to the Russia–Syria–Iran alliance rather than a global superpower. In addition, the assault on the positive narrative of the US may give ammunition to opponents of secularism in Arab societies. Modern Arab debates about the establishment of just and allegedly authentic Arab societies have settled into a split between proponents of secularism and Islamists. To a much greater extent, Arab secularists have developed their visions in conversations with Western secular societies like the US. Ambiguity in the US about the value of democracy as a global system may lead to a tipping of the scale in Arab societies towards Islamists and also eventually to the erosion of one of the bases for US influence in the Middle East.

Within the overall argument of this book, the Arab case demonstrates that looking at US resources alone to assess its influence can be misleading. How important global audiences such as the Arabs perceive the wielding of these resources by the US is as important. The US sees itself as an advocate for democracy and human rights, yet the Arab media sample showed little evidence that US resources for influence such as the presidential elections translated into an actual influence on Arab perceptions. In fact, scholars of public diplomacy have already registered the opposite effect. According to William Rugh, the Trump Administration's strong Islamophobic statements "make it very difficult for American diplomats working with Muslim leaders abroad to explain American policy and argue that America is a tolerant nation that wants cooperation with the Muslim world" (Rugh, 2018, n.p.).

Although it is important to register the perceptions of international audiences, it is also necessary to interpret them in context. Arab negative perceptions of US democracy during the election, therefore, yield a different meaning from those among Russian and Chinese audiences; after all, the Arab world does not see itself as a true rival to the US and a leader of a new global order.

Notes

1 According to William Rugh (2004), before the satellite era, the nature of the political system in each Arab country defined the role of its media. In most Arab states, the regime had full monopoly of power over the media, which could not criticize the regime's members or its policies, but instead actively mobilized popular support for them.

2 BBC Arabic radio was established in 1938, while the Voice of America broadcast between 1942 and 1945 and later between 1950 and 2002.

3 *Al-Arabiya*. (2016, October 19). Data captured by Texas A&M's Media Monitoring System. Unpublished raw data.

4 *al-Dustur*. (2016, September). Data captured by Texas A&M's Media Monitoring System. Unpublished raw data; *al-Jazeera*. (2016, September 27). Data captured by Texas A&M's Media Monitoring System. Unpublished raw data; *al-Dustur*. (2016, September 28). Data captured by Texas A&M's Media Monitoring System. Unpublished raw data.

5 *al-Dustur*. (2016, October 15). Data captured by Texas A&M's Media Monitoring System. Unpublished raw data.

6 *al-Jazeera*. (2016, October 13). Data captured by Texas A&M's Media Monitoring System. Unpublished raw data.

7 *Al-Arabiya*. (2016, October 16). Data captured by Texas A&M's Media Monitoring System. Unpublished raw data.

8 *al-Ahram*. (2016, November 5). Data captured by Texas A&M's Media Monitoring System. Unpublished raw data.

9 *al-Jazeera*. (2016, November 9). Data captured by Texas A&M's Media Monitoring System. Unpublished raw data.

10 Ibid.

11 *al-Mustaqbal*. (2016, November 11). Data captured by Texas A&M's Media Monitoring System. Unpublished raw data; *al-Jazeera*. (2016, November 10). Data captured by Texas A&M's Media Monitoring System. Unpublished raw data; other sources also reported that there was an increase of settlements building, e.g., *al-Alam*. (2016, November 12). Data captured by Texas A&M's Media Monitoring System. Unpublished raw data.

12 *al-Jazeera*. (2016, November 9). Data captured by Texas A&M's Media Monitoring System. Unpublished raw data.

13 *al-Arabiya*. (2016, November 12). Data captured by Texas A&M's Media Monitoring System. Unpublished raw data.

14 *al-Dustur*. (2016, October 10). Data captured by Texas A&M's Media Monitoring System. Unpublished raw data.

15 *al-Ahram*. (2016, October 18). Data captured by Texas A&M's Media Monitoring System. Unpublished raw data.

16 *al-Hayat*. (2016, October 21). Data captured by Texas A&M's Media Monitoring System. Unpublished raw data.

17 *al-Jazeera*. (2016, October 20). Data captured by Texas A&M's Media Monitoring System. Unpublished raw data.

18 *al-Ahram*. (2016, October 21). Data captured by Texas A&M's Media Monitoring System. Unpublished raw data.

19 *al-Sabah*. (2016, October 5). Data captured by Texas A&M's Media Monitoring System. Unpublished raw data.

20 *al-Sabah*. (2016, September 26). Data captured by Texas A&M's Media Monitoring System. Unpublished raw data.

21 Ibid.

22 *al-Mustaqbal*. (2016, November 13). Data captured by Texas A&M's Media Monitoring System. Unpublished raw data; *al-Anbaa*. (2016, November 13). Data captured by Texas A&M's Media Monitoring System. Unpublished raw data.

23 *al-Thawra*. (2016, November 3). Data captured by Texas A&M's Media Monitoring System. Unpublished raw data; *SANA*. (2016, November 3). Data captured by Texas A&M's Media Monitoring System. Unpublished raw data.

24 *al-Thawra*. (2016, November 10). Data captured by Texas A&M's Media Monitoring System. Unpublished raw data.

25 *al-Arabiya*. (2016, November 9). Data captured by Texas A&M's Media Monitoring System. Unpublished raw data.

26 *al-Thawra*. (2016, November 15). Data captured by Texas A&M's Media Monitoring System. Unpublished raw data.

27 *al-Thawra*. (2016, November 10). Data captured by Texas A&M's Media Monitoring System. Unpublished raw data.

28 *al-Jazeera*. (2016, September 28). Data captured by Texas A&M's Media Monitoring System. Unpublished raw data.

29 *al-Ahram*. (2016, October 2). Data captured by Texas A&M's Media Monitoring System. Unpublished raw data.

30 Ibid.

31 *al-Jazeera*. (2016, September 28). Data captured by Texas A&M's Media Monitoring System. Unpublished raw data.

32 *al-Ahram*. (2016, October 2). Data captured by Texas A&M's Media Monitoring System. Unpublished raw data.

33 *al-Ahram*. (2016, October 18). Data captured by Texas A&M's Media Monitoring System. Unpublished raw data.

34 *al-Ahram.* (2016, October 2). Data captured by Texas A&M's Media Monitoring System. Unpublished raw data.
35 *al-Ahram.* (2016, October 2). Data captured by Texas A&M's Media Monitoring System. Unpublished raw data.
36 *al-Shuruq.* (2016, November 12). Data captured by Texas A&M's Media Monitoring System. Unpublished raw data.
37 *al-Manar.* (2016, November 10). Data captured by Texas A&M's Media Monitoring System. Unpublished raw data.
38 *al-Qabas.* (2016, November 12). Data captured by Texas A&M's Media Monitoring System. Unpublished raw data.
39 *al-Mustaqbal.* (2016, November 13). Data captured by Texas A&M's Media Monitoring System. Unpublished raw data; *al-Anbaa.* (2016, November 13). Data captured by Texas A&M's Media Monitoring System. Unpublished raw data.
40 Ibid.
41 *al-Ahram.* (2016, October 18). Data captured by Texas A&M's Media Monitoring System. Unpublished raw data.
42 *al-Jazeera.* (2016, November 22). Data captured by Texas A&M's Media Monitoring System. Unpublished raw data.
43 Emily Shugerman, "Jared Kushner 'Tried and Failed to Get a $500m Loan from Qatar before Pushing Trump To Take Hard Line against Country,'" *Independent,* July 10, 2017.
44 *al-Ahram.* (2016, October 2). Data captured by Texas A&M's Media Monitoring System. Unpublished raw data.
45 Ibid.
46 *al-Watan.* (2016, November 12). Data captured by Texas A&M's Media Monitoring System. Unpublished raw data.
47 Ibid.
48 *al-Ahram.* (2016, October 21). Data captured by Texas A&M's Media Monitoring System. Unpublished raw data.
49 *al-Arabiya.* (2016, November 60). Data captured by Texas A&M's Media Monitoring System. Unpublished raw data.
50 *al-Jazeera.* (2016, November 7). Data captured by Texas A&M's Media Monitoring System. Unpublished raw data.
51 *al-Ahram.* (2016, November 4). Data captured by Texas A&M's Media Monitoring System. Unpublished raw data.
52 *al-Jazeera.* (2016, November 7). Data captured by Texas A&M's Media Monitoring System. Unpublished raw data.
53 *al-Jazeera.* (2016, November 5). Data captured by Texas A&M's Media Monitoring System. Unpublished raw data.
54 *al-Thawra.* (2016, October 9). Data captured by Texas A&M's Media Monitoring System. Unpublished raw data.
55 Ibid.
56 Lebanon has been a consociational democracy for decades, with the exception of the civil war of 1975–1991. Tunisia, Kuwait, and Morocco are also considered democratic states with differing degrees of freedom.
57 *al-Jazeera.* (2016, October 11). Data captured by Texas A&M's Media Monitoring System. Unpublished raw data.

References

Amine, L., Chao, M., & Arnold, M. (2005). Executive insights. Exploring the practical effects of origin, animosity, and price-quality issues: Two case studies of Taiwan and Acer in China. *Journal of International Marketing*, 13(2), 114–150.

Aqqad, W. (2018). Taqyyim Asatidha al-"Ilam li-Ada" al-Fada'iyat al-Masriyya fi Taghtiyat Intikhabat al-Ri'asa al-Amerikiyya li-'Am 2016". *Arab Media & Society*, 24(Summer/Fall/Fall).

Arab American Institute (2012, November 1). US presidential election: The Middle East factor. Arab American Institute. Retrieved from: http://www.aaiusa.org/us-presidentia l-election-the-middle-east-factor.

Arab Center Washington DC (ACW), & Arab Center for Research and Policy Studies (ACRPS), Doha, Qatar. (2016). Arab public opinion and US presidential elections 2016. Retrieved from http://arabcenterdc.org/survey/arab-public-opinion-and-us-presi dential-elections-2016/.

Bayoumi, A. (2008, October 22). Is Arab support for Obama fading?Al Jazeera. Retrieved from https://www.aljazeera.com/focus/uselections2008/2008/10/200810211844168488.html.

Bekhait, A. (1998). *Al-Qiyam al-Ikhbariyya fi al-Sihafa al-Masriyya*. Cairo: Arabi.

Berger, L. (2011). The missing link? US policy and the international dimensions of failed democratic transitions in the Arab world. *Political Studies*, 59(1), 38–55.

Berger, L. (2014). Foreign policies or culture: What shapes Muslim public opinion on political violence against the United States? *Journal of Peace Research*, 51(6), 782–796.

Caris, C. (2014). The Islamic State announces Caliphate. Institute for the Study of War. Retrieved from http://iswresearch.blogspot.com/2014/06/the-islamic-state-announ ces-caliphate.html.

Charney, C., & Yakatan, N. (2005). A new beginning: Strategies for a more fruitful dia-logue with the Muslim world. New York: Council on Foreign Relations. Retrieved from https://www.cfr.org/report/new-beginning.

Dagli, C. (2013). Jihad and the Islamic law of war. In HRH PrinceGhazib. Muhammad, G. I. Kalin, & M. Kamali (Eds.), *War and peace in Islam: The uses and abuses in Jihad* (pp. 56–98). Cambridge: Islamic Texts Society.

Freeman, C. (2009). US–Arab relations: Forks in the way forward. *Middle East Policy*, 16(4), 68–75.

Funk, M., & Parkes, R. (2016). Syrian refugee flows—and ebbs. European Union Institute for Security Studies. Retrieved from https://www.iss.europa.eu/sites/default/files/ EUISSFiles/Alert_5_Refugee_flows.pdf.

Furia, P., & Lucas, R. (2008). Arab Muslim attitudes toward the West: Cultural, social, and political explanations. *International Interactions*, 34(2), 186–207.

Guaaybess, T. (2008). Orientalism and the economics of Arab broadcasting. In K. Hafez (Ed.), *Arab media: Power and weakness* (pp. 199–231). New York: Continuum.

Hafez, K. (2002). Journalism ethics revisited: A comparison of ethics codes in Europe, North Africa, the Middle East and Muslim Asia. *Political Communication*, 19(2), 225–250.

Hafez, K. (2008). The unknown desire for "objectivity": Journalism ethics in Arab (and Western) journalism. In K. Hafez (Eds.), *Arab media: Power and weakness* (pp. 147–164). New York: Continuum.

Hallin, D. C., & Mancini, P. (2004). *Comparing media systems: Three models of media and politics*. Cambridge, UK: Cambridge University Press.

Hinnebusch, R. (2007). The American invasion of Iraq: Causes and consequences. *Perceptions*, 12(1), 9–27.

Khatib, D. (2017). US–Arab gulf relations amidst regional and global changes. *The International Spectator*, 52(2), 102–114.

Kraidy, M., & Khalil, J. (2009). *Arab television industries*. London: Palgrave Macmillan.

Kurlantzick, J. (2007). *China's charm: Implications of Chinese soft power*. Policy Brief 47. Washington, DC: Endowment for International Peace.

Lock, E. (2010). Soft power and strategy: Developing a "strategic" concept of power. In I. Parmer & M. Cox (Eds.), *Soft power and US foreign policy: Theoretical, historical and contemporary perspectives* (pp. 32–50). London: Routledge.

Makdisi, U. (2002). "Anti-Americanism" in the Arab world: An interpretation of a brief history. *The Journal of American History*, 89(2), 538–557.

Makdisi, U. (2014). After Said: The limits and possibilities of critical scholarship of US–Arab relations. *Diplomatic History*, 38(3), 657–684.

Matar, H. (2016). Limits of US soft power in the Arab world (2003–2015). *Contemporary Arab Affairs*, 9(3), 428–444.

Mattern, J. (2007). Why soft power isn't so soft: Representational force and attraction in world politics. In F. Berenskoetter & M. J. Williams (Eds.), *Power in world politics* (pp. 98–119). New York: Routledge.

McAlister, M. (2005). *Epic encounters: Culture, media, and US interests in the Middle East 1945–2000*. Oakland, CA: University of California Press.

Nye, J. (2004). *Soft power: The means to success in world politics*. New York: Public Affairs.

Patrick, A. (2011). Faith misplaced: The broken promise of US–Arab relations: 1820–2001. *British Journal of Middle Eastern Studies*, 38(3), 441–443.

Pejman, P. (2004, November 2). Middle East: Many Arabs see little difference between Bush and Kerry. Radio Free Europe Radio Liberty. Retrieved from: https://www.rferl.org/a/1055647.html.

Qutb, S. (2000). The America I have seen. In Abdel-Malek (Ed.), *America in an Arab mirror: Images of America in Arabic travel literature: An Anthology*. London, UK: Palgrave Macmillan.

Ramaprasad, J., & Hamdy, N. (2006). Functions of Egyptian journalists: Perceived importance and actual performance. *International Communication Gazette*, 2, 167–185.

Robichaud, C., & Goldbrenner, R. (2005). Anti-Americanism and violence. Princeton project on national security. Princeton Project on National Security, Working Group Paper, June 30, 2005, 1–52.

Rugh, W. (2004). *Arab mass media: Newspapers, radio, and television in Arab politics*. Westport, CT: Praeger.

Rugh, W. (2018). Challenges for US public diplomacy in the Age of Trump. *Arab Media & Society*, 25, Winter/Spring.

Sabry, T. (2010). *Cultural encounters in the Arab World: On media, the modern, and everyday*. London, UK: I.B. Tauris.

Said, E. (1979). *Orientalism*. New York: Vintage Books.

Stokes, B. (2014). Which countries don't like America and which do?Pew Research Center, July 15.

Tomlinson, S. (2015). US scraps its $500 million programme to train "moderate" Syrian rebels after producing fewer than 80 soldiers, most of whom were either shot or ran away. *MailOnline*, October 9, 2015. Retrieved from: http://www.dailymail.co.uk/news/article-3266509/US-scraps-500million-programme-train-moderate-Syrian-rebels-producing-fewer-80-soldiers-shot-ran-away.html.

Yaqub, S. (2002). Imperious doctrines: US–Arab relations from Dwight D. Eisenhower to George W. Bush. *Diplomatic History*, 26(4), 571–591.

Zaharna, R. (2010). *Battles to bridges: US strategic communication and public diplomacy after 9/11*. New York: Palgrave Macmillan.

Zogby, J. (2017). US–Arab relations in the Age of Trump. *The Jordan Times*, February 13.

5

THE CRUMBLING FACADE OF US DEMOCRACY

Russian Resurgence Amidst US Moral Decay within Russian Media Coverage of the US Election

Introduction

As noted in the Chapter 1 of this volume, the outcome of a 2016 US presidential election, at least post-World War II, holds significance for nations across the globe as US policy typically guides most of the Western world and implicates virtually all sovereign nations across a broad spectrum of factors relating to global security, economics, trade, immigration, and humanitarian aid, to name a few. Despite their quadrennial importance, for leaders of the Russian Federation few US elections in recent memory have had the potential for such enormous impacts on their nation than that of the 2016 presidential contest between Hillary Clinton and Donald Trump.[1] While the role of Russian interference in the 2016 election process is, as of the time of writing this chapter, still an issue of unknown depth, strategy, and scandal, Russian media went to significant lengths to communicate and construct narratives about the US election in ways challenging US soft power and democracy, while positioning Russia's own images of strength in the global order. As such, Russian media portrayals of the 2016 election offer sincere points of contestation, and thus important consideration for citizens of the Western world interested in understanding what the election meant for Russian citizens. These constructed narratives serve to not only call into question the fundamental process by which the ideals of democracy are met in the US, they also serve to place a moral equivalence between the US and Russia that serves well in justifying the regime of Vladimir Putin; the narratives come together to form an overall argument that the US is in a state of decline, and, consequently, there is an emergence of a new multipolar world order that Russia is a part of.

One can understand the severity with which Russians viewed the outcome of the US election, and the opportunity the event provided for challenging US soft power, through the rising tensions between the US and Russia in the closing years of the Obama administration, with Russians consistently complaining of mistreatment from a historically aggressive and expansionist US into former Soviet territories, as well as the outright destruction of functioning state systems in the Middle East aligned with Russia. As Hinck, Kluver, and Cooley (2018) noted, Russian media in 2015 already showcased increasing anti-Western rhetoric, describing the US as an aggressive actor waging extensive propaganda wars against Russia and of violating international law in power projected across Eastern Europe and the Middle East. The impacts of the US-led sanctions against the Russian economy, mounting tensions over wars in Syria and Ukraine, a spiraling migration crisis in which Russians blamed on Obama-led policies, and a suspicion of Western attempts to disrupt the functioning of the Russian state made the 2016 US presidential election a critical juncture for Russians.

Thus, fears of a continuation of Obama administration policies, seen as aimed at undermining Russian sovereignty and crippling the Russian economy, motivated deep attention to the outcome of the US election. The Russian administration viewed Clinton as a nightmare scenario for its regime, and as this chapter will show, as equivalent to war; on the other hand, Trump was presented as a complete unknown with the possibility to re-set relations and restore a semblance of balance to relations between the two nations. Across Russian media, the outcome of the 2016 US presidential election carried with it both the possibility of global world war or restored relations, continued sanctions or increases in trade, and an endless list of other spectrum swinging, polar opposite potentialities depending on the victor. Needless to say, the election was a highly covered event in Russian news media and provided a perfect opportunity to construct narratives on US democratic practices in favorable contrast to the Russian regime. Taken together, the stories constructed by Russian news media on the US election provides us with insight into not only how Russia views the US, but also Russian views of its own insecurities as a sovereign state.

Policies, Perceptions, and Images of US–Russian Relations: A Shifting Pendulum

The path down which both nations have traveled to arrive at such dramatic shifts towards one another based on who assumes the office of US President, is a long one and is filled with incoming US administrations continually seeking a reset of relations with the Soviet Union, and now the Russian Federation (of note, the same can be said of incoming Russian leadership; simply not in the context of this discussion). Since the close of the Cold War, both the perceptions of and relations between Russia and the US have fluctuated through moments of sincere cooperation to that of genuine mistrust, and the public opinion of citizens from both nations has fluctuated equally as an ever-altering political landscape filled with significant military challenges have presented themselves to each nation.

Through much of the twentieth century US policy towards Russia was built upon the idea that the liberal elites of the country were sympathetic to US interests, though both the masses and conservative elites in Russia remained hostile towards the US (Shlapentokh, 2001). Through the 1980s and 1990s, US belief in a rising, intellectually liberal ruling class in Russia led to the promotion of liberal democracy and capitalism in order to generate favorable perspectives of the West and shift the Soviet-era dogmas of the population. Evans (2010) contended that US optimism on the imitation of American democracy by other nations was a consistent theme in US popular culture dating back to the late eighteenth century and helped to fuel former president Bill Clinton's administration's emphasis on transitioning post-Cold War Russia into a democratized, free-market case study as a top policy priority (Evans, 2010).

However, by the mid-1990s Russia's ruling class became increasingly jaded by US self-promotion and liberalism within its borders, seeing US actions as more self-serving than genuine (Shlapentokh, 2001). Emerging Russian narratives centered on the notion that the West had systematically taken advantage of the Soviet collapse to expand its institutions and security interests at the expense of Russia under a banner for promoting democracy and cooperation (Dempsey, 2016). The wound of Western-led NATO expansion following the change in US presidents from George H.W. Bush onwards, who had made assurances to the contrary to Soviet leader Gorbachev, to the Bill Clinton administration and shocks to the post-Cold War Russian economic system allowed for the Yeltsin-appointed President Vladimir Putin to begin a campaign of Russian revitalization under the banner of nationalism and Soviet era nostalgia. Putin promoted a narrative that would vilify "NATO expansion as an unjust Western strategy of entrapment" (O'Malley, 2014).

Yet the vacillation between trust and mistrust would continue with another US presidential transition from the Bill Clinton administration to that of the younger George W. Bush. An initial propinquity between the early years of both of the Bush Presidential administrations and that of President Putin's was seemingly solidified following the attacks of September 11, 2001 on the US. The two nations engaged in historic intelligence sharing and cooperation with one another (Roberts, 2013) with President Bush praising Putin as an "honest, straightforward man" as both agreed to confront historic challenges between the nations concerning spheres of influence, economics and security (Milbank, 2001). The attacks of September 11, 2001 also provided an opportunity for Russia to cast the war in Chechnya as part of a larger campaign against Islamic terrorism and allow them to once again play a leading role in world affairs (Cross, 2004). Gallup polls at the time showed historic favorability ratings by US citizens towards Russia (Gallup, 2017).

However, the extension of the US-led war on terror into Iraq following President Bush's now infamous "axis of evil" speech and later invasion placed tremendous strain on this new-found cooperation (Cross, 2006). The invasion of Iraq marked what would be a steady decline in relations over the coming years as Russia engaged in a war in Georgia, despite Western opposition, disputes over Western military defenses in Europe erupted, and the 2008 global financial crisis put economic strains on the entire global system. Increasing suspicion and mistrust of one another continued through the remainder of Bush's tenure with the US viewing Russia as increasingly authoritarian and anti-Western and Russians viewing the US as attempting to topple Russia's historic sphere of influence with intentional force (Gerber, 2015).

Once again, a change of leadership for both nations in 2009 offered hope for a new beginning that would focus itself on the progresses made at the early start of the century. President Obama's and President Medvedev's pledge of cooperation hoped to overcome what were seen by the two as ideological disagreements and focus on practical policies towards collaboration (Gerber, 2015). The creation of the Obama–Medvedev Commission to strengthen communication between the two nations, the new START agreement and reductions in nuclear missile launchers and deployed warheads, and agreements on supply route access to Afghanistan through Russian territory for NATO were tangible manifestations of the pledged renewal of friendship between the two countries (Kaphle, 2013).

The attempted reset led Obama to be criticized in the US as too willing to appease Russian leaders, while Medvedev was accused in Russia of selling out to Western democratic meddlers (Cohen, 2011). Medvedev's miscalculation in agreeing with the West to establish a no-fly zone in Libya, which ultimately led to Qaddafi's overthrow and murder, assured the return of Putin (who had disagreed publicly with Medvedev's passive actions towards the West over Libya) to the Russian presidency (Zygar, 2016). Things would only get significantly worse between the two nations as protests in Russia over voter fraud in the Russian election were blamed by the Kremlin as being incited by the West and encouraged by Western leaders such as Hillary Clinton (who had criticized the Russian elections and President Putin) (Crowley & Ioffe, 2016). Putin's view that Western leaders had attempted to undermine the Russian election results and his own position as leader led to increasingly anti-Western rhetoric and populist policies (Zygar, 2016).

What followed was a complete fallout of all good relations as the US Congress placed sanctions on Russian leaders accused of human rights violations, Russia responded by issuing a ban on the adoption of Russian children by US citizens and the granting of asylum to NSA contractor Edward Snowden, and both President Obama and President Putin had public disagreements over how to deal with the war in Syria. Furthermore, Putin blamed the US for the protests against and eventual ousting of Ukrainian President Yanukovych and both annexed Crimea and supported offensives in eastern Ukraine as a result (Zygar, 2016). These last actions by President Putin led to US-led sanctions against Russia, amidst a backdrop of an increasing East vs. West military escalation in Syria. A 2017 report by the Rand Corporation noted that relations between Russia and the West post–Ukrainian crisis had become irremediable and that fault lines between the West and Russia now existed over spheres of influence and their relation in the global order (Pezard, Radin, Szayna, & Larrabee, 2017).

Russian Strategic Narratives: Defining a National Identity and Attacks on the West

Reflective of the political developments covered above, Russian media has recently become an active force attempting to shape domestic and international audiences' images of Russia itself, as well as the US-led international order. Key elements of these narratives defining Russian identity through media took notable turns following economic sanctions placed on Russia by the West. These sanctions, declining oil prices, and souring relations between the US and Russia not only made middle-class Russians doubt their future economic outlook, but also challenged Putin's notion that "managed democracy" could functionally compete in the open global marketplace. New narrative elements were needed to justify the regime, and virtually nothing was off the table, even likening the Putin Government to that of the Russian czars and reviving the Russian Orthodox Church's role in validating Russian rulers (Damm & Cooley, 2017). As Roselle (2014) noted,

> Russian system narratives that emphasized US overreach or entrapment found resonance in some circles, as did identity narratives about "Christian" values. These narratives could be used to support domestic political ambitious of political actors, even as they threatened European cohesion (108).

This shifting of narrative elements, attempting to keep the justification of the regime intact, had several focal points but largely attempted to cast a Western-led (by the US) globalism as a sort of abstract antagonist that could morph into different forms, from different nations, through different policies, and was casted as attacking and undermining Russia and other nations across the globe that disagreed with its ideology, all while Russia itself was constructed as forging ahead with partners for a new, fairer and more moral global order.

Indeed, there are numerous articles analyzing Russian strategic narratives supporting these basic themes, albeit in different contexts, with all of them finding that Russian strategic narratives have been employed to bolster Russian identity and challenge US global leadership (Szostek, 2017; Miskimmon & O'Loughlin, 2017; Roselle, 2017; Irvin-Erickson, 2017; Skalamera, 2018; Suslov, 2017; Tsygankov, 2017). For instance, Suslov (2017) argues that Russian media has recently tried to promote a culturally-produced, political-territorial brand around the idea of a "new Russia" or *Novorossiya*. Constructed from building blocks of historical traditions and framed by metaphors of geographical and popular imagination, the narrative construction of Novorossiya shows the characteristics and imbrication of historical and cultural legacies and memories associated with Russia. This narrative, however, was not solely domestically oriented, but closely linked to Russia's divergence from the politics of the West due in part to the decline of the Russian economy and altered the way in which these narratives depicted the story of Russian strength. Consequently, Suslov (2017) concludes that these narratives make the West an enemy of Russia with Russia's national identity tied to Western antagonism.

Likewise, Skalamera (2018) claimed Russian authorities pursued an active policy of "narrative building" around 2013–2016 to support Russian global economic ties with China as Russia distanced itself from European politics. These narratives drew upon Russian culture to help bolster and attract large portions of the Russian population still upset at the loss of status accorded by the rapid crack-up of Soviet power and concentrated on Russian nationalism. In doing so, these narratives presented the US and the West as a representative of global imperialism which, by 2014, had become politically expedient and persuasively potent to fully portray the US/West as an enemy of the Russian state and its people.

Furthermore, Szostek's (2017) study of Russian narrative construction found a similar juxtapositioning of branding positive images of Russia with negative portrayals of the West/US. While Russian media presented the Russian state as a friendly, welcoming, non-threatening actor on the world stage, it frequently described the US as risible, foolish, criminal, and immoral. Common plotlines of these narratives depicted Western interference as causes of state instability; the West was viewed as seeking dominance without due consultation with others.

Finally, further evidence of this narrative divide can be seen through Miskimmon and O'Loughlin's (2017) strategic narrative analysis of Russian state speeches and government policy documents. These authors argue that as far back as 2000 Russian strategic narratives sought to reinforce Russia's global prestige and authority, while promoting multilateral and institutional constraints on other actors, specifically the US. These narratives were remarkably consistent and produced more contestation, making alignment with the US an unlikely possibility even prior to the calamities in relations to come.

Context of the 2016 US Presidential Election and US–Russian Relations

It is within this context of "irremediable" relations and notions of Western antagonism that the 2016 US presidential election took place and was presented to the Russian population by Russian media. The highly centralized, and state monitored, Russian news media had presented the US as a mismanaged failure and anti-Russian aggressor throughout the closing years of the Obama administration (Hinck et al., 2018). In fact, Russian anti-Western rhetoric through the 2012 US presidential election was described as refocusing on the US as a Cold War adversary in order to shore up domestic support for Putin, pushing the pendulum swing in relations arguably too far in a direction of mistrust to be quickly reconciled (Elder & Amos, 2012). Hutchings and Szostek (2015) claimed that through the Ukrainian crisis, Russian state-controlled media featured anti-Western narratives tied to Russian national identity and a call for solidarity, projecting the US as a historic Russian enemy seeking global dominance (Hutchings & Szostek, 2015).

However, the uniqueness of the US election in 2016, thanks in large part to the unlikely and unorthodox candidacy of Donald Trump, offered an opportunity for the Russian regime to utilize Trump's anti-establishment rhetoric to simultaneously present damning presentations of anti-Western democracy and point towards a new balance of potential relations. During Trump's presidential run, then candidate Trump offered praise towards Russian president Putin as a leader and went so far as to dismiss Russian suppression of journalism and political opponents, arguing in seeming defense of Putin's tactics "I think our country does plenty of killing also" and claiming his presidency would start a new era of US–Russian relations (Diamond, 2015). The conservative–liberal political faults lines in the US unfurled during the election process opened up a new narrative channel for Russian news media to exploit. Not only could it present its prescriptive, virtually continuous negative coverage of the US system as a hypocritical aggressor, it could further argue the US presidential election as a case study in Western societal collapse with a populace, and presidential front-runner, calling for massive and sometimes shocking institutional governance overhaul. If relations between the US and Russia were to again swing towards more cooperative relations, it would be the US doing the bulk of the movement. It is critical to note here that there was no strong love affair between Russian news media and then candidate Trump. Rather, the disruption that Trump's candidacy presented was simply capitalized on in ways to further the aforementioned narratives.

In essence, the US presidential election and its fiercely focused, and widely broadcasted, internal disputes concerning US-led globalism gave Russian news media ammunition from which to construct narratives bolstering its own system, while continuing efforts to diminish US soft-power and any appeal towards Western democracy, the damages of which will be focused on at the conclusion of this chapter. The potential power of such coverage, however, bears further explication here.

As noted in Chapter 1, the projection of soft power through strategic media narratives is a powerful weapon for modern state systems. While perhaps too cumbersome and potentially double-edged at times to wield for more authoritarian-based media systems, when aligned properly with the internal discourses and national myths of the population the efforts can bear undeniably beneficial fruits. According to Jankovski (2016), the US and Russia have unceasingly, despite all crises and points of friction in the modern era, seen themselves as bound by a common set of rules towards one another in relation to the workings of international society. This binding has a preset condition rooted in some shared notion of a pluralist global order and shared common interests, if not also common values (Jankovski, 2016). The question thus arises as to how to alter the status quo of the existing notion of that pluralist order towards one's own advantage? Our argument here is that constructed strategic narratives on the US presidential election through Russian news media was the process by which this alteration of perception was attempted and, plausibly, accomplished.

Quantitative Results

This study was guided by a desire to understand how the US was being presented to Russian citizens by Russian news media during coverage of the 2016 US presidential election. Our belief was that, because of the gravity of the outcome that the US election would potentially have on US Russian relations, the event would be highly covered and that the narratives laced throughout that coverage concerning the US would be telling in what image Russian citizens have of the US and its role in global affairs. The study also sought insight into how the legitimacy of the US democratic process was discussed, as well as the legitimacy of US leaders.

Researchers conducted an initial inductive narrative analysis with two trained coders on 200 randomly selected articles from the data examining discussions on legitimacy, the democratic process and its desirability, presentation of the political candidates, metaphors on the election and democracy, and overall themes presented through narratives in order to create and test the initial code book. Following the initial pilot codes and reliability checks, a stratified random sample of 523 articles was pulled, ensuring that data was taken equally across time periods and news sources.

Exploring Presentations of the US and Candidates across Russian Media Sources

The differences across the various types of Russian news media in their coverage of the election provides a number of useful insights, including the scope of how the concept of the US as a nation, the election and democratic process are presented to Russian audiences; particular leanings towards one candidate or another and towards Western practices; and also demonstrates, to some extent, a composite sketch of the narratives available to Russian citizens concerning the US. Perhaps more importantly, noting the differences across Russian news media in election coverage makes the areas of convergence more compelling. The segmentation of Russian news sources follows previous research by the authors in which the stated position and/or financing of the new sources was used to categorize them as either pro-government (state-sponsored or directly endorsing the positions of the Kremlin) such as the broadcast news channel *Rossiya 24* or the news website *Izvestia*, stated-neutral (those news agencies claiming objective independence) such as *Ino-Pressa* and *Kommersant*, as well as news sources with stated oppositional views to the

Russian regime such as *Izvestia* (Cooley & Stokes, 2018). While the state-owned Russian broadcast channels are considered the main vehicles from which Russians get their news (Mickiewicz, 2008; Schenk, 2012), the scope of this study sought to examine the full diversity of narrative discussions taking place across the Russian media-scape in order to more fully understand the pliability and potential limitations to the strategic narratives presented to Russian citizens.

Thus, while the major sources of news information were an obvious part of the data collected, voice is also given here to more marginal sources. The intention is not necessarily to present sources of vastly diverging viewership on an equal footing, but rather to explain to a Western audience the full possible range of the narratives constructed concerning the US democratic process. A full source listing is provided in Chapter 2 of this volume.

Pro-Government

Pro-government Russian news sources (n=211) were overwhelmingly critical of Hillary Clinton, with 33 (15%) articles directly criticizing her actions and only 3 (1%) articles offering praise to Clinton (two of which were reports on President Obama's remarks concerning her ability to lead). Clinton is largely shown as a corrupt candidate, with a laundry list of scandals following her from previous posts. She is labeled as an outright liar and manipulator, and the very legitimacy of her candidacy was questioned after revelations of her actions against rival Senator Bernie Sanders were made public. Pro-government sources show Clinton as an enemy of Russia and warn of her victory in the election leading to increasingly strained US–Russian relations and a virtually inevitable war.

The pro-government sources, perhaps unsurprisingly, gave more praise to Donald Trump throughout the election process, 12 (6%) stories directly praised Donald Trump. However, perhaps more surprisingly to citizens outside of Russia, 26 (12%) articles directly criticized Trump. There were more than double the number of critical news articles related to Trump than there were positive ones. This was largely because Trump was completely unknown as a political actor and was thus presented as an absolute wild card. His actions throughout the campaign inspired much to the imagination in terms of what a Trump Presidency would look like for Russia, particularly related to the economic sanctions, and a general cautious optimism that Trump would be a better alternative than Clinton prevailed in the coverage.

Of tremendous importance to the conceptualization of the US by Russian citizens, pro-government sources were merciless in their criticisms of the state of American democracy. The legitimacy of the US democratic system and its candidates were called into question in 50 (23%) articles, while 39 (18%) were critical of the election process and its workings. Only a small handful of stories showed US democracy in a positive light, but they were far overshadowed by those showing the system as desperate and failing. The US and its election processes were shown as hypocritical, given the amount of corruption in the US system, and as representing the failures of Western-led globalism. Trump's eventual election victory demonstrates how much the US system has failed to meet the demands of its own citizens and Russian pro-government sources are keen to point out that all Russians have to do is sit back and watch as the US implodes on itself.

Neutral

Neutral news articles (n=156) were less critical of Clinton than pro-government sources, with 10 (6%) stories directly critical of Clinton, but only 2 (1%) in direct praise. A majority of the coverage of Clinton offered by neutral sources was in fact neutral towards Clinton herself. Articles focused mainly on poll numbers, lead changes and similarities between her and President Obama. Clinton is shown as coming under a lethal three-pronged attack from Donald Trump, Wikileaks, and Russian officials and affiliated cyber-hacking affiliates.

Of notable difference from the pro-government sources as well, 44 (28%) of the neutral articles were directly critical of Donald Trump and only 4 (2%) were in direct praise. Neutral articles presented Trump as a Putin sympathizer, an immoral businessman, as representing the blowback from the failures of globalism. Trump's admiration for Putin and ties to Russia are shown primarily in negative terms, his policies towards Russia, the Baltics, and Ukraine are shown as dangerous and recklessly naive. Neutral stories make the case that Trump is likely to make the lives of Russians, Americans, and others worse as he increasingly mirrors Putin.

The conceptualization of the US and its democratic process presented by neutral sources is a bleak one for Russian citizens to take in; 47 (30%) articles were critical of the election process and its workings and 43 (28%) questioned the legitimacy of US democracy and the candidates. Ultimately, neutral sources presented to Russian citizens the notion that mismanagement of elite, capitalist-driven globalism has caused the US system to begin to collapse from a surge in populist pushback from US citizens. The culmination of this is the election of Donald Trump, a figure that neutral sources claim will lead the US to the same type of authoritarianism found in Russia. One very telling article notes that Moscow is both happy for Trump and laughing at the catastrophe engulfing the Western liberal world. Neutral sources claim the US ideology of globalism became vulnerable because of its own corruption and greed, and now it has been undermined by internal, and some external, forces to become captured by authoritarianism.

Oppositional

Oppositional news articles (n=155) struggled to present the election to Russian citizens in ways that could speak to the need for more such democracy in Russia, nevertheless these sources did offer a very different take on the election. Principally these articles warn of an authoritarian manifestation taking place in the US as a result of the election chaos. In coverage of Clinton, 12 (8%) of the articles were directly critical of Clinton, while 7 (5%) articles offered direct praise. Most coverage focused on her strategies to defeat Trump (using the "woman card," alliances with the media, alliances with the Republican Party and other Democrats) and her ineffective, and unfounded, reliance on Russian hacking claims to save face. An assumption of certainty in Clinton's victory is presented throughout, a focus on her victory in the first debate, and the importance of her appeal to women and African Americans is mentioned regularly. However, Clinton is also presented as an extremely flawed candidate: corruption, scandal, false accusations and dangerous policies concerning Russia, and a candidate whose socialist policies could potentially ruin the US system.

Oppositional articles seemed confused in how to present Trump to their audience. Of the stories, 32 (20%) were directly critical of Trump, while 14 (9%) were in direct praise of Trump. Coverage on Trump ranged from that of an unintelligent, foolhearted buffoon, to a burly game show host figure, a racist tax-evader, a future dictator, to that of the real voice of the American people. He was cast as both a legitimate representative of concerned US workers and as a charlatan ready to work with Putin to divide the spoils of the world. Oppositional sources offered a perplexing perspective of Trump: on one hand, he was presented as a toxic poison to the GOP and US democracy, yet, on the other, still a legitimate representation of populism in the US.

The conceptualization of the US and its democratic process presented by oppositional sources seemed equally confused. On 23 (14%) occasions oppositional stories questioned the legitimacy of US democracy and of its candidates, yet 13 (8%) stories showed US democracy as a legitimate voice of the American people. Only 9 (6%) stories, however, were critical of the US the election process and its workings. Oppositional sources, though perhaps uncertain how to explain to Russian citizens what exactly was taking place in the US election, were keen to respect and legitimize the process itself far more than other sources.

Qualitative Narrative Analysis of the 2016 US Presidential Election

The strategic narratives in the Russian media took the harshest anti-US stance with specific commentary drawing upon how each candidate came to represent two very different paths for US–Russian relations. As such, Clinton symbolized US establishment politics representative of the larger "globalist" agenda that promoted a US-led liberal order dedicated to spreading democracy abroad and in opposition to Russia. Trump was contrasted as symbolizing both the American electorates' turning against these globalist policies, as well as a future whereby Russia and the US could ease tensions and work together, albeit through the legitimation of Russian interests. On the whole then, the larger geopolitical setting of the US election was constructed as proof regarding US decline and the reasonability of Russian policy, all within the notion of a growing multipolar world order where Russia was needed and succeeding in providing global leadership.

Issue and National Level Narratives

While Russian news media included informational descriptions of the US election process, more significant attention was placed on issue-specific narratives focused on the flaws and personal failings of the candidates, accusations of Russian hacking into the US election, the US-led sanctions imposed on Russia, and the Syrian civil war. These issue narratives, both about the candidates and their policies, come together to depict Clinton as an unabashed critic of Russia who represented US establishment politics which promoted a failed globalist agenda out of touch with US citizens' needs and in opposition to Russian interests. Trump, on the other hand, was presented as a flawed candidate representative of the weakness of the US system, albeit with the potential for a new direction in US–Russian relations. Taken together, the candidates and their policies were narratively constructed as corrupt, poor decision makers who have unjustly targeted the Russian nation because of Russia's resistance to their aims. Issue level narratives then coalesced to reinforce national level narratives projecting evidence of US failure with defenses of Russian policies and identity.

Issue Narratives: Candidates' Personal Failings and the Failings of the US Election Process

Informational narratives within Russian media explained how and when the debates took place, frequently cited polling data indicating who was winning,[2] the importance of the electoral college and the critical battleground states each candidate needed to win. In doing so, articles placed the US election process in context to the Russian election process, stating that "US electoral system is significantly different from the Russian"[3] and "[f]or Russians, the US presidential election rules are unusual. They are indirect and two-stage. First, citizens in each state cast their votes for the electoral college. That, in turn, selects the candidate directly."[4] Within this description of how the US president was elected were elements stressing the fierce competition and drama regarding who will ultimately win. As *Gazeta Russian* noted, "there is a war for every vote, and the election result is unpredictable."[5] This discussion even included how many electoral votes were needed and how close the two candidates were to reaching them, especially in battle ground states:

> Throughout the pre-election period Hillary Clinton maintained a significant lead in the "guarantee votes." It is now much closer to the secret of his opponent in the number of 270 electoral votes, which guarantee victory. Donald Trump in the last days of the race makes the election sprint. He needed the air in victory "wavering" states: Pennsylvania, Ohio, Iowa and Florida. In Utah and Arizona, the situation looks better for him, but the victory is not guaranteed and there.[6]

This competition, however, was not viewed positively. Instead, the debates and the candidates' policy discussions were seen as vacuous, with too many personal attacks more akin to political theatre. Following the first debate, *Novaya Gazeta* opined how the discourse "turned mildly scandalous, sometimes boring and—ultimately—useless" whereby "the candidates talked past each other."[7] In doing so, the article claimed that the purpose of the candidates' discourse was to "abuse details" so as to not bore the audience, because "[i]n the age of Twitter—psychologists say—we have the attention span, like aquarium fish."[8] Not only, then, were the candidates and the US electorate mocked, but so was the process, with the article suggesting that instead of journalists covering the election the US should employ "theater critics."[9]

The theme of the debates as political theater or entertainment continued with articles noting the large number of individuals who tuned in. For instance, one article noted that the debate between "Hillary Clinton and Donald Trump outdid Jimmy Carter and Ronald Reagan. According to Nielsen, the live broadcast of the debates ... [was] watched [by] more than 84 million people—a record in the history of American television debate" with further comparisons drawn to the Super Bowl.[10] Other articles even reported that many Americans were actually being taken to movie theaters streaming the debates and imbibing presidential candidate-inspired alcoholic beverages. As a *Kommersant* journalist sent to Ohio witnessed,

> Much more free atmosphere in the evening was in the homes of Americans, many bars and even a cinema showing the debate ... the foyer of the cinema [sold] special alcoholic drinks whose names refer to the presidential race, so everyone can choose their candidate to taste.[11]

Entertainment was offered not only by the big screen, but also through the belittling comments made throughout the debates and the quirky nicknames assigned by Trump such as "Lying Ted" and "Crooked Hillary" being referenced across Russian news media. *Novaya Gazeta* quipped that the only reason Americans tuned in was in the hope that "Trump will throw out something they can tell their grandchildren about."[12] The relative gamesmanship of the election was also drawn out, such as Trump inviting Cruz to speak at the GOP convention after having gone so far in the primaries as to insinuate that Cruz's father was "involved in the murder of President Kennedy"[13] and through opinion polls suggesting who "won" and "lost" the debates. An article from *Gazeta Russian* shared how, "Opinion polls have awarded victory in the US election debate [to] Hillary Clinton ... Her confidence and tranquility looked more advantageous than the loud arrogance of Donald Trump."[14]

While the election process and its debates were seen primarily as entertainment, the candidates themselves were constructed in colorful ways, with narratives drawing attention to various reports of candidate corruption, mis-dealings, legal battles and controversies, missteps, misstatements, and general unfitness for leadership. Donald

Trump was presented with the largest range of characterizations, from an inexperienced political buffoon, an uncouth and potential unqualified showman to, in a notable article in *Kasparov*, a dangerous demagogue compared to the likes of George Wallace and Mussolini, noting that Trump's campaign focused on painting a bleak future for American democracy and insisting in a tyrant-like fashion that only he could possibly save it.[15]

While more positive characterizations of Trump came from Russian articles discussing his implications for US–Russian relations, many negative characterizations were included, with the Russian media picking up the US outrage over his "unfitness for the office of president." For instance, *Gazeta Russian*, citing *Politico*, noted how "Trump [was] accused of raping a woman [and] has drawn a lawsuit,"[16] while more sources cited how Americans protested his election, holding "banners with slogans condemning racism, sexism and xenophobia."[17] Other characterizations of Trump's character revolved around his unfitness for the office of US president. For instance, after the first debate, one article reported how "Trump is not suitable for the post of President" because he "shows the vocabulary of a 13-year-old boy and behave[s] in accordance with this age",[18] while another explained how "he behaved like a schoolboy, dropouts material before the exam first, [then] he complained of a malfunctioning microphone."[19] Furthermore, Russian reports picked up on US disillusionment with Trump, including an at length discussion of the US newspaper *USA Today*'s editorial, explaining that Trump "does not have the temperament, knowledge, fortitude and integrity, which are necessary to the American president" going on to state how he "'betrayed the foundations' laid down by past leaders of the country, including the commitment to support NATO and opposition to the 'Russian aggression.'"[20]

Other key issues narrating Trump's character within Russian media included his business experience, with numerous articles tracking his wealth and tax returns.[21] While it was shared that his wealth had declined and did so because of his "inefficient management of the three casinos in Atlantic City, failing to do business in the airline industry and the failure of the acquisition of Plaza Hotel in Manhattan,"[22] these losses were reported as justifying the lack of taxes paid over the past decade as these were all business losses; as one article explained, "because of [his] huge losses the state granted Trump the right not to pay income tax … for 18 years. In 1995, Trump suffered a loss of nearly 916 million dollars."[23] Republican backers of Trump were extensively cited as defending his tax evasion with both former New York City mayor Rudy Giuliani and New Jersey governor Chris Christie suggesting that this "demonstrates the talent [of] Trump" calling him "a genius, because he failed to pay income tax so long."[24]

Clinton received consistent coverage presenting her as mired in scandals with the most recurring issue by far being her use of a private email server to handle classified materials and the ensuing FBI investigation. Relentless reminders of her as under investigation and quotes from then FBI Director James Comey noting Clinton had "violated the rules for handling classified information"[25] projected Clinton as untrustworthy, sloppy, and deeply flawed. This theme of Clinton's inability to handle classified information continued with multiple articles discussing accusations that "during a visit to Moscow as Secretary of State Clinton [had] forgotten in the room a secret document" and from this, "according to the head of the FBI, the investigation revealed that the former secretary of state behaved extremely careless in the handling of information of national importance."[26]

Less frequent attacks on Clinton included her health and her actions during his husband's infidelities with Monica Lewinsky. *Rossiya 24* commented that her attacks on Trump for his sexual infidelities were for "ironically, exactly [the same as] twenty years ago [when] her husband retire[d] in the Oval Office with Monica Lewinsky."[27] Russian media also picked up on US media and some Democrats' concerns that following her collapse after a campaign event "the news of Clinton's disease and canceling some activities with her participation frightened supporters of Democrats and raised the question of what would happen if the candidate's health did not allow her to continue the race."[28]

In addition to her various scandals, however, Hillary Clinton was uniquely portrayed as disliked by President Putin with more hawkish policies related to Russian interests. According to one report, "Hillary Clinton and Vladimir Putin distrust [each other] mutually." As such, during one debate, it was reported that "Hillary Clinton voiced [her] long-standing suspicions against Vladimir Putin" with the article continuing to state how Putin "often spoke of Clinton, the Democratic candidate, in the scornful tone" with "[i]nsiders in the Russian government and former diplomats say the Kremlin believes that Clinton [is] a threat to its existence" because "Clinton—is the embodiment of absolute unique school of liberal interventionism."[29] Clinton's views became tied to national identity narratives of the US, as she was thus seen as reflective of the US political establishment, not only disliked by the Russian government, but also by US citizens themselves. As one article explained, "The former first lady, Senator and the head of the State Department ... personifies the most hated establishment, and it is slippery as an eel, professional resourcefulness rather repels many."[30] As *Kommersant* explained, this establishment politics and the success of Trump and Sander's proved, "a clear failure of the establishment and party leadership"[31] suggesting that a change in US policy was needed.

Both candidates, taken together with the negative depiction of the US election process, coalesced then into a narrative whereby the US democratic system had failed to produce quality candidates. Russian media concluded that Clinton and Trump "prove the mutual unfit for work as a head of state and commander in chief" because "[b]oth candidates have flaws. In fact, these defects are so serious that in the old days, and Hillary, and Trump would have long since forced to withdraw from the election campaign, but now everything is not as it once was."[32] The article goes on to explain, "We have two candidates with the largest negative-rating in history" with US "voters undecided due to the fact that this time they will have to vote against, not for."[33] These flaws then become an indictment on the US system, suggesting that:

> The current election race in the United States held in violation of all the laws and traditions of the American political process. All this suggests that something went wrong in the American system. Or, on the contrary, it demonstrates the ability to adequately respond to the political changes.[34]

Issue and National Level Narratives: Key Issues in US–Russian Relations

While Russian media reported extensively on both candidates' personal failings and emplotted their inadequacies onto a failing US democratic system, discussion of three key issues related to US–Russian relations went further into mapping issue level narratives onto national ones critical of US policy and in support of Russian strength through contrasting Clinton in negative ways, while more optimistically suggesting that Trump could warm US–Russian relations.

First, Russian media reported extensively on accusations leveled against Russia for manipulating the US election, and thus in defense of Russian national identity. These narratives focus on demonstrating the innocence of Russia in any guilt relating to the hacking of Clinton's campaign and accuse Clinton herself of attempting to obfuscate her guilt by blaming Russia for her problems, serving as a parallel to US involvement throughout the world likewise scapegoating Russian actions for policy failures caused by the US.

In defending the Russian state from accusations leveled by Clinton and the Democratic National Committee that Russian hackers aided in any way in hacks and leaks of private emails of the DNC, numerous articles quoted famous hackers asserting Russian innocence, as well as definitive statements from Russian political leaders and internet specialists claiming that the accusations against Russia were not only false but being put forward to mask the incompetence of both Hillary Clinton and the DNC in protecting their own information. For instance, *Arguments and Facts* reported that "Presidential press secretary Dmitry Peskov said Russia has nothing to do with hacking database US Democratic National Committee," going on to state "I completely rule out the possibility that the (Russian) government or government agencies were involved in this."[35] Instead, the article suggested that these accusations were a "weak" explanation attempting to scapegoat enemies of the US.[36]

Furthermore, the Russian media constructed a narrative whereby the hacking accusations were neatly packaged into preexisting conceptions of Clinton as adamantly anti-Russian, claiming that her latest rounds of accusations against Russia for her own mishandling of information and misdeeds were simply a continuation of her anti-Russian campaign rhetoric.[37] Again, another article citing Putin's spokesperson, Dmitry Peskov, explained, "Hillary Clinton's words are 'part of the pre-election rhetoric.' In this case the attacker Guccifer 2.0, who was involved in the breaking of the Democratic Party to the US, denied reports that he was acting on behalf of the Russian government." This was then placed in context, whereby the article insinuates that Clinton's accusations came when she was beginning to lose support, stating: "Recall, according to recent reports, Hillary Clinton ahead of Donald Trump by only 2% in popularity. Earlier, billionaire noticeably behind in the presidential race, but seven weeks before the vote began to strengthen its positions."[38]

Trump on the other hand, supported this narrative and his statements doubting Clinton's accusations of Russian hacking were frequently reported within Russian media. For instance, an article explained that "Trump doubt[s] that the attacks on the US servers is Russia," going on to quote Trump stating the perpetrators could be "'anyone', 'even 180-pound man from his bed.'"[39] Going further, another article picked up on Trump suggesting that even China could be responsible for the hacking, and turned blame away from the US's enemies to President Obama: "'It could be Russia, it could be China or any other country,'—says the billionaire. According to him, the incidents with the attacks of hackers suggest that the US under President Barack Obama 'lost control of cyberspace.'"[40]

Second, in addition to defenses of Russian hacking of the 2016 election, Russian media discussed at length the candidates' policies on US–Russian relations related to the Obama administration's sanctions placed on Russia due to its annexation of Crimea. Here again Clinton was viewed as an enemy towards Russia and willing to continue Obama-era policies which dangerously threatened Russia–US relations. Trump, on the other hand, was portrayed as contemplating the lifting of Russian sanctions to resolve tensions between the two countries.

Clinton's policies in support of Ukraine and sanctions against Russia came to negatively symbolize an establishment view of US foreign policy identity revolving around the spreading of democracy. While Clinton was reported as having "never liked to deal neither Putin, nor with Russian Foreign Minister Sergei [Lavrov]" with the "feeling [being] mutual,"[41] her personal disdain towards Russia was reported as "a threat to its sovereignty" because it centered around a globalist, "democratization policy, which he [Putin] sees as a threat to its [Russia's] existence."[42] Clinton's policy, then, stood in contrast with Russian interests, as "The Russian government has long been critical of the pro-democracy revolutions in the Middle East and neighboring Ukraine," and "Russian officials have often accused Washington of following the policy of 'regime change', which they claim is directed against Moscow, and the US and openly, and secretly funded pro-democracy organizations."[43]

These fears were discussed at length with Clinton's policy towards economic sanctions against Russia and support for the Ukrainian government. For instance, as one article noted, Clinton "became an avid supporter of the adoption of sanctions that would have a negative impact on the Russian economy. She also advocated the need to take all possible measures in order to slow down the establishment and expansion of the Eurasian Union."[44] The explanation for Clinton's policies was, again, that she distrusted Putin, with reports picking up how in the debates she said, "Putin was a KGB agent, he had no soul by definition" and therefore concluding that "Many experts have long called Hillary Clinton a major Russophobe."[45] Further evidence of Clinton's support of sanctions against Russia came from articles explaining how Ukrainian president "Poroshenko said about the effectiveness of anti-Russian sanctions and thanked Hillary Clinton for the constant and firm support for Kiev."[46] Even worse for Russians, Clinton's support of Ukraine and US sanctions against Russia were described as going further in escalating relations through the supply of weapons to Ukraine. An article discussed the importance of the US election in relation to a congressional debate over a bill "including the supply of lethal weapons [to the] ATO [anti-terrorist operation] zone, as well as a number of other actions aimed at further escalation of relations with Russia," which the winner of the election would need to sign. The article then explains the consequence of the election, reporting that because Clinton was likely to sign the bill, "If Clinton wins—this is a war."[47]

As for Trump, Russian media frequently reported his willingness to relax US sanctions. Russian media noted that: "The US position, according to Trump, generally does not involve any special interest in Ukraine. If the situation has developed in such a way that at the expense of the territory will be something to bargain with Russia, he intends to compete."[48] Thus, "[r]eporters noted that if Trump takes over as president, [Trump would] then hasten to lift the sanctions against Russia."[49] However, they were cautious: "As for Trump, then here it is difficult. He has repeatedly said in his pre-election campaign of the desire to stabilize relations with our country. Perhaps upon becoming US president, he will choose [such] a policy."[50]

Taken together then, Clinton's statements against Russian advancement of the Eurasian Economic Union, her comments about Putin as having no soul, and her avid support of the 2014 sanctions against Russia aiming to cripple the Russian economy were used as evidence of Clinton's wanton hopes for Russian destruction. While Clinton was cast and confirmed, through the sanctions, by Russian news media as a globalist who could not see anything other than an enemy when looking at Russia, Trump's comments on removing the economic sanctions on the regime were construed as evidence of their inherent wrongfulness and callously vindictive intent. As the Russian media explained, the differences in policy and character between Clinton and Trump's approach towards Russia was the following: "Clinton, like a true politician, is trying to win the sympathy of voters calling to unite against the 'Russian threat', and Trump like a real businessman, playing on people's fatigue from hunting 'foreign witch' and a desire to focus on the well-being of their own country."[51]

Finally, the contrasting positions of the two candidates continued in discussion of US–Russian relations regarding the conflict in Syria. Issue and national level narratives came into play in discussion of US and Russian policy towards Syria, where the conflict was projected by Russian news media as evidence of Putin's success over the West as President Assad remained in power. Putin was thus shown as a level-headed peacemaker in the face of an escalatory globalist US, and once again, comments by candidate Trump were often used in support of the Russian position. The securing of Assad's control on power in Syria was celebrated as flying directly in the face of Washington, with *Izvestia* reporting that "Assad is going to remain in power for another six years ... this runs counter to Washington's plans and in contrasts to the statements of Barack Obama, which he stated on a regular basis that 'Assad must go.'"[52]

Comments by Trump contrasting his position to that of Obama and Hillary Clinton were capitalized on as supportive of the Russian position in Syria. As one article discussing the policy options regarding Syria explained, "It is also important to consider the position of the next US administration" with it being "[h]ard to say what will be done in Syria [if] Donald Trump became president." However, Clinton's policy was known and seen as in contrast to Russia's aims. As the article continues to explain, Clinton's likely winning of the US election means that "Putin will have to deal with President Clinton, which has long been in favor of a no-fly zone over Syria and consistent support of the opposition, are skeptical about the intentions of Russia in Syria."[53]

Further examples of Russian disdain towards Clinton's Syria policy included Russian media quoting a letter Clinton wrote to Obama when she stepped down as Secretary of State:

> Before leaving the State Department in early 2013, Hillary Clinton wrote to President Obama farewell note about Russia She said [the] "Reset" [of] relations with Moscow, which had hoped [White house] was ultimately unsuccessful Clinton urged Obama to set a "new course", starting tougher to deal with Russian President Vladimir Putin.[54]

As a result, the article continues by stating how today "the Syrian conflict has already begun to emerge as a new tectonic fault line in the conflict between the US and Russia." The article then showcased Clinton's hawkish stance towards Russia, citing her as saying: "It is also important that the US make very clear to Putin that his party is not acceptable to be in Syria, to create even more chaos, bomb the people, being on the side of Assad."[55]

Clinton's position was then compared to Trump's position on Syria. Here, Clinton was seen as, again, likely to start a war with Russia, whereas Trump called for collaboration and thus normalizing Russian policy in the region. This comparison was made clear in an article explaining, "The aggressive approach Clinton to Moscow is very different from the cozy relationship Trump" going on to warn how Clinton's position "requires it [US] to conduct a much more confrontational policy in Syria ... Moscow already sees Clinton's call to create a no-fly zone in Syria, a signal that it is ready to start a war with Russia."[56] On the other hand, Trump's policy was shown as demonstrating the effectiveness of

Russia's approach and its criticism of the US through Trump's warning of a third world war occurring because of US military actions in Syria and his claims that Clinton "was reckless with e-mail, with the change of regimes and with the lives of Americans. Our people are humiliated abroad ... compromised by radical Islam, which got to our shores."[57] Thus, for Trump, the solution was a change in US policy primarily through cooperation with Russia in Syria. After Trump won the election, an article noted how during a phone conversation between Putin and Trump, the two sides "agreed that the current state of Russian–American relations 'extremely poor' and in need for 'active' collaboration in their normalization and ... constructive cooperation on a wide range of issues."[58] These issues included economics, trade, fight against terrorism and "the settlement of the crisis in Syria" where "Trump declared sympathy for the Russian leader and the intention to improve relations with them," despite the "number of European politicians [calling] for him to take a tough stance against Russia."[59]

The narrative construction, then, of Clinton and Trump's policy regarding Syria bolstered Russia's claims that the US was a global aggressor out to challenge Russia with Trump's statements used as supporting Russia's narrative that US–Syria policy was ineffective, losing to the Russians in Syria, and that stability in Syria required Russian support. In doing so, these issue narratives demonstrate a worldview whereby Russians were under attack by US establishment policy-makers, as seen through Clinton, US strength was declining, through its failure in overthrowing Assad and destabilizing the region, and in support of Russian prestige and strength through the US's calling upon Russia to help it solve the crisis in Syria.

International and National Level Narratives: The End of US Exceptionalism, Failed Globalism, and Collapse of Western Democracy

In reporting on the events of the 2016 US presidential election, Russian news media presented international level narratives that showed a fractured world order whereby national level narratives projected Russia as a sane alternative to US and Western immorality and globalism. In doing so, three narrative themes emerge: the US at the end of its exceptionalism, failed globalist policies, and the collapse of Western democracy.

The Strength of US Populist Movements Is a Result of Failed Globalization

Russian media explained Trump's ascendance, and eventual victory, as a tale of US citizens' unrest leading them to turn against the establishment polities of globalization. Thus, the drive by Western nations towards globalism was shown as in crisis, with the US election pointedly demonstrating the internal struggles of the masses against liberal elitism. This explanation also aided in legitimizing the strong, nationalistic, leadership style of Vladimir Putin, as well as explaining the break between Russia and the globalist West.

The structure of this narrative sets up strong Russian nationalism, explaining Western rejection as being a result of its refusing to cave into a Western-run world government, and ultimately attempts to demonstrate that globalist policies are not in the interests of the common people. For instance, as *Izvestia* explained, "America is torn between two political trends—globalism, the national ideology of the last few decades, and isolationism."[60] The article goes on to juxtapose what a Clinton and Trump presidency would be, citing Trump as saying "Hillary Clinton [wants] to be president of the world. I choose to be president of the US. And to protect the interests of US citizens."[61] Finally, the suggestion is made that Americans do not care about US establishment foreign policy, represented by a Clinton presidency, and instead care about issues affecting their daily lives: "ordinary Americans are hardly interested in international politics, they prefer to vote for a candidate who formulates coherent economic program, which includes social transformation, and most importantly—health insurance and affordable fuel prices in the nearest gas station."[62]

This renouncing of globalist policies is also projected onto the world stage. As an article from *Kasparov* explains, "The sensational triumph of Trump dictated by political shamanism ... it is a response to the rejection of the masses of the world establishment [which] methodically enriching caste elected by washing out the budgets of all the other strata."[63] From this statement there is evidence of a conspiratorial tone to those with globalist agendas as corrupt and taking advantage of ordinary citizens' economic wellbeing, a narrative Putin has likewise used in combatting US economic sanctions against his nation. Further support of Russian views comes from Trump's attack on globalists' policies reported as analogous to Putin's platform in Russia, with an article explaining:

> Many people in Russia see Donald Trump American [as an] "analog" of Vladimir Putin. He, too, he speaks the language of ordinary people. And if Putin tried on the role of a champion of a new just world order, Trump puts upside down the established structure of the political elite of America. Both want to look like that kind courageous outsiders.[64]

Finally, within the same article, part of Trump's "championing of a new just world order" are his foreign policy positions which justify Russian actions in Crimea and objection to NATO enlargement: "Trump has promised to consider the recognition of the Crimea, and Russia, in principle, not opposed to the abolition of the anti-Russian sanctions" all the while "NATO partners [are] disappointed with [Trump's] statements to the effect that [he] sees no urgent need to protect the Baltic countries."[65]

As one can see, Russian media narratives construct Trump's victory as resulting from US populist movements viewing establishment politicians, as represented by a Clinton candidacy, as deaf to their economic plight which is the result of a failed globalization. This movement by the US is reflected on the international stage, connecting it to Putin's narratives of his actions in Russia, as well as serving as justification and support for Russian foreign policy goals. Thus, the casting of the US election of Trump comes to be seen as a rejection of globalism and demonstrating a failure for so-called liberal democracies that had looked down on Russia, reinforcing Putin's managed democracy and strong nationalistic intimations.

The US at the End of the Era of Exceptionalism

In addition to showcasing Trump's electoral success as coming at the hands of globalist movements, Russian media also constructed a narrative centered on the election of Trump as epitomizing the end of US global dominance. Whereas the US had championed and advocated the supremacy of its democratic, liberal world order, American's election of Trump showcased a clear decision to go down a new path. According to this story, at best, the US nation would be so divided and in turmoil in the wake of the election that it forced introspection and required internal focus; at worst, the election result was the last gasp of the US as a global leader championing freedom and the values of a US-led liberal order. These narratives simultaneously diminish US moral leadership, while also helping to establish validation for the posturing of the Russian regime and reinforce the national identity of a strong and re-emerging Russia.

For instance, Russian media narrated the implications of American's election of Trump as proving that global liberalism was a failed notion and those who perpetuated it, that is, US elites, were now out of touch with the majority of Americans. Accordingly, Trump won because "Trump contributed to the accumulated anger and frustration in relation to the political elite" with Americans choosing Trump because "Americans want change."[66] Indeed, Trump's campaign and foreign policy was viewed as in contrast to the typical values undergirding the US-led liberal world order reflective of US establishment politics. As *Slon* reported, citing Trump foreign policy adviser Carter Page, the liberal worldview, based "on ideas such as democratization, inequality, corruption and regime change" was not only "hypocritical" but "liberal" in name only. Instead, the argument was made that US policy should reflect "[a]nother group of countries, such as China and Russia" as they "base their foreign policy on the principles of mutual respect, mutual benefit and equality."[67] Therefore, Trump's victory symbolized American's support of Russian and Chinese foreign policy, while Clinton's loss was a loss for liberal values.

Even in oppositional media, as best illustrated in an article by liberal independent *New Times* the election of Trump demonstrated that the US was no longer unique, and thus removed cover for anyone in the US to criticize the Russian political system. The article begins by gleefully attacking the US establishment, including its political commentators, as well as the loss of Clinton, as well criticizing the US electorate through its election of Trump. As the article explains, Trump's victory on election night demonstrated how "highbrow analysts" had incorrectly projected a Clinton victory. Instead, "the American people confidently chose a populist demagogue in Donald Trump, who appeals to the basest of feelings—vulgar sexism, racial prejudice, and the most primitive ideas about international relations." The Russian commentators continue by discussing the implications of Trump's victory, stating that:

> I do not consider this gloating, but I remember our conversation, which took place a year ago. You confidently said that here [in Russia] is a populist and demagogue in Putin, and [that] in America, Trump is impossible. Alas, it turned out that it is possible.

The explanation that follows argues that America's choosing of Trump demonstrated that a "gap in values occurred between the elites of developed countries and their peoples" which debunks the "popular" "globalist theory" whereby "human rights—regardless of gender, race, social origin and sexual orientation, as well as in tolerance and political correctness" proved not to be shared by all, but instead "divided them, overwhelming majority of their populations" for a Trump victory. The importance of this establishment, liberal, globalist world view was that Russians felt it had been deployed against them in the past, explaining how supposedly, according to this globalist ideology, "'backward' Russia, with its history of the Tatar yoke and centuries of slavery was [supposedly] doomed to trail behind the developed countries with their enlightened nations." The authors conclude that, with the election of Trump: "Alas, my friend, today, after the election of Trump, it turned out—we are in the same boat."[68]

As this article shows, not only did Trump's election discredit the values undergirding the US-led liberal order, it also functioned to support Russia's own national identity as equivalent to that of the US. The hypocrisy of the liberal US system and its pretentious treatment of other "corrupt" and not-democratic-enough nations had proved itself, despite propagandized promotion of an easy Clinton victory, as a tragic democratic failure,[69] with Trump's victory cast as an act of a desperate populace to rid itself of Western-led globalism and liberalization, marking a bookend to America's era of exceptionalism.

Collapse of Western Democracy

Finally, in building upon the idea that anti-globalist sentiment propelled Trump to victory and the US-led liberal order no longer provided America with a sense of exceptionalism to pontificate to the rest of the world, Russian news media also constructed an international level narrative that showed a fractured world order. This broken, liberal-leaning globalist-led order is summarized as a collapse of Western democracy, building upon the previous two narratives, where the manipulations of greedy, corrupt, elite globalists under the guise of democracy were shown as finally being undone by their own miscalculations and Russia.

Now, Russia and other strongly nationalist focused nations were projected as being freely able to reshape a more honest global system. This narrative, then, focused on demonstrating to Russian citizens that the Western democratic system had become so corrupt, hypocritical, and out of touch with its own population that its foundations were crumbling around itself. Once more, these narratives lend support to Putin's model of managed democratic rule and fit within existing political myths of the Russian population with Trump and the Brexit vote being constructed as manifesting a literal retreat of globalism.

The overspread and exhausted US was portrayed as in retreat from its tendencies to global extension, with Trump's campaign of "America First" made as a direct illustration of this withdraw. As one article noted, anyone voting for Trump "risks plung[ing] US into isolation, plunge them into provincialism and lead to the brink the world power, which itself Trump allegedly wants to 'once again make [America] great' ... jeopardizing the security of the world."[70]

Even before Trump's election, Russian news media argued the damage had already been done, with an article from *Slon* reporting how "Even if the eccentric billionaire is to lose ... the American political system [has] a long time to comprehend and digest the election crisis [of] 2016" due to the fact that "from two flanks, populists and demagogues [in] Donald Trump and Bernie Sanders tore to shreds the house of cards of American party politics."[71] Indeed, virtually every place the US had intervened to spread it liberal democratic cause were depicted as failing, from the Middle East to the Asia Pacific region, as well as Europe, also shown as recoiling from its globalist agenda, as both the US and Europe were dealing with popular riots and challenges to the legitimacy of their very structures of governance. As *Kommersant* reported:

> The demonstrators were beating shop windows and set fire to trash cans, threw stones at police. Law enforcement in response used pepper gas and rubber bullets. 26 people were detained ... Mr. Trump is not prepared for this role, his favorite thing is shifting responsibility to other people, his impulsiveness, cockiness, the constant lies, proven cases of sexual violence and lack of experience—all this shows that he is a threat to the republic the signatories argue.[72]

Likewise, the presentation of Europe followed similar harsh treatment in these narratives.

> Brexit and Trump specter is haunting Europe, the specter of populism. No sooner had supporters of Brexit, driven by nationalist and anti-European rhetoric, celebrated this victory in the referendum on June 24 as the latest news came from Austria, where on July 1 of the Constitutional Court overturned the results of the last presidential elections in May and appointed to a new date in October 2016. They have an excellent chance of far-right Austrian Freedom Party.[73]

Hence, Trump's candidacy and ultimate election in the US was tied to a much larger rejection of globalism by the very populations from which it had arisen.[74] If the world had been run by Western-led globalist before, Russian news media was keen to tell its viewers that, with the election of Donald Trump in the US, such was no longer the case. As *InoPressa* stated: "The current global order—a liberal, rules-based system, formed in 1945 and extended after the end of the Cold War—is now subjected to the unprecedented pressure of Globalization and in retreat."[75]

Implications of Russian Strategic Narratives

What comes into focus from these media narratives is a concept of US democracy as a failing experiment. There is a focus on presenting a claimed backlash against Western globalism (led by the people of the US) as one of the fundamental failures of US democracy. This is tied to a presentation of globalization being driven by an elite subset of hypocritical Westerners. The goal is not necessarily to believably bolster the claims of the superiority and functionality of the Russian system to that of democracy, but rather to show that a greater moral equivalence exists there than meets the eye between Russia and what the West now calls democracy. By casting hypocrisy as the gravest of sin, the individual with no moral pretense seems almost pure, and thus globalism at the hands of self-serving elites is no better than auto-cracy and perhaps it is even worse given the duplicity with which it is delivered. This is not an argument against democracy per say, only that the practicalities of the existing global system to which it has been deployed, developed, and allowed to flourish has bastardized its ideals into something much harsher and shrewd; so much so that the populations are turning against it.

This directly serves the interests of the Russian regime, as it demonstrates that Russian exclusion by the West is coming from the same self-serving elites disinterested with the lives of their own people and serves to validate Putin's cultivation of strong national identity tied to historic national myths held by the population of their own resilience. But more still, it serves to recast Putin as a sort of honest villain who has lived long enough to see himself become a hero. The story of a hero necessarily involves an antagonist with plans against it, and in this story the hero is winning.

The US political system is painted as corrupt and over-extended and its citizens are given a sideshow that mirrors reality television in substitute for meaningful political conversations. Ultimately, Russians are given a picture of US democracy that shows little more than a demolished night at the movies. Russian news media shows that rather than genuine discussions on issues related to world affairs or domestic policy, US political conventions, debates, and election riddled insults are all entertainment festivals led by extremely corrupt and flawed candidates. The rise of Donald Trump is highlighted as the cherry on top to the failures of globalism and demonstrative of the unrest brewing in the country among and between citizens. All of the Russian news sources make clear that, for better or worse, the US is no longer a model of democracy that others should readily follow with devastating presentations of US soft power arising from even the most liberal and oppositional of Russian news sources.

The manifestations and construction of these narratives certainly do have differences among sources. For example, pro-government sources construct the rise of Trump as an opportunity for Russia to have a greater role in world affairs and signaling a splintering of the West and its constant spread of democracy with tanks and color-revolutions. The neutral sources use the same material to issue warnings of the authoritarian nightmare coming to the US, while oppositional sources do their best to show a system in shock but still able to represent its people—even if their choice is an incredibly surprising one.

Russian citizens are given a concept of the US through the election coverage that informs them that democracy-led, capitalist globalism is either at its end or at an incredibly vulnerable stage. While there is indeed some optimism about Trump from some of the sources (e.g., he will take pursue Russia-friendly, he will be inwardly focused and thus halt the spread of globalism, and/or he will completely destroy the US system) that is not the larger focus and the points of cooperation coming from Trump are not drawn out in detail that would assume anything close to normative relations. Trump is certainly not cast as a character capable of somehow magically flipping the switch towards mutual affinity. The common narrative is about the collapse of the US system. Ultimately, and most importantly, the legitimacy of the office of the US presidency and of the entire US democratic process is called into question and presents Russian citizens with an extremely poor image of the US from which to form a concept of and gives them a reaffirming lens with which to view their own government.

While some Russian media sources acknowledged a potential for collusion and attempted cyber-hacking, by and large, Russian news media covered the accusations of Russian manipulation of the US election in ways that were very specifically damning to the image of Hillary Clinton and the Democratic Party. Clinton was presented as typifying the Western global elite system. Russian officials, particularly in pro-government sources, deny all claims of wrongdoing and claim themselves to be victims of Clinton's obfuscation or her own corruption. Clinton is shown as someone literally willing to risk causing a panic between the US and Russia, stoking a new Red Scare, rather than lose an election. Virtually all of the sources show the accusations of election manipulation by Russians as overblown by Democrats and doing damage to US–Russian relations. Pro-government sources, following Trump's victory, bring an increased cooperative tone to this narrative and express a want to work with the new administration.

The narratives created around the US-led economic sanctions imposed on Russia also had common elements across the various news sources. All focused significantly on comments made by Donald Trump concerning Russia's territorial claims to Crimea, NATO, and the sanctions themselves. There is also a common element of a concern for war, or at least conflict, over increasingly dissolving US–Russian relations, particularly related to the imposed sanctions. The scrambling and chaotic effect Trump's election victory had on NATO, and the Western world, and what it might mean for the united front currently sanctioning Russia was also a common feature across all new sources. While intuitive distinctions arose in discussions of the sanctions based on whether the news source was pro-government or oppositional, the narratives constructed on the sanctions showcased to Russian citizens a clear partisan split in the US that related directly to Russia: Democrats were shown as globalists and in support of anti-Putin measures at almost any cost to themselves or others; Trump (and to some degree Republicans supporting Trump) were much more positive towards the Putin regime and could potentially bring about radical changes to the current global system.

Similarly, the narratives concerning the Syrian war were constructed by all Russian news sources to show Russian citizens how dramatically US partisan politics could swing US–Russian relations. This construction was more prevalent in pro-government sources but was shown across all sources as a micro-representation of the differing macro-foreign policy agendas between the West and Russian leadership. Pro-government sources tended to present the Russian regime as an honest broker of peace in the region, while presenting Obama and his administration with a short-term focus on resolving the conflict quickly for their own political gain. Across all sources, Russian weapon technology being used in the Syrian conflict and the potential escalation points between the US and Russia are articulated to Russian citizens. The Syrian war, and US involvement, across all sources is constructed most descriptively as a call on the US to act in more cooperative ways with others to accomplish meaningful peace. Russian citizens are given a presentation of a US foreign policy as one that is disjointed, short-sighted, confused, potentially catastrophic in terms of war, and swinging tremendously depending on the outcome of one election.

Conclusion

Looking back to Fisher's (1984, 1989) narrative paradigm and the idea that we understand, and interact with, our world through story, there are several conclusions that stand out from this analysis. First, the US election gave plenty of ammunition to the Putin regime to justify its positions on a number of fronts and validate its nationalistically focused identity. The globalist versus populist dynamic served well in illustrating Putin's, and therefore Russia's, ongoing battle with the West, linked neatly by casting said globalists as corrupt hypocrites. These elements gave Russian news media the opportunity to construct narratives showing Putin as both correct in his judgements and, at least in contrast, a rather palatable leader. Importantly, this narrative construction showed Putin as the better option in a story that basically boils down in a lot of ways to good versus evil. Did the election ultimately hurt the US soft power in the minds of Russian citizens? That is a question this particular analysis can only speculate on and theoretically imply.

However, what is evident is that these narratives reaffirmed, rather than challenged, an already negative, or, at the very least, disenchanted impression of the US tied intrinsically to the use of strategic narratives the Putin regime has for so long capitalized on in affirmation of the regime.

For those in Russia hoping to see their country one day become a free and open democracy, the US election and the narratives Russian news media were able to generate from it were surely a bitter disappointment. And if the population did in fact look towards these constructed narratives as indications of US soft power, it saw a very weak nation indeed.

Furthermore, these narratives give us interesting insight into how Russia views itself and the myths on which the current regime relies to present the story of itself and its legitimacy to its population. Embattled, castigated, accused, but ultimately in the historic right and vindicated. These narratives have an unmistakable underdog characteristic, a rebellion against an empire-type story coming from a nation that has seemingly always been on the outside looking in at Western Europe; yet always there and always able to endure and retain its strength. It is also important to note that the July 2018 summit between Trump and Putin underscores much of the political success of the narrative positioning of Russia throughout the election, in demonstrating that the notion of an idealist and incorruptible Western democracy was pure fantasy as then President Trump seemingly deferred to Russian positions and leadership. It was a remarkable scene, arguably perhaps a capstone moment in the success of Russian strategic narratives both domestically and abroad.

Understanding that these narratives arose from a political system with vast state control of the news media also points to the notion that such regimes are very cognizant of their own fragility, using every single opportunity to win over the citizenry by using narratives to recast events to match those national myths on which their life source is dependent. And, in the case of the 2016 presidential election, the US gave the Russian regime the perfect story to tell.

Notes

1 The importance of the 2016 presidential election for the Russian government is evident, in part, from the extent to which the Russian government was willing to meddle in the 2016 US election.
2 *Gazeta Russian*. (2016, November 6). Data captured by Texas A&M's Media Monitoring System. Unpublished raw data.
3 *Arguments and Facts*. (2016, November 9). Data captured by Texas A&M's Media Monitoring System. Unpublished raw data.
4 *Gazeta Russian*. (2016, November 7). Data captured by Texas A&M's Media Monitoring System. Unpublished raw data.
5 Ibid.
6 Ibid.
7 *Novaya Gazeta*. (2016, September 30). Data captured by Texas A&M's Media Monitoring System. Unpublished raw data.
8 Ibid.
9 Ibid.

10 *Kommersant.* (2016, October 1). Data captured by Texas A&M's Media Monitoring System. Unpublished raw data.

11 *Kommersant.* (2016, September 27). Data captured by Texas A&M's Media Monitoring System. Unpublished raw data.

12 *Novaya Gazeta.* (2016, September 30). Data captured by Texas A&M's Media Monitoring System. Unpublished raw data.

13 *Arguments and Facts.* (2016, September 22). Data captured by Texas A&M's Media Monitoring System. Unpublished raw data.

14 *Gazeta Russian.* (2016, September 27). Data captured by Texas A&M's Media Monitoring System. Unpublished raw data.

15 *Kasparov.* (2016, July 28). Data captured by Texas A&M's Media Monitoring System. Unpublished raw data.

16 *Gazeta Russian.* (2016, November 5). Data captured by Texas A&M's Media Monitoring System. Unpublished raw data.

17 *Grani.* (2016, November 8). Data captured by Texas A&M's Media Monitoring System. Unpublished raw data.

18 *InoPressa.* (2016, September 28). Data captured by Texas A&M's Media Monitoring System. Unpublished raw data.

19 Ibid.

20 *NEWSru.* (2016, September 30). Data captured by Texas A&M's Media Monitoring System. Unpublished raw data.

21 *Arguments and Facts.* (2016, August 3). Data captured by Texas A&M's Media Monitoring System. Unpublished raw data.; *Izvestia.* (2016, September 28). Data captured by Texas A&M's Media Monitoring System. Unpublished raw data.

22 *NEWSru.* (2016, October 2). Data captured by Texas A&M's Media Monitoring System. Unpublished raw data.

23 *NEWSru.* (2016, October 3). Data captured by Texas A&M's Media Monitoring System. Unpublished raw data.

24 Ibid.

25 *Kommersant.* (2016, September 24). Data captured by Texas A&M's Media Monitoring System. Unpublished raw data; *Slon.* (2016, July 30). Data captured by Texas A&M's Media Monitoring System. Unpublished raw data.

26 *Kasparov.* (2016, September 24). Data captured by Texas A&M's Media Monitoring System. Unpublished raw data.

27 *Rossiya24.* (2016, October 3). Data captured by Texas A&M's Media Monitoring System. Unpublished raw data.

28 *Slon.* (2016, September 19). Data captured by Texas A&M's Media Monitoring System. Unpublished raw data; *Moskovskij Komsomolets.* (2016, October 2). Data captured by Texas A&M's Media Monitoring System. Unpublished raw data.

29 *InoPressa.* (2016, September 29a). Data captured by Texas A&M's Media Monitoring System. Unpublished raw data.

30 *InoPressa.* (2016, September 28b). Data captured by Texas A&M's Media Monitoring System. Unpublished raw data.

31 *Kommersant.* (2016, October 1). Data captured by Texas A&M's Media Monitoring System. Unpublished raw data.

32 *Moskovskij Komsomolets.* (2016, August 2). Data captured by Texas A&M's Media Monitoring System. Unpublished raw data.

33 *Gazeta Russian.* (2016, September 30). Data captured by Texas A&M's Media Monitoring System. Unpublished raw data.

34 *Kommersant.* (2016, October 1). Data captured by Texas A&M's Media Monitoring System. Unpublished raw data.

35 *Arguments and Facts.* (2016, July 28). Data captured by Texas A&M's Media Monitoring System. Unpublished raw data.

36 Ibid.
37 *Izvestia.* (2016, August 1). Data captured by Texas A&M's Media Monitoring System. Unpublished raw data.
38 *Kommersant.* (2016, September 27). Data captured by Texas A&M's Media Monitoring System. Unpublished raw data.
39 *Slon.* (2016, September 27). Data captured by Texas A&M's Media Monitoring System. Unpublished raw data.
40 *Kommersant.* (2016, September 27). Data captured by Texas A&M's Media Monitoring System. Unpublished raw data.
41 *InoPressa.* (2016, September 29). Data captured by Texas A&M's Media Monitoring System. Unpublished raw data.
42 Ibid.
43 Ibid.
44 *Arguments and Facts.* (2016, July 26). Data captured by Texas A&M's Media Monitoring System. Unpublished raw data.
45 Ibid.
46 *Izvestia.* (2016, September 20). Data captured by Texas A&M's Media Monitoring System. Unpublished raw data.
47 *Moskovskij Komsomolets.* (2016, September 22). Data captured by Texas A&M's Media Monitoring System. Unpublished raw data.
48 *Izvestia.* (2016, September 22). Data captured by Texas A&M's Media Monitoring System. Unpublished raw data.
49 *Arguments and Facts.* (2016, September 22). Data captured by Texas A&M's Media Monitoring System. Unpublished raw data.
50 *Moskovskij Komsomolets.* (2016, September 22). Data captured by Texas A&M's Media Monitoring System. Unpublished raw data.
51 *Moskovskij Komsomolets.* (2016, July 28). Data captured by Texas A&M's Media Monitoring System. Unpublished raw data.
52 *Izvestia.* (2016, November 4). Data captured by Texas A&M's Media Monitoring System. Unpublished raw data.
53 *Moskovskij Komsomolets.* (2016, September 30). Data captured by Texas A&M's Media Monitoring System. Unpublished raw data.
54 *InoPressa.* (2016, September 23). Data captured by Texas A&M's Media Monitoring System. Unpublished raw data.
55 Ibid.
56 *InoPressa.* (2016, September 23). Data captured by Texas A&M's Media Monitoring System. Unpublished raw data.
57 *Izvestia.* (2016, August 3). Data captured by Texas A&M's Media Monitoring System. Unpublished raw data.
58 *Grani* 11/14/2016 11:01:25 PM
59 Ibid.
60 *Izvestia.* (2016, September 30). Data captured by Texas A&M's Media Monitoring System. Unpublished raw data.
61 Ibid.
62 Ibid.
63 *Kasparov.* (2016, November 11). Data captured by Texas A&M's Media Monitoring System. Unpublished raw data.
64 *InoPressa.* (2016, November 2). Data captured by Texas A&M's Media Monitoring System. Unpublished raw data.
65 Ibid.
66 *InoPressa.* (2016, September 28). Data captured by Texas A&M's Media Monitoring System. Unpublished raw data.

67 *Slon.* (2016, July 20). Data captured by Texas A&M's Media Monitoring System. Unpublished raw data.
68 *Newtimes.* (2016, November 9). Data captured by Texas A&M's Media Monitoring System. Unpublished raw data.
69 *Slon.* (2016, November 14). Data captured by Texas A&M's Media Monitoring System. Unpublished raw data.
70 *InoPressa.* (2016, September 28). Data captured by Texas A&M's Media Monitoring System. Unpublished raw data.
71 *Slon.* (2016, July 21). Data captured by Texas A&M's Media Monitoring System. Unpublished raw data.
72 *Kommersant,* 11/12/2016.
73 *Slon.* (2016, July 21). Data captured by Texas A&M's Media Monitoring System. Unpublished raw data.
74 *InoPressa.* (2016, September 22). Data captured by Texas A&M's Media Monitoring System. Unpublished raw data; *Kommersant.* (2016, November 12). Data captured by Texas A&M's Media Monitoring System. Unpublished raw data.
75 Ibid.

References

Cohen, S. (2011). *Soviet fates and lost alternatives: From Stalinism to the new Cold War.* New York: Columbia University Press.

Cooley, S., & Stokes, E. (2018). Manufacturing resilience: An analysis of broadcast and Web-based news presentations of the 2014–2015 Russian economic downturn. *Global Media and Communication,* 14(1), 123–139.

Cross, S. (2004). Putin's turn toward the West: Russia, US/NATO and the war on terrorism post-September 11. In K. Khudoley (Eds.), *Post-communist countries in the globalizing world.* St. Petersburg, Russia: St. Petersburg State University Press.

Cross, S. (2006). Russia's relationship with the United States /NATO in the US-led global war on terrorism. *Journal of Slavic Military Studies,* 19, 175–192.

Crowley, M. & Ioffe, J. (2016, July 25). Why Putin hates Hillary. *Politico.* Retrieved from https://www.politico.com/story/2016/07/clinton-putin-226153.

Damm, E., & Cooley, S. C. (2017). Resurrection of the Russian Orthodox Church: Narrative analysis of the Russian national myth. *Social Science Quarterly,* 98(3), 942–957.

Dempsey, J. (2016, January 18). The clash of narratives between the West and Russia. *Carnegie Europe.* Retrieved from https://carnegieeurope.eu/strategiceurope/62489.

Diamond, J. (2015, December 18) Donald Trump lavishes praise on "leader" Putin. *CNN Politics.* Retrieved from https://www.cnn.com/2015/12/18/politics/donald-trump-praises-defends-vladimir-putin/index.html.

Elder, M. & Amos, H. (2012, November 5). Russia's views on the US elections. *The Guardian.* Retrieved from https://www.theguardian.com/world/2012/nov/05/russia-view-us-elections.

Evans, A. (2010). The failure of democratization in Russia: A comparative perspective. *Journal of Eurasian Studies,* 2(1), 40–51.

Fisher, W. F. (1984). Narration as a human communication paradigm: The case of public moral argument. *Communication Monographs,* 51(1), 1–22.

Fisher, W. F. (1989). *Human reason as narration: Toward a philosophy of reason, value, and action.* Columbia, SC: University of South Carolina Press.

Gallup (2017). Russia. In depth: topics a to z. Retrieved from https://news.gallup.com/poll/1642/russia.aspx.

Gerber, T. (2015). Foreign policy and the United States in Russian public opinion. *Problems of Post-Communism*, 62(2), 98–111.

Hinck, R., Kluver, R., & Cooley, S. (2018) Russia re-envisions the world: Strategic narratives in Russian broadcast and news media during 2015. *Russian Journal of Communication*, 10(1), 31–37.

Hutchings, S., & Szostek, J. (2015, April 28). Dominant narratives in Russian political and media discourse during the Ukraine crisis. *E-International Relations*. Retrieved from http s://www.e-ir.info/2015/04/28/dominant-narratives-in-russian-political-and-media-dis course-during-the-crisis/.

Irvin-Erickson, D. (2017). Genocide discourses: American and Russian strategic narratives of conflict in Iraq and Ukraine. *Politics and Governance*, 5(3), 130–145.

Jankovski, A. (2016). Russia and the United States: On irritants, friction, and international order or what can we learn from Hedley Bull? *International Politics*, 53(6), 727–751.

Kaphle, A. (2013, August 7). Timeline: Highs and lows in US–Russia relationship. *The Washington Post*. Retrieved from https://www.washingtonpost.com/apps/g/page/ world/timeline-highs-and-lows-in-us-russia-relationship/382/?noredirect=on.

Mickiewicz, E. (2008) *Television, power, and the public in Russia*. Cambridge, UK: Cambridge University Press.

Milbank, D. (2001, June 17). Bush and Putin set cordial tone. *The Washington Post*. Retrieved from https://www.washingtonpost.com/archive/politics/2001/06/17/bush-and-putin-set-cordial-tone/61d6396e-b30b-44af-bd00-f0a78f69ab35/?utm_term=.9608ae42dd75.

Miskimmon, A., & O'Loughlin, B. (2017). Russia's narratives of global order: Great power legacies in a polycentric world. *Politics and Governance*, 5(3), 111–120.

O'Malley, D. (2014, November 3). The power of the story: Vladimir Putin and the rise of the Russian Federation. *War on the Rocks*. Retrieved from https://warontherocks.com/ 2014/11/the-power-of-the-story-vladimir-putin-and-the-rise-of-the-russian-federation/.

Pezard, S., Radin, A., Szayna, T., & Larrabee, F. S. (2017). *European relations with Russia: Threat perceptions, responses, and strategies in the wake of the Ukrainian crisis*. Santa Monica, CA: RAND Corporation. Retrieved from https://www.rand.org/pubs/research_reports/RR1579.html.

Roberts, K. (2013). Putin's choice: The Russian president and the reset. *St. Antony's International Review*, 8(2), 127–148. Retrieved from http://www.jstor.org/stable/26228742.

Roselle, L. (2017). Strategic narratives and alliances: The cases of intervention in Libya (2011) and economic sanctions against Russia (2014). *Politics and Governance*, 5(3), 99–110.

Schenk, C. (2012). Nationalism in the Russian media: Content analysis of newspaper coverage surrounding conflict in Stavropol, 24 May–7 June 2007. *Nationalities Papers*, 40(5), 783–805.

Shlapentokh, V. (2001). Russian attitudes toward America: A split between the ruling class and the masses. *World Affairs*, 164(1), 17–23.

Skalamera, M. (2018) Understanding Russia's energy turn to China: Domestic narratives and national identity priorities. *Post-Soviet Affairs*, 34(1), 55–77.

Suslov, M. (2017) The production of "Novorossiya": A territorial brand in public debates. *Europe-Asia Studies*, 69(2), 202–221.

Szostek, J. (2017) Defence and promotion of desired state identity in Russia's strategic narrative. *Geopolitics*, 22(3), 571–593.

Tsygankov, A. P. (2017). The dark double: The American media perception of Russia as a neo-Soviet autocracy, 2008–2014. *Politics*, 37(1), 19–35.

Zygar, M. (2016, December 9). The Russian reset that never was. *Foreign Policy*. Retrieved from https://foreignpolicy.com/2016/12/09/the-russian-reset-that-never-was-putin-o bama-medvedev-libya-mikhail-zygar-all-the-kremlin-men/.

6

COMPELLING NARRATIVES AND THE IMPLICATIONS FOR US SOFT POWER AND THE GLOBAL ORDER

Comparative Analysis of Chinese, Arab, and Russian Narratives of the US Election

Introduction

This project set out to understand how non-Western news media packaged and constructed US politics and political processes to their citizens in order to affirm, contest, and alter perceptions of US soft power through narrative. As the previous chapters have shown, this is accomplished both by making US practices of democracy appear as unattractive, while also bolstering national identities and/or making their own systems of governance appear more attractive to domestic audiences. In this sense, from the framework of strategic narratives, we come to understand how influence is contested and constructed through local media ecologies' interpretations of the 2016 US presidential election. In this concluding chapter, we focus on comparing the three data sets to understand both the similarities and differences in their narrative constructions, their implications for how media ecologies construct and legitimize strategic narratives more broadly, elements of what makes such narratives compelling, and draw out the implications for US soft power relative to that of the global order.

Convergent Global Narratives of the 2016 US Presidential Election

As we noted at the start of this book, the three regions chosen for our analysis, Russian, Chinese, and Arabic news media systems, share two similar characteristics. First, all three cases operate in a context in which there is a relatively closer media–state relationship relative to Western media systems; second, all three regions are currently perceived as somewhat antagonistic to US values and policies. From Boudana and Segev's (2017) study of "provocation" narratives, we would expect that these nations, although having varying national press cultures and political orientations, might share similar narrative structures challenging US policy and visions of democratic leadership. Indeed, that is, in part, what we found.

First, in all three regions, issue narratives frequently took the form of informational narratives explaining the US electoral and debate process, the candidates' campaign and debate rhetoric, and citations of US news sources and polling data. However, outside of these neutral stories were constructions of the candidates and US democratic process that were predominately negative. These negative constructions provide the larger narrative context from which audiences are to make sense of the informational content reported to them. Thus, the qualitative narrative reading of these stories converged in showing Clinton and Trump as both being out of touch with US audiences' wants and needs, possessing numerous failings in character, and, overall, inadequate candidates to lead the US. This inadequacy stemmed from the US democratic system's failure to produce quality candidates and served as a major indictment of US-styled democracy. Media in all three regions portrayed a system that was corrupted, dominated by elites and the political establishment, tainted by money, resultant in civil strife and polarization. The debate process was shown as failing to produce meaningful discussions on policy and values, instead turning into a media spectacle, a cage-match competition. What might have been a moment of serious analysis of the virtues or vices of democracy instead focused primarily on the candidates' failings and scandals.

Second, in all three media systems, the issue narratives contributed to national and international level narratives defining US values, which implicated US global leadership and its liberal, rule-based order. Through the policies espoused by the two candidates, the US was described as possessing self-serving, uninformed interests and policies across the world, whether it be in the Middle East or the Asia Pacific region. Importantly, the US was portrayed as in a state of decline, marked by social strife at home, a growing multipolarity in global economics and politics, and poor foreign policies. The US is shown as a failing hegemony, collapsing under the weight of its own over-extension, misguided notions of exceptionalism, and an inability of its ruling class to alter a system that has contributed to their own enrichment.

The portrayal of the collapse of the US system is accentuated by the portrayal of its hypocrisy, its inability to deliver upon its democratic ideals to its own citizens by failing to produce a campaign based on serious policy-driven, informed candidates who represented the will of the US citizenry. As the system itself fails, only a pretentious shell of democracy, put on by clown-like candidates making a mockery of the very ideals they are intended to personify, remains. The US's inadequacy in fulfilling even the minimum of its own grandiosely defined requirements for functional democracy was a fact that stood in direct contrast with the US's rationale for why other nations would want to adopt a similar system. Similarly to the candidates' policies, US interests were described as self-serving, and failing to support a fair and just global order. Thus, through the presentation of issue, national, and international level strategic narratives we can see the coalescing of a shared narrative among Chinese, Russian, and Arabic audiences that US democracy is not something worth following, and that the US itself is not a country worth emulating. The US system is laid bare in these presentations, having stripped itself of the vestiges of democratic ideals in order to maintain the dominance and power of its political elite; the system has cannibalized its very foundations. The audiences are left to take away that in the current global milieu, Western states are not only self-interested, they do not live up to the democratic ideals which they espouse towards others. Meanwhile, non-Western nations' grow in strength and prestige thereby presenting alternative models for governance and global leadership.

The convergence in negative narratives of the 2016 election by Chinese, Russian, and Arabic media likely stems from two interrelated reasons: first, all three regions are the targets of US socialization discourse; and second, they each have their own socio-cultural, situational aspirations distinct from US-Western norms which lead to diverging narratives relative to those told by the US. Thus, the strategic narratives present in Chinese, Russian, and Arabic news media demonstrate a contestation of US narratives detailing the supposed benefits of the US-led international order by constructing their own alternative sources of international norms and values from which emerging powers can influence the evolution of norms within the larger international community for their own strategic benefit. From a constructivist standpoint, "shared ideas, perceptions, and beliefs are what give the world structure, order, and stability" (Finnemore & Sikkink, 1998, 894), and in recent history it has been Western nations that have taught and persuaded non-Western nations of the values and policies to which they should conform (Acharya, 2004; Xiaoyu, 2012). Indeed, US officials have for decades attempted to press upon Chinese and Russian leaders, and their citizens, the importance of democratic governance and the benefits of a liberal-rule based international order; similarly, the US has promoted a policy of spreading democracy in the Middle East.

In the Russian, Chinese, and Arabic media reporting of the 2016 US election, we see a clear narrative convergence challenging those norms; instead of US intrusions, these regions' narratives, as reported by their news media, unravel US societal norms. This demonstration illustrates the importance of strategic narratives as a form of soft power, challenging traditional theories of international influence as a one-way diffusion of norms and values, from Western nations to developing or non-Western countries. As Xiaoyu (2012) points out, state socialization is a two-way process whereby "people are not only the targets of socialization but also active agents that influence the content and outcomes of the process" (344). As part of this process, emerging powers have challenged the notion that Western ideas and culture are superior to those of the rest of the world, emphasized their own sovereignty and independence, used multilateral forums to influence the evolution of international norms, and defined what kind of norms should be regarded as legitimate in international society. These themes are largely echoed in the narratives found in Arabic, Russian, and Chinese news media, and function to help open up the discursive space for these nations to legitimately define their own identities, values, and perceptions of world order, while implicating current global norms through the challenging or delegitimatizing of US leadership. Indeed, according to Wiener (2004) we should expect greater norm contestation as we move among different socio-cultural contexts and across state borders, and this would especially be true when considering Chinese, Russian, and Middle Eastern audiences.

However, these narrative critiques of the US election do more than just allow Russian, Chinese, and Arabic nations to voice their own values; they also form a stigmatizing discourse. As Adler-Nissen (2014) argues, stigmatization rhetoric plays a central part in the process of state socialization. Stigma clarifies norms and promotes conformity by distinguishing between "us" and "them," or the normal states and the transgressive ones. While typically it has been Western nations that define the "pariah" states in world politics, the narratives within Russian, Chinese, and Arabic media flip the criticism onto the US. Here the 2016 US election, with its candidates' character and policies, reflect malapropos US behavior in the world, and thus attempts to stigmatize US politics as a means to legitimate alternative values and policies. The importance of this converging stigmatization rhetoric will likely have lasting impacts on the credibility of US narratives into the future. As Krebs and Lobasz (2007) and Subotić (2016) argue, strategic narratives reduce the political space for debate by making alternative narratives sound incoherent and uncompelling, and as Jackson (2003) and Mattern (2005) explain, strategic narratives limit the potential for political contestation when they are accepted as societal fact. In this sense, future US claims to moral authority and arguments extolling the value of democratic governance will stand in contrast to how Russian, Chinese, and Arabic audiences came to experience the 2016 election through their news media's colorful coverages of the event, and make US narratives of democracy less coherent, and thus less attractive and persuasive.

Divergent International, National, and Issue Narratives in Russian, Chinese, and Arabic Media

Despite these common themes of US decline and democratic failure, these three regional media ecologies also demonstrate divergent narratives, specifically in the focus and manner in which they critique US democracy and US values. The primary difference among our three cases is that the Chinese and Russian cases are both national media ecologies, whereas the Arabic case is a regional one. In this sense, if media ecologies play a key role influencing strategic narratives we would expect differences in the strategic narratives constructed about the 2016 election, especially in the case of national narratives in China and Russia versus the Arabic region. Furthermore, because each region has different cultural and political histories and aspirations, both for themselves, but also in relation to the US, we would expect differences in the priorities and interests their media systems employ in their respective narratives on each issue, national, and international level. These three narrative forms, however, stand less on their own, and, as we detail below, work together in weaving narratives about each nation's identity and role in the world vis-à-vis the US. As Roselle, Miskimmon, and O'Loughlin (2014) note, the extent to which issue, national, and international level narratives mutually support and enforce each other plays an important role in their ultimate resonance by target audiences.

Differences in National Level Narratives

The most significant divergence regarding the narrative constructions of the 2016 election can be found at the national level. In both the Russian and Chinese cases, there is a much clearer juxtapositioning of US strength to that of their own than in the Arabic case. Russian national narratives most strongly characterize US decline and use issue level narratives to demonstrate the US's immorality. As a consequence, Russian media suggests that Russia is the nation with the moral clout to lead the world and further emphasizes Russian global influence both through the loss of US influence and the mentioning of Russian regional importance. In this case, Russian national narratives take more of a realist, win–lose mentality whereby US failings lead to Russian strength. This likely springs from the recent history of US–Russian relations, particularly the Russian conviction that the nation "lost" its great power status due to pernicious US actions.

Similarly, national narratives told by Chinese news media juxtaposed Chinese strength to US decline but did so in less of a zero-sum orientation. For instance, Chinese media tended to report ambivalence as to the victor of the election, because regardless of who led the US, China has confidence that their recently gained international power is enough to withstand US pressure, irrespective of any new administration. Instead, the democratic failings of the US were shown to debunk the universality of Western style democracy, which was then shown to demonstrate the Chinese Communist Party (CCP)'s success in establishing itself as a world power. The Chinese were thus confident in their own identity and believed that they would continue to gain greater clout in the current order, rather than needing to displace or fully discredit US global leadership.

In Arabic news media, however, a pattern of national level narratives of specific Arabic countries was hard to find, outside of national narrative characterizations that demonized Israel and criticized the US. Instead, the US election, and its candidates' policies, focused on the recent history of the US's relationship with the region as a whole, arguing that the candidates were ignorant of the region which was a reflection of American institutions' naivete about the Middle East. The concerns of the Arabic media were whether US policy would cause further destabilization of the region as a whole, suggesting a common interest or, at the very least, a loosely woven common identity among Arabic nations. This identity showed a common concern regarding just solutions to the Palestinian cause and the US' military struggle with ISIS.

Differences in International Level Narratives

The national level narratives implicated each regions' international understanding of world order in similar but diverging ways. While all three depicted a world of declining US influence, as well as the rise of globalism and nationalism, the implications for each region were different. Russian media narratives took the harshest, anti-US stance. According to their narratives, the US, and the West, were seen as setting up global institutions designed solely to advance their immoral and self-interested policies, at great cost to all other nations, and to Russia in particular. The US election was used as an exemplar to emphasize the fracturing and collapse of the US-led order, with the rise of populism and authoritarianism being the foremost evident consequence. Russia, however, was portrayed as the one nation with the moral clout to lead in the reconstruction of international institutions that would better serve the world, based on principles of mutual respect and equality. Western democracy was ridiculed as merely an elite-managed device which hampered the development and success of other nations. Thus, the 2016 US presidential election showcased the hypocrisy of US policies and the failings of its international rule-based order premised on democracy, and Russia's resurgent influence in world affairs.

The Chinese media's international narratives were less prevalent and harsh. While some international narratives did claim that the US-led liberal order's values and universal belief in democracy were tools for global US hegemony, these aspersions were far less prevalent than in the Russian media. Instead, the Chinese saw a global order that their already established influence would allow them to continue to grow within and ascend. The key element of their understanding of the world order was that there was not one universal mode for governance from which success was derived. Within the international system, nations still had to compete for power and prestige, and the Chinese were confident in their ability to do so.

This is perhaps one of the most striking and consequential of the findings of this study: that, while Russian narratives largely sought to displace US leadership, Chinese narratives sought to fit China's own national strength alongside that of the US, rather than replacing it. In other words, *Russian narratives sought the replacement of the current global order, while Chinese narratives argued that China should take its rightful place within the global order*, given its long history. The geopolitical worldview of the Russian media stressed the total inadequacy of the existing system of geopolitics, economics, and cultural influence, while Chinese media sought to find China's place within the existing system.

Arabic news media narratives describing the global order diverged most from those of the Russian and Chinese in their positive evaluations of the ideals of democracy. While their narratives still argued that the US itself, and its practice of democracy, was a poor standard to follow, they still affirmed the value of democracy in general and rhetorically judged the US based on that ideal. Inherent in the ideals of democracy is a standard of cooperation, but the US election process and its discourse did not produce this cooperative element. Furthermore, Arabic media, like the Russian, emphasized the chaos in the international order and did so by likewise recognizing the decline of US influence due to the multipolarization of geopolitical power. However, unlike both the Russian and Chinese media, the Arabic media recognized that the Russian and Chinese states were themselves contributing to this decline through their media attacks on the US. Thus, they understood that China and Russia were competing with the US and were using the US election as a means to advance their own prestige and influence. Within this conceptualization of increased competition and waning US dominance, the Arabic media suggested the solution was for a more pragmatic reevaluation of the US's relationship with the region, with Arab publics and governments needing to specify their own interests in order to safeguard their security. Thus, their image of world order was that multipolarization required states to cooperate and define their interests to gain influence and that the ideals of democracy were still worth living up to, and for the Arabic region to develop better relations with the world by forging a set of common interests.

Differences in Issue Level Narratives

Finally, we can understand the varying levels of resonance of the national and international level narratives told by each nation by considering the different issue narratives that came to form them. Issue narratives within the Russian media focused much more on Hillary Clinton as a poor candidate for Russian interests with, not surprisingly, much more pro-Trump coverage. Other issues most commonly discussed were US sanctions towards Russia, US involvement in Syria, European unity, or lack thereof, and the rise of global populism as evidenced by the Brexit vote. The two common themes throughout these issues concerned US antagonistic policies towards Russia and the US system failing apart. In both instances, negative characterizations of Hillary Clinton served to symbolize this failed, anti-Russian globalist policy, while Trump symbolized the efficacy of Russian interests and the potential to reset relations between the two nations. Thus, the issues that manifested themselves the most served to support the national and international level narratives of immoral and unfair US leadership, the morality and "correctness" of Russian policy, and the need for Russia to stand up and take charge in creating a new world order.

The Russian issue narratives are in most stark contrast to the Arabic issues. In the Arabic media, Donald Trump, not Hillary Clinton, represents the symbolic failings of US democracy. Trump is portrayed as undermining democratic values through his coarse statements and claims of the US system being corrupt, while also representing a threat to the Arabic region through his support of right-wing Israeli politics. Clinton, on the other hand, is praised for being the first female candidate. Though Clinton is more positively covered, Arabic news media narratives nevertheless remain cynical of both candidates' proposed policies, and both candidates come to represent the Arabic media's national narrative portrayal of enduring US narcissism and lack of understanding of issues important to the region more generally. Other issue narratives prevalent in the Arabic media discourse include US interventions in the Arab world, such as US policy in Syria, Iraq, plans to fight ISIS, and the Palestinian–Israel conflict. The common theme around these issues is of a more humanitarian concern regarding how US leadership and values may, or may not, support the people of the region rather than being an argument for US inaction or isolationism. These issues feed into then the need for Arab nations to better articulate their interests.

Issue narratives within the Chinese news media tended to focus more on US–China-related topics and the US political system's specific failings. Chinese media provided the most informational content to its audiences to explain the rationale for US democratic processes and its shortcomings. However, this appears to have been done in order to give the Chinese strengthened faith in their more authoritarian governance model as led by the CCP; thus, a stronger emphasis appeared to be placed on US domestic discord as a consequence of the election and the US democratic system. Whereas Russian issue narratives tied establishment politics to more global policies, Chinese narratives stressed how money and establishment interests rendered the US model of democracy ineffective. In this sense, both candidates' personal drama came to represent the inability of the system to produce strong candidates and reasoned discourse within US society and, consequently, to demonstrate how US politics not only fails to promote social harmony, but actively contributes to political polarization, racism, and economic inequality. More regional issues, rather than global ones, were also discussed such as US policy and alliances in the Asia Pacific region (including the South China Sea in particular), as well as US–China trade relations. These issues were portrayed in such a manner as to reassure Chinese audiences of how far China has come in being a successful and strong nation. Unlike the Russian narratives, this was less an indictment of the US led international order and more a sign that China was succeeding in displacing and insulating itself from US influence and power.

Constructing Compelling Narratives

As the analysis above has shown, the 2016 US presidential election similarly challenged and critiqued the efficacy of both US democracy and US global leadership. However, in doing so, the event came to mean different things within Russian, Chinese, and Arabic news media. Furthermore, despite each region investing in communication infrastructure to enable its own media ecology to portray the event outside of a historically dominant Western media lens, they nevertheless still compete internationally with alternative explanations of the 2016 US election. As such, constraints are placed on how each heavily, state-influenced media system crafted credible portrayals of the event to their respective audiences. In this section we discuss what makes these narratives likely, or unlikely, to resonant with their own domestic audiences as well as foreign ones.

According to Roselle et al. (2014), strategic narratives function as a form of power resource by providing compelling narratives which draw audiences to certain descriptions of the actors, events, and explanations describing the history of a country or specific policy and as a process to understand how power resources work broadly. In doing so, one can see how actors use narrative strategically in contesting other narratives in complex media ecologies. But the question remains as to which narrative wins out and why? Both Roselle et al. (2014) and Szostek (2017) argue that it is through a process of imbuing attraction and unattraction of political actors' values, policies, and identities that leads another to accept one's narrative, while rhetorical theorist Walter Fisher (1984, 1989) contends that narratives must contain "narrative fidelity" and "narrative coherence," with the former corresponding to the lived experiences and values of the audiences, and the latter referring to the internal consistency of the narratives. This perspective is likewise reflected in Schmitt's (2018) work on narrative whereby he proposes that "the degree to which an external strategic narrative resonates with local political myths determines the effectiveness and impact of the strategic narrative" (2). Thus, the mechanism through which a strategic narrative can be made attractive to foreign audiences is the extent to which appeals to the values, interests, and prejudices of a target audience contributes to the target community's political myths.

To understand how this process works more specifically, we turn to Dimitriu and De Graaf's (2016) conception of strong versus weak narratives. While their model focuses on the contestation of strategic narratives within a political community in support of continued use of military force abroad, their criteria are nevertheless useful in understanding what makes a strategic narrative compelling. They list five such criteria: strong narratives a) articulate a clear, realistic, and compelling mission purpose; b) gain legitimacy through both judicial/procedural and subjective/political values; c) promise success; d) are consistent by providing persistent reinforcement by political elites paired with real live events and media reporting; and e) fit within an overall strategic plan in harmony with major national themes, ideas, images, and actions.

In considering these criteria, we see that in all three of the regions under analysis, narratives of the 2016 US election are rather compelling. In Russian, Chinese, and Arabic news media, the narratives focused extensively on the drama and characters of the 2016 US presidential election. The scandals of both Hillary Clinton and Donald Trump were discussed profusely, the debates and polling data were characterized in lively terms, such as soap operas or cage matches, internal party politics and strife among Democrats—between Bernie Sanders' supporters and those of Hillary Clinton—and Republicans through their questioning of Donald Trump's maverick campaign tactics and rhetoric. All appeared to draw in readers and generated numerous news reports on the event. However, anyone following US news coverage of the election would realize that this was true, as well, of US media. In this sense, the 2016 presidential election might be a unique case in that the raw material provided to news outlets more easily made the election entertaining and full of strife. Indeed, perhaps a notable vulnerability for the US in projecting its soft power through its news media system, both domestically and abroad, is the partisan and commercially competitive nature of the news programming itself; which offers stinging rebukes of parties within its own political framework and must take on live event formatting similar to that of sport to compete for domestic audiences against entertainment-based programing. The entertainment structure of the election as an event exchanges the cooperative element underpinning democratic deliberation towards meaningful resolution on issues for that of competitive-oriented sound-bites, which can more readily be repackaged by other media systems to fit within the aims of their own strategic narratives.

Thus, the narratives constructed by Russian, Chinese, and Arabic news media can be considered uniquely compelling in that they each offered audiences what the US election meant for their respective regions. For Russians, the candidates, their policies, and the US process came to represent more than just an episodic depiction of US politics, and instead tied in narratives of US efforts to constrain Russian interests globally and historically, going as far back as the end of World War II and the birth of the US liberal order. Additionally, this was narrated as reflecting a larger plot perpetrated by Hillary Clinton and US establishment politicians to constrain Russia. This narrative form reflects, in part, what Sakwa (2012) calls conspiracy narratives in which malign forces and conspiratorial groups have caused calamitous events and was likewise employed during the 2008 Russia–Georgia war. Furthermore, Russian narratives pitted US hypocrisy, as shown through the issue narratives of the candidates and their policies, against resurgent Russian strength and US decline. In doing so, this plotline contributed to Russia's local political myths as the world's moral leader, supporting its resurrection of state backing for the Orthodox Church, as well as supporting narratives of Russia as a Great Power; suggesting that the world was becoming more multipolar and that the Russian state played a significant role in leading that rising multipolarity. Whether or not these myths are true or are even likely to materialize does not matter. What does matter is how they graft over to the existing myths and identities of the population, even if they are pure fancy. As Eberle (2019) argues, fantasy plays an important role in crafting effective narratives in that narratives utilize fantasy to translate an object of desire into discourse. These fantasy narratives serve to help their subjects make sense of their ontological incompleteness by providing narrative subjects with an ideal and obstacle to overcome. In the case of Russia, US policies, economic sanctions, and its liberal-democratic values are all obstacles that Russia is overcoming in its return to greatness. Rather than a concern with objective truth, the reality created through such fantasy lies simply in the coherence of the story itself.

The Chinese media narratives similarly draw upon local mythologies and narratives as well. The Chinese narratives' informational analysis of US democracy served to justify the CCP's narrative of authoritarian governance by debunking US accounts of the universality of Western democracy, thereby legitimizing China's unique governance model. Its account of the election drew in Chinese audiences by most frequently analogizing the US election to the popular television show, House of Cards (widely available to Chinese viewers through online video sharing sites), as well as popular Chinese soap operas depicting palace intrigue. Here the characters and their settings help to delegitimize the seriousness of democracy as a model of governance. The key claim, then, is that the spectacle of democracy, especially in the case of the US debates, serves just to entertain, not inform audiences. This attack is particularly important in that China practices an authoritarian model of deliberation whereby it eschews political debate outside of the parameters it defines for itself (He, 2006; He & Warren, 2011). With regards to national level narratives, the juxtaposition of US to Chinese strength helps support CCP mythologies of its national rejuvenation of China's historical strength and its objective of doing so by the CCP's 100-year anniversary in 2021 and the founding of the PRC's 100-year anniversary in 2049. The narratives of the 2016 US election were used to make good on the CCP's promise that through its leadership China would no longer be victimized at the hands of foreign powers and would reassert its historical influence in the Asia Pacific region once again. This presentation in essence liberates the Chinese system from the need to conform to the demands of West in order to have a meaningful voice in the global order, and shows that the strength of its own culturally-defined model of governance is worthy to stand within that order on its own accord; and, that its system is perhaps necessary to forge a more equitable global order.

Whereas the Chinese and Russian narrative accounts of the 2016 US election can be considered as possessing compelling constructive, identity-forming narratives through the "othering" of the US, the Arabic media narratives took a different form, that of cynicism. Arabic media focused on demonstrating the candidates' ignorance of the region and superficial understanding of its needs. In this sense, both candidates represented previous US administrations' militarism in the Middle East. Transcendent depictions of their interests were limited to issue-specific policies such as the Palestinian–Israel relationship, and US involvement to combat ISIS in Syria, rather than overarching visions of their own identities. This is perhaps due to our research design with the focus not on a single country, but rather the media ecology of the whole region. Alternatively, this could be because the Middle East, as a region, has less power to unilaterally form and affect global affairs, limiting it to issues of regional concern. Nevertheless, a pan-Arabic identity took some form, albeit a more rational understanding of state-influence by calling on Arabic countries to come together to better articulate their needs and interests in the region.

Our analysis of regional media's narrative constructions of the 2016 US election provides a unique understanding of the role of local media ecologies in contesting strategic narratives implicating their relative "strength." As Dimitriu and De Graaf (2016) noted, strong narratives need clear and compelling mission purposes, must legitimate themselves using the public's cultural and political norms, promise success, provide consistency, and fit the overall national themes, ideas, images, and actions of the nation. Likely due to the close state–media relationship enjoyed by our three cases, we see that their narratives depict rather strong and consistent narratives challenging the image of US democracy. Furthermore, they frequently cite and challenge the legitimacy of the US election, both by explaining what it is supposed to accomplish and how it fails to do so, as well as challenging the legitimacy of US values such as humanitarian aid in the Middle East, US moral authority in the world, and the universality of US democracy.

However, the Chinese and Russian narratives can be seen as especially "strong" in two ways. First, they most clearly narrated the 2016 US election in terms of their overall national themes—Russian Great Power narratives, moral supremacy, and the fracturing of the US-led order and China's model of authoritarian government and national rejuvenation/return to strength. Second, they discuss the success of their respective governments in augmenting their influence and prestige, whether it be under the influence of Russian President Putin or the CCP. The Arabic narratives, on the other hand, typically do not depict the election in a context of US vs Arabic success, and thus, do not use the failures of US democracy to highlight the relative success or universal appropriateness of Arab values and systems. As van Noort (2017) argued in her analysis of BRICS strategic narratives, the lack of causal implications of tangible indicators and achieved successes contributes to an inability to craft a strong narrative justifying their worldview as an alternative to the Western-led order. Thus, with China and Russia, their narratives create a stronger alternative to the US-led order than the Arabic media narratives.

One further observation can be made when regarding the relative strength and weakness of the narratives told of the 2016 US election. With regards to contestation, strategic narratives are most susceptible to change, or open for interpretation, when there is division among elites (Krebs, 2015; Ringsmose and Børgesen, 2011; Dimitriu & De Graaf, 2016). In the case of the 2016 US election, while we see consistency within Russian, Chinese, and Arabic media, the division among US political elites regarding the election provided significant leeway for Russia, Chinese, and Arabic news media to cite Western news reports, as well as Western leaders, in ways that fit their narratives regarding the shortcomings of the US election, thus making it easier for foreign media to legitimate claims of Western decline. This tactical use of Western media is discussed in more detail below as a mode for legitimizing Russian, Chinese, and Arabic news media narratives.

Legitimation of Russian, Chinese, and Arabic Media Narratives

After assessing the similarities and differences among Russian, Chinese, and Arabic news media narratives of the 2016 US election and the extent to which they can be considered compelling, or strong, our analysis provides one further advancement of the understanding of strategic narratives: their legitimation within regional media ecologies. As Arsenault, Hong, and Price (2017) argue, key questions for advancing our understanding of strategic narratives includes analysis of the role mainstream media plays as the site in which strategic narratives are not only disseminated but gain legitimacy. Accordingly, they argue that critical components of what makes a narrative strategic include the characteristics of sponsorship, the narrative themes, the strategies of promotion, and legitimizing agents, and ask who and what are the emerging sponsors of narratives and their themes and how do legitimizing agents work, vis-à-vis the ecology of strategies of promotion?

In answering these questions, our analysis of regional media ecologies among nations with close state–media relationships and their narrative themes suggest that, in part at least, their reporting was not wholly about the US election, but about their own national visions and domestic soft power. The juxtapositioning of the US election and its implications to the national mission or purpose of their own state might thus help inoculate any reading of these narratives as pure propagandizing of their own values and lends further credence and adherence to their own national and international level narratives. According to Skuse and Gillespie (2011), when considering how strategic narratives are received and interpreted one must consider how meaning or attractiveness is made through the audience's engagement and experience of those narratives. The drama and constant reporting of the 2016 US election thus enables foreign audiences to voyeuristically experience the election through their media, as well as making tangible and real the problems the US witnessed. From a narrative perspective, this lays the scene and emplots the actors and problems they face. Doing so in conjunction with local narratives suggests the resolution is not democracy, but continued application of their own national project.

On a discursive level, the inclusion of historical allusions and national mythologies and narratives used to make sense of the US election provide further cultural resonance and narrative coherence to the national stories told. Here again, and perhaps unsurprisingly, the national media ecologies drew upon their own cultural understandings and experiences to interpret the election. While citizens of countries with close state–media relations likely learn how to distinguish blatant propaganda content from more realistic depictions of their political surroundings, our inclusion of a wide range of media sources across a broad ideological and topical spectrum suggested a collective discursive understanding of the US election. No one media outlet dominated the discourse or unilaterally voiced the narratives we found, and they still were largely critical of the US election and shared elements in support for their home nation's policies. Indeed, US policies and candidates were not discussed in a vacuum but made coherent by focusing on the implications for each respective region. Thus, we might conclude that the sponsors of these narratives did not appear to be politically motivated but rather reflective of the societies' cultural understandings and collective experiences. Our study suggests that strategic narratives can become especially important when discussing large, foreign events without obviously inherent political objectives such as military engagements or invasions where there is a clearer separation between ally and non-ally states.

With regards to who the specific legitimizing agents of these narratives were, we found that all three regions' media relied substantially on citing outside, Western sources. As a specific legitimation technique, this inclusion of polling data and reporting conducted by the US media can be seen as aiding in the formation of more credible narratives through the use of sources emanating directly from the US itself. This aids in the credibility of their narratives as its comes across to the viewer as non-state driven or biased, but rather as accurately transmitting what US media has to say about its own nation. Furthermore, analysis of the news stories collected showed that the media did not overly rely upon Russian, Chinese, or Arabic political leaders' descriptions of policies or critiques on the US, but instead on what the candidates and US reporters were saying. Through analysis of multiple news sources, a plethora of foreign reporting, as well as native journalism, one gets a sense that these narratives created about the US election were more organic and reflective of how these political collectives made sense of the event.

Finally, considering the quantitative frequency of stories coded as informational or neutral, we find that in general, the vast majority of articles focused on providing informational content and explanations regarding how the US election process worked and how it unfolded. Only a few articles clearly and obviously critiqued the US and ideas of US democracy. Not until one looks more closely at the qualitative level does one find the strategic implications these narratives hold for each respective region's understanding of the US and their own national identities. Despite the larger number of more neutral, informational narratives, when taking all the stories into account, one can see how the informational narratives come to support the larger contextual cues the critical articles provide. In this sense, when audiences read about what the candidates said during their debates and polling data citing US audiences' dissatisfaction with the candidates, these pieces of "objective" data and news reporting cohere with the stories that the US democratic system is failing. Thus, again, one can see the importance of regional media ecologies' collective discursive formation of narratives; indeed, it might even suggest that, when looking across a broad spectrum of news media and media reports, these narratives might necessarily arise, providing a larger structure and clarity of how politics functions in the world.

Conclusion

Our goal in the study was to demonstrate the implications of contesting strategic narratives to soft power within media ecologies regarding news reporting on the 2016 US presidential election. In doing so, our analysis focused on how non-Western media systems within countries possessing closer state–media relationships perceived as more antagonistic to US aims constructed and contended US notions of the universality and value of democracy more broadly and US interests specifically. The consequences of this are important not just for US national prestige, and soft power, but at a theoretical level, for demonstrating how the contestation of strategic narratives emerges not just in explicitly geopolitical conflicts, but also in how nations comment upon the political processes of others (Kluver, Hinck, & Cooley, 2019). This process implicates nations' soft power in that, from our analysis of Russian, Chinese, and Arabic media, we find these regions depicting not only the US process as unappealing, but also building up their own political values and culture as more appealing by translating and making more tangible these values through media to the political community's citizenry. Thus, we see how soft power, being more than just a resource for nations to attract others, unfolds in both common and uniquely local ways in building up the relative attractiveness of one's national identity and social cohesion, as well as making unattractive the rhetoric, behavior, policies, and identity of others, or in this case, the US.

If soft power serves to persuade others to adopt the policies, values, and beliefs of another nation, a key element then is strategic narratives. Indeed, the persuasive force soft power provides is in the articulation of where political communities see their future and the political discourse they use to mobilize support of that aspirational "world to be." In this sense, narrative, not framing or public opinion polls, provides the community with a sense of direction. Narrative's ability to take past values, stories, myths, etc., and emplot them onto the present all serve to project, then, the direction of where one is going. In this sense, the 2016 US presidential election showed that US soft power, or the promise of democracy based on the US model, was not the direction other nations should follow.

For Arabic audiences, the past was constructed as one whereby US politicians had previously and continued to ignore their plight. The present was viewed as one where US power alone cannot solve the geopolitical realities of their region with future US action more likely to take an isolationist approach. The future then, is to come together, define their own collective goals and policies, and struggle along to figure out how to enact their form of democratic governance in a region full or authoritarian politics and increasing geopolitical contestation. For the Chinese, the past was full of Western meddling and preaching of how best to adopt Western practices of governance at the hands of a weakened China. However, the present came to represent a new faith in the Chinese government's ability to effectively guide its citizens into a future where they no longer have to kowtow to Western values, beliefs, and interests, but reclaim their role in the current world order through Chinese strength. Indeed, for the Chinese, their future was presented as bright, with a functioning government and greater ability to shape the current world order in ways supportive of their own interests. Finally, for the Russians, narratives of the 2016 US election came with descriptions of the past full of Western interference and attempts to undermine their social, political, and economic system and frequent criticism of their policies. This was reaffirmed in their descriptions of the present, with US establishment politics seen as likewise designed to challenge Russian interests. However, with the election of Trump, Russian interests were confirmed, with a future vision of an increasingly multi-polar world needing Russian leadership as an alternative to the failed and declining US-led world order. In all of these imagined futures, US authority and values are placed in sincere doubt.

In addition to describing the narratives constructed by Russian, Chinese, and Arabic media, this study also advances our understanding of strategic narratives more broadly by showcasing the importance of media systems in making real foreign political events. The 2016 election included vastly different political visions, and personalities, contesting the election, providing a tremendous number of narrative resources for media around the globe to comment critically on the US, its political processes, and its role in the global order. Narratives of a failed US political system were legitimized by foreign media, not only through their own narrative constructions of them through the drawing upon of their local narrative interpretations, but also through the citing of US news reports detailing the candidates' personal failings and subsequent US voter dissatisfaction with them. These narratives became compelling as they cohered within the larger narrative projects of each political community, most notably Russia and China, and this suggests that nations with closer state–media relations in particular are able to wield strategic narratives effectively to bolster domestic support and legitimacy for their governments.

However, for international audiences too, the narrative construction of the US election appears to have converged in negative ways for US soft power. Soft power ranking systems, such as Anholt-GfK "nation-brands" index and McClory's 2017 Soft Power 30 rankings, both indicated a fall in US soft power following the 2016 election. In this sense, multiple audiences, whether more typically Western-aligned nations as well as antagonistic ones, found resonance with a declining US. As our study suggests, the delineation of issue, national, and international level narratives can be messy as they can, at times, implicate and draw upon each other to help audiences see the larger narrative picture an event like the US election holds. Furthermore, these elements can diverge in their specific manifestations, such as what policies are deemed important or how national identities are drawn, and yet still manage to come back together over the larger conclusions and meaning of the event, which for the US election, was one of declining global leadership and political strife at home. While this analysis only revealed narratives in published and broadcast media, which cannot directly substitute for public opinion polling in understanding the perceptions of global audiences, media coverage is nevertheless important in that it helps to drive political knowledge when taking a narrative form to help audiences place in context the informational content their media systems report, and in this context, creates opinions and beliefs about the US.

With this in mind, it is important to note that, while the US election was the topic of media coverage, the stories told about it were not solely about the US in and of itself. The election provided an opportunity for these regions to reflect upon their political systems, whether it be their own political processes for choosing leaders or their limited ability to engage with politics themselves. Unfortunately for the US, however, for many of them, this introspection confirmed the superiority of their less democratic system of governance, or in the Arabic case, a form of democracy different from that prescribed by the US.

Finally, because the election is the embodiment of US political processes and values, which the US actively propagates as a model for the world, it provides a unique opportunity for governments, media outlets, and individuals around the world to reflect upon, critique, or affirm US politics and the order that it implies. In fact, it seems that outside of actual warfare involving multiple state actors, the election is probably the most significant stage for contestation to occur. This is, perhaps, best illustrated by the fact that in both the Russian and US media, conversations on election interference, the legitimacy of the outcome, and malfunctions of the US election process continue unabated. Indeed, as the world continues to become more closely interconnected through advances and greater investment in information technologies, we can expect greater narrative contestation and future research examining its consequences.

References

Acharya, A. (2004). How ideas spread: Whose norms matter? Norm localization and institutional change in Asian regionalism. *International Organization*, 58(2), 239–275.

Adler-Nissen, R. (2014). Stigma management in international relations: Transgressive identities, norms, and order in international society. *International Organization*, 68(1), 143–176.

Anholt-GfK Nation Brands Index (2017). Available online: https://nation-brands.gfk.com/.

Arsenault, A., Hong, S., & Price, M. (2017). Strategic narratives of the Arab Spring and after. In A. Miskimmon, B. O'Loughlin, & L. Roselle (Eds.), *In forging the world: Strategic narratives and international relations* (pp. 190–217). Ann Arbor: University of Michigan Press.

Boudana, S., & Segev, E. (2017). The bias of provocation narratives in international news. *The International Journal of Press/Politics*, 22(3), 314–332.

Dimitriu, G., & De Graaf, B. (2016). Fighting the war at home: Strategic narratives, elite responsiveness, and the Dutch mission in Afghanistan, 2006–2010. *Foreign Policy Analysis*, 12(1), 2–23.

Eberle, J. (2019). Narrative, desire, ontological security, transgression: Fantasy as a factor in international politics. *Journal of International Relations and Development*, 22(1), 1–26.

Finnemore, M., & Sikkink, K. (1998). International norm dynamics and political change. *International Organization*, 52(4), 887–917.

Fisher, W. F. (1984). Narration as a human communication paradigm: The case of public moral argument. *Communication Monographs*, 51(1), 1–22.

Fisher, W. F. (1989). *Human Reason as narration: Toward a philosophy of reason, value, and action*. Columbia, SC: University of South Carolina Press.

He, B. (2006). Western theories of deliberative democracy and the Chinese practice of complex deliberative governance. In E. Leib & B. He (Eds.), *The search for deliberative democracy in China* (pp. 133–148). New York: Palgrave Macmillan.

He, B., & Warren, M. E. (2011). Authoritarian deliberation: The deliberative turn in Chinese political development. *Perspectives on Politics*, 9(2), 269–289.

Jackson, P. T. (2003). Defending the West: Occidentalism and the formation of NATO. *Journal of Political Philosophy*, 11(3), 223–252.

Kluver, R., Cooley, S., & Hinck, R. S. (2019). Contesting strategic narratives in a global context: The world watches the 2016 US election. *International Journal of Press and Politics*, 24(1), 92–144.

Krebs, R. R. (2015). How dominant narratives rise and fall: Military conflict, politics, and the Cold War consensus . *International Organization*, 69(4), 809–845.

Krebs, R. R., & Lobasz, J. K. (2007). Fixing the meaning of 9/11: Hegemony, coercion, and the road to war in Iraq . *Security Studies*, 16(3), 409–451.

Mattern, J. B. (2005). *Ordering international politics: Identity, crisis and representational force.* New York: Routledge.

McClory, Jonathan. (2017). *The Soft Power 30.* The Portland Group. Retrieved from http://softpower30.portland-communications.com/.

Ringsmose, J., & Børgesen, B. K. (2011). Shaping public attitudes towards the deployment of military power: NATO, Afghanistan and the use of strategic narratives. *European Security*, 20(4), 505–528.

Roselle, L., Miskimmon, A., & O'Loughlin, B. (2014). Strategic narrative: A new means to understand soft power. *Media, War & Conflict*, 7(1), 70–84.

Sakwa, R. (2012). Conspiracy narratives as a mode of engagement in international politics: The case of the 2008 Russo-Georgian war. *The Russian Review*, 71(4), 581–609.

Schmitt, O. (2018). When are strategic narratives effective? The shaping of political discourse through the interaction between political myths and strategic narratives. Contemporary Security Policy, 39(4), 1–25.

Skuse, A., & Gillespie, M. (2011). *Drama for development: Cultural translation and social change.* New Delhi: Sage India.

Subotić, J. (2016). Narrative, ontological security, and foreign policy change. *Foreign Policy Analysis*, 12(4), 610–627.

Szostek, J. (2017). Defense and promotion of desired state identity in Russia's strategic narrative. *Geopolitics*, 22(3), 571–593.

van Noort, C. (2017). Study of strategic narratives: The case of BRICS. *Politics & Governance*, 5(3), 121–129.

Wiener, A. (2004). Contested compliance: Interventions on the normative structure of world politics. *European Journal of International Relations*, 10(2), 189–234.

Xiaoyu, P. (2012). Socialisation as a two-way process: Emerging powers and the diffusion of international norms. *The Chinese Journal of International Politics*, 5(4), 341–367.

INDEX

Note: Information in figures and tables is indicated by page numbers in *italics* and **bold**.